What Is Antiracism?

What Is Antiracism?
And Why It Means Anticapitalism

Arun Kundnani

VERSO
London • New York

First published by Verso 2023
© Arun Kundnani 2023

All rights reserved

The moral rights of the author have been asserted

1 3 5 7 9 10 8 6 4 2

Verso
UK: 6 Meard Street, London W1F 0EG
US: 388 Atlantic Avenue, Brooklyn, NY 11217
versobooks.com

Verso is the imprint of New Left Books

ISBN-13: 978-1-83976-276-5
ISBN-13: 978-1-83976-278-9 (UK EBK)
ISBN-13: 978-1-83976-279-6 (US EBK)

British Library Cataloguing in Publication Data
A catalogue record for this book is available from the British Library

Library of Congress Cataloging-in-Publication Data

Names: Kundnani, Arun, author.
Title: What is antiracism? : and why it means anticapitalism / Arun Kundnani.
Description: London ; New York : Verso, 2023. | Includes bibliographical references and index.
Identifiers: LCCN 2022054491 (print) | LCCN 2022054492 (ebook) | ISBN 9781839762765 (hardback) | ISBN 9781839762796 (ebook)
Subjects: LCSH: Anti-racism. | Racism. | Capitalism.
Classification: LCC HT1563 .K86 2023 (print) | LCC HT1563 (ebook) | DDC 305.8—dc23/eng/20230109
LC record available at https://lccn.loc.gov/2022054491
LC ebook record available at https://lccn.loc.gov/2022054492

Typeset in Sabon by Biblichor Ltd, Scotland
Printed and bound by CPI Group (UK) Ltd, Croydon CR0 4YY

Contents

Introduction	1
1. How to Hide a Genocide	8
2. The Liberal Theory of Antiracism	26
3. Imperialism and the Uses of Diversity	41
4. Marxists Confront Colonialism	54
5. Racism Is a Structure	74
6. Internationalists	92
7. Antiracism Means Anticapitalism	113
8. What Is Racial Capitalism?	127
9. The Neoliberal Idea	155
10. Policing the Wastelands	183
11. A War on the Urban Dispossessed	206
12. Why Neoliberals Build Borders	223
13. A Darker Red	241
Acknowledgments	253
Notes	255
Index	287

Introduction

In the summer of 2020, the people of the United States declared their broad support for burning down police stations. Polling by Monmouth University found that a majority of Americans believed the setting ablaze of a police precinct in Minneapolis was fully or partially justified as a method of antiracist protest.[1] At least 15 million people participated in the Black Lives Matter insurrection across the US that summer, after the murder of George Floyd by Minneapolis police officer Derek Chauvin.[2] As with any movement, its participants were motivated by various viewpoints and experiences. But the aims of defunding the police, abolishing prisons, and abolishing Immigration and Customs Enforcement (ICE) were central. The activists accused policing, carceral, and border agencies of not reducing violence but adding to it; they were not organizations that made us safer but infrastructures of racist violence and inequality. The problem was not just individually biased police officers, corrections officers, and deportation officers deviating from the rules of appropriate professional behavior, but the character of those rules themselves. The people on the streets understood racism as a structural force. They did not call for these infrastructures of violence to be reformed through better officer training or increased diversity; they demanded their dismantling.[3]

As the protests swept the US, the institutions of liberal America responded with what they called a racial reckoning. Everywhere you looked, white liberals were talking about how to challenge unconscious biases, reduce micro-aggressions in interpersonal relationships, better represent diverse identities, educate away individual prejudices, and stop right-wing extremism. An unending stream of news articles, podcasts, and documentaries offered endless opportunities for personal reflection. Universities, corporations, and government departments intensified their programs of antiracist workshops and diversity training for their employees. One of the best-selling books of that year, Robin DiAngelo's *White Fragility*, was subtitled "Why It's So Hard for White People to Talk about Racism." And liberal households placed placards on their porches demanding an end to white silence. But white people were doing a lot of talking about racism, albeit anxiously.

Few noticed that, in their response to what was happening on the streets, liberals had substituted one definition of racism for another. Instead of the macro-aggressions of police, prison, and border infrastructures, they focused upon the micro-aggressions of individual biases. This substitution was obscured somewhat because everyone talked about the need to address "structural racism" and "systemic racism." But in using these phrases, liberals did not mean what the people on the streets meant. This mismatch reached its apotheosis in the vapid efforts of corporations to take up the antiracist cause. Walmart, for example, announced that it would invest $100 million in creating a Center on Racial Equity to "address the drivers of systemic racism." But, for the center, the word "systemic" did not mean racism was part of a broader social system that needed to be examined; rather, it meant it was something that could be remedied through "eliminating bias and fostering positive relationships with law enforcement"—in other words, by focusing on changing individuals rather than social structures.[4]

Similarly, in a 2020 letter to colleagues, Larry Fink, the billionaire CEO of BlackRock, the most powerful financial organization in the world, controlling assets of over $6 trillion, wrote that racism was a "deep and longstanding problem in our society and must be addressed on both a personal and systemic level." Was this to be done through the cancelation of his donations to the

New York City Police Foundation, an organization that enables the very wealthy to fund the police department and undemocratically influence its priorities? Or perhaps by ending BlackRock's investment in arms manufacturers like Boeing, General Dynamics, Lockheed Martin, and Raytheon, which supply the weapons for the US wars in the Middle East? Maybe even by redistributing the wealth he controls to address the vast racial inequalities of the world? No, his solution to "systemic" racism was not to focus on systems at all but, as he put it, to "talk to each other and cultivate honest, open relationships and friendships" so that we can "heal these wounds" and build "a more diverse and inclusive firm"—in other words, the usual corporate program aimed at changing individual attitudes.[5]

The following year, the Biden White House announced that it was tackling "systemic racism" by initiating a study of "domestic violent extremism" movements and their "biases against minority populations," and by creating a "chief diversity and inclusion officer" at the State Department to create "opportunities for the improvement of communities that have been historically underserved."[6] Asking how more people of color could be promoted in the US military got more attention than asking how fewer people of color could be killed by the US military. Underpinning all these responses was the belief that the solution to structural racism is to tackle individual biases and diversify the people who preside over the US's most powerful institutions—as those institutions carry on with basically the same policies and practices.

The confusion extended to some of the most prominent writers on antiracism. Robin DiAngelo writes that racism is "a far-reaching system that functions independently from the intentions or self-images of individual actors." But her invocation of racism as a system is not so much a substantial part of her analysis as a device to make it easier for white readers to reflect on their unconscious biases without feeling too guilty about them—because they can be seen as the work of larger social forces over which her audience has limited control. She gives her readers no explanation of how these systemic forces function, and all her proposed remedies involve white individuals delving into their personal assumptions.[7] The idea is to educate one mind at a time—move pebbles to start an avalanche. Except all it does is simply move pebbles around.[8]

In a host of similar texts, writers treat racism as an individual malady operating through the unconscious. Structural racism is either a sort of hidden and unexamined force that somehow introduces these biases, or a term referring to the cumulative effects of many personal biases. But "structural racism" does not just denote a situation where there are many individuals with racist attitudes, unconsciously or otherwise. Structural racism circulates through individual attitudes and behaviors, sometimes unconsciously, but its analysis requires us to go beyond that level. Without an explanation of what the *structure* in structural racism is, these accounts cannot explain what sustains the unconscious biases they see as so damaging. The racially differentiated effects of COVID brought this home in an especially forceful manner. As the journalist Gary Younge wrote:

> Notwithstanding the handful of cases where nonwhite people were spat at, sometimes while being showered with racial epithets, there is no suggestion that anyone tried to deliberately make them ill with Covid. In other words, they were not disproportionately affected because individual people with bad attitudes did bad things to them. Their propensity to succumb to the virus wasn't primarily the result of people's uncouth behaviour, bad manners, mean spirits, crude epithets or poor education. For while all of those things are present, it is the systemic nature of racism that gives it its power and endurance.[9]

Only after we understand how racism's "systemic nature" operates will we be able to imagine the kinds of collective action that would disassemble it. Without such an understanding, antiracism is more an exercise in personal development for white people than genuine structural change.

Liberals have been arguing for a century that racism is fundamentally an individual problem of irrationally held beliefs and prejudiced attitudes. In the 1930s, this claim accompanied new ideas about the value of cultural diversity, replacing the scientifically discredited doctrine of racial superiority. Liberal antiracists developed their ideas in response to Nazism, which, to them, showed the danger of political extremists capitalizing on mass prejudices and bringing about the collapse of liberal democracy. In response, they called upon US elites to lead a process of teaching people to be less prejudiced, especially among the uneducated and economically insecure. In these ideas from the 1930s lies the origin of how liberals think about antiracism today, from the enthusiasm for diversity training to the hope that better representation in Hollywood movies can educate us out of our racist attitudes.

Alongside the growth of this liberal antiracism, a more radical antiracism flowered. It first sprouted among peoples dominated by European colonialism. The root argument was that racism had to be understood in terms of the broad economic and political structures through which societies were organized. These radicals saw racism as closely tied to colonialism and capitalism; a central question focused on the racial distribution of resources. And only with the organized collective action of Black and Third World peoples could these structures be changed. In the 1960s, the Black freedom movement popularized these kinds of radical antiracist arguments in the US. But in the 1970s, ruling classes mobilized a neoliberal conception of market forces to defeat mass movements for the redistribution of wealth, reconfigure Western domination of the Third World, and erect new structures of racism. By this time, liberal antiracism could claim to have succeeded in achieving something of a reduction in the extent to which racial prejudices affected interpersonal relationships—progress in this sphere, at least. But liberal antiracism was powerless against the new forces of structural racism. What's more, its venerations of diversity and individualism were easily co-opted to shore up the new racist system.

Thereafter, to look to liberal antiracism as the solution, with whatever good intentions, was to aid the system in sustaining new forms of racism. It was not simply that racism had become more subtle or unconscious after its overt forms had been defeated. It was more that there had been a shift to a new configuration of power that did not need to routinely make explicit assertions of racial superiority; it could function through the abstractions of the market alongside newly intensifying infrastructures of violence, carried out in the name of seemingly race-neutral concerns about security—"law and order," "counter-narcotics," "border protection," and "counter-terrorism" were the watchwords. Liberal notions of diversity and inclusion were completely compatible with these forms of racist structural violence. White liberals could heroically confront their own whiteness all they wanted, yet these structures would remain.

This book attempts to tell the story of the two antiracisms and their fates as neoliberalism reordered the world in the last decades of the twentieth century. It does so by tracing a history of ideas, movements, and policies. The central characters are Anton de Kom, Manabendra Nath Roy, C. L. R. James, Aimé Césaire, Frantz Fanon, Kwame Nkrumah, Claudia Jones, Martin Luther King Jr., Coretta Scott King, Jamil Al-Amin, Cedric Robinson, Stuart Hall, and A. Sivanandan. These figures each gave shape and expression to ideas of antiracism that had been forged in the heat of collective struggle. The list, of course, is somewhat arbitrary: there are many names one might substitute to equal effect. Figures as important in the US as W. E. B. Du Bois and Angela Davis make only occasional appearances, in part because they are already somewhat familiar to many. The point, however, is not to erect a pantheon but to draw on these radical antiracists as a way to see how neoliberalism reinvented racism and imperialism, how "diversity" supports the violence of racial capitalism, and why we need an antiracism that is socialist in its outlook, internationalist in its scope, and insurrectionary in its methods.

1

How to Hide a Genocide

In the summer of 1942, the Nazi occupiers of the Netherlands began the construction of a concentration camp in the forests near the small town of Vught. Run by SS officers, including Dutch recruits, the camp's initial purpose was to act as a transit center to hold Dutch Jews temporarily before their transportation to the death camps in Germany and Poland.[1] The first prisoners arrived at Vught in January 1943. Three months later, Jews in all the provinces outside Amsterdam were rounded up and most of them were sent to Vught. Several hundred lost their lives in the first few months of the camp's operation, owing to starvation, disease, and summary executions. The Jews who survived Vught itself were slated for deportation trains. More than 34,000 were transported from the Netherlands to the Sobibór extermination camp in Poland between early March and the end of July 1943.[2] In June alone, the Nazis transported almost 1,300 Jewish children from Vught to the death camps.[3] There were 140,000 Jews living in the Netherlands before the Nazi occupation. Only one in four survived.[4]

The construction of the camp at Vught was a consequence of the meeting at Wannsee near Berlin on January 20, 1942, at which fifteen Nazi leaders and German government officials agreed on what they called the "final solution of the Jewish question in Europe." But the SS also found other uses for the camp. The Dutch corporation Philips opened a workshop there to manufacture flashlights and radios with forced labor. Roma, LGBTQ people, Jehovah's Witnesses, homeless people, and people accused of ordinary crimes were also imprisoned at Vught. So, too, were communists and other activists in the anti-Nazi resistance. Among them was Anton de Kom, who had been a leader of the struggle against Dutch colonialism in Suriname. His 1934 book *We Slaves of Suriname* is a landmark work of Caribbean anticolonial literature. Written in Dutch, it traces the long history of resistance to European rule in Suriname, from the Indigenous "red slaves," through to the guerrilla wars waged by bands of escaped African slaves against the plantation system, and the struggles of indentured workers from India and Indonesia—all these resisters were the "slaves" of the book's title.[5] De Kom demonstrated that slavery did not end with its abolition in 1863 but continued in new forms: the Dutch arranged emancipation "in such a way that the freed slaves had no other choice but to voluntarily take up the slavery which had just been legally abolished." Under the colonial system, the various categories of workers were not truly free because they were still "forced to sell their labor-power, albeit in a different way than during the days of slavery." As such, the plantation system's "physical pains have mostly been replaced by mental torture, poverty, and deprivation." The history De Kom wrote was a history he knew intimately. His father had been born enslaved. "Better than in the history books of the whites," De Kom wrote, "the abuse of our fathers has been imprinted on our own hearts. Never did the suffering of slavery speak more strongly to me than from the eyes of my grandmother, when she told us children, outside the hut in Paramaribo, stories from the olden times." At the colonial school De Kom attended, history lessons inculcated in him a sense of Black inferiority. He hoped his book would help others free themselves from such attitudes so that a movement to overturn Dutch colonialism could emerge. There was, he wrote, no better way "to slowly create an inferiority complex in a race than through history lessons in which the sons of another people are exclusively named and praised." It took a long time, De Kom wrote, to "free myself from the obsession that a Negro must always and unconditionally be the inferior of any white."[6]

Anton de Kom, 1924
Family archive

A year before the book's publication, De Kom had organized a protest of Black and Asian workers at the governor's office in Suriname, which led to his arrest by the Dutch colonial authorities. A mass uprising in the capital city, Paramaribo, followed. Police officers fired at the crowd, killing two demonstrators and injuring twenty-three. The authorities imprisoned De Kom for three and a half months without trial before exiling him to the Netherlands, where, they thought, he would not stir up further trouble. But, despite his unemployment and struggle to make ends meet, he continued his anticolonial organizing, collaborating with Indonesian students in the Netherlands who were also fighting for their country's liberation from Dutch rule. He became close to the Dutch communist movement and joined the underground resistance after the Nazi invasion. In August 1944, he was betrayed by an associate, and German police arrested him. After a period at Vught, he was transported to the camp at Sandbostel, an annex to the Neuengamme concentration camp in Germany, where he died of tuberculosis in April 1945, aged forty-seven.[7] He was one of perhaps 2,000 Black people who died in the Nazi camps.[8]

Another prisoner at Vught was my grandfather, Henricus van Herten, a Dutch Catholic who worked as a bookkeeper at the town hall in Roermond. He was arrested for "unlawful dealings with ration cards," sentenced without a trial, and, after two months in other prisons, was taken to Vught on January 18, 1943, when the camp was still being built. The Nazis placed him in the "asocial" category and listed his crime as "economic deceit." They made him work in the Philips workshop. By March, he had fallen ill with malnutrition and was sent to the camp hospital. In a letter to his mother that month, he wrote: "I am okay in spite of the circumstances and I have made many friends here." (The guards would have censored any negative statements about the camp.) The letter included a request to receive the permitted "small parcel with bread, cheese, etc." By then, most of the camp's inmates were dependent on food packages sent from outside. On May 11, he was released. He never fully recovered his health and died in 1962. In the years after the war, he never spoke to his children about what happened. My grandmother told them that he had been in the resistance and had stolen ration cards to help Jews in hiding. However, years later, when an aunt of mine investigated her family history, she met the daughter of another deceased Henricus van Herten who had lived in the same region and had talked to his family about his assistance to Jews in hiding during the war. This discovery suggested the possibility that the Nazis had mistaken my grandfather for someone else with the same name. There is nothing in the archives to confirm one or another version of what happened.

Today, a national memorial exists at the site of the Vught concentration camp. The memorial is spread out over several buildings and outdoor areas; the main building is a museum with exhibits on the history of the camp and Nazism in Europe. Outside are life-size reconstructions of the camp's living quarters, watchtowers, and barbed-wire fences. Various components of the memorial commemorate those killed at Vught or murdered after passing through it. The final part of the memorial is a reflection room where several short films aim to tie the camp's history to the "here and now." Written on the wall in large type is the question: "How do you make a difference?" The films answer with the message that you should not be a bystander when you see others needing help. The examples the films choose have nothing to do with racism, with the exception of one film, entitled *Not Everything Is What It Seems*. It presents three characters discussing stereotypes. A blond woman talks about how people assume she is unintelligent. A white man with tattoos explains that people sometimes think of him as "white trash." A North African man says people are surprised by how well he speaks Dutch. In the memorial's understanding of antiracism, we all make unfounded assumptions about others based on their appearances, but education can help us overcome these prejudices.[9] It is a message that seems designed to make no one feel uncomfortable in a place that should be discomforting—and thereby nullifies the possibility that what happened at Vught might be more than superficially instructive in understanding Dutch racism today.

But more significant is the lack of discomfort at another aspect of the Vught site. Walking around the grounds of the memorial, it is impossible not to notice that, alongside one of the memorial's walls, is a much taller wall, topped with barbed wire and closed-circuit TV cameras. On the other side of that wall are prison buildings, their arrangement mirroring that of the memorial's reconstructed camp buildings. The memorial, in fact, takes up only a small part of the original concentration camp site. A larger part is occupied by a functioning prison. If you look left from the memorial's main entrance, the tall metal doors of the prison entrance are visible, flanked by lines of people waiting to visit inmates. Many are women wearing hijabs and niqabs, a result of the fact that the Vught prison includes a high-security unit where anyone suspected or convicted of being a terrorist or "Islamic radicalizer" is automatically separated from other prisoners and held under especially punitive conditions. Because almost all of those imprisoned there are Muslims, the unit has come to be known informally as a "Muslim detention center."[10]

Dutch prison authorities opened the high-security unit in 2006 at the behest of the domestic intelligence agency, the Algemene Inlichtingen- en Veiligheidsdienst (AIVD).[11] These agencies organized a regime in the unit to prevent its prisoners from having any meaningful contact with other human beings. Prisoners are isolated and confined for up to twenty-two hours per day. One woman imprisoned there, who was eventually acquitted of all charges, spent two full stretches— one for ten consecutive weeks and the other for three—cut off from anyone else.[12] This kind of isolation has been a focus of research for Craig Haney, a psychologist at the University of California, Santa Cruz, who writes that prisoners held in long-term solitary confinement suffer "appetite and sleep disturbances, anxiety, panic, rage, loss of control, paranoia, hallucinations, and self-mutilations," as well as cognitive dysfunction, a sense of impending emotional breakdown, and suicidal ideation and behavior. The effects, he writes, "are analogous to the acute reactions suffered by torture and trauma victims."[13] Former United Nations special rapporteur on torture Juan E. Méndez has said that, based on the medical evidence, solitary confinement for longer than fifteen days can amount to torture when used during pre-trial detention or as a punishment, and therefore should be absolutely prohibited.[14]

Adding to this mental torture in the Vught high-security unit are the regular and invasive full-nudity strip searches of inmates. So humiliating are these measures that, when they are allowed to have visitors, many prisoners choose to meet them separated by a glass barrier because that option does not require such a search. Physical contact with loved ones then becomes impossible. Prison officials concede that they've never discovered contraband in these searches. Even without the glass barrier, family visits are monitored to such an extent that they become superficial encounters. Indeed, every word and movement of the prisoners outside their cells is observed and recorded.

Approximately 170 prisoners were held in the high-security unit at Vught in its first ten years of operation. The majority were not convicted of a crime but were awaiting trial, which can take up to twenty-seven months. Among those at Vught who had been convicted were a woman found guilty after retweeting a single tweet that allegedly encouraged people to fight in Syria, and a man convicted for giving a thousand Euros to a childhood friend who had traveled to Syria—these are terrorism offenses under the Dutch counter-terrorism system that emerged in the first decade of the twenty-first century.[15] Soon after the unit opened in 2006, a group of prisoners held there publicly complained that the "Muslim detention center" had treated them worse than animals and went on hunger strike. They said they received punishments for speaking Arabic, for trying to shout to prisoners in neighboring cells, and for refusing to cut short their prayers. Because they were denied any contact with outside agencies, they had to arrange for their handwritten letter to be smuggled out.[16]

"A new form of death"

The regime of extreme isolation, humiliating searches, and continuous monitoring at the Vught high-security unit is modeled on those that operate at so-called supermax prisons in the United States. The emergence of supermax prisons began in 1934 with the opening of Alcatraz Island in San Francisco Bay. FBI chief J. Edgar Hoover directed that the military prison previously operating there be repurposed as a "maximum custody–minimum privilege" penitentiary where well-known organized crime figures could be concentrated. It was more a spectacle for public consumption than a response to a specific criminal problem. By the 1950s, its regime of severe separation combined with so many deprivations had become outdated in people's minds. Alcatraz ceased operations in 1963.[17] But two years earlier, academic psychologists had begun to work with the Federal Bureau of Prisons to propose a new method of "behavior modification" that included the use of isolation. Among them was Edgar Schein of the Massachusetts Institute of Technology, who studied how US prisoners of war were treated by the Chinese after capture in the Korean War. At a meeting with the Bureau of Prisons in 1961, Schein laid out the communist "brainwashing" techniques he believed he had discovered, and recommended they be applied to troublesome prisoners in the US. Another psychologist at the meeting, Bertram S. Brown of the National Institute of Mental Health, suggested the Bureau of Prisons ought to "undertake a little experiment of what you can do with Muslims." Black Muslims were at the time organizing strong resistance to prison authorities and for many had become a major source of disruption. From 1961, the California Department of Corrections and Rehabilitation had already been placing Nation of Islam activists in "adjustment centers," where they were isolated to prevent their recruiting other prisoners.[18] Isolate as a punishment, the psychologists recommended, and grant rewards and privileges for acceptable behavior. A mix of manipulation and coercion, they said, could break inmates down to a kind of blank slate, upon which a new, more docile personality could be constructed. Officials began implementing these techniques on an experimental basis at the federal penitentiary at Marion, Illinois, in the early 1960s.[19]

A decade later, prison rebellions erupted across the United States, from San Quentin in California to Attica in New York. Prisoners formed clandestine study groups, produced newspapers, organized labor strikes, and filed legal briefs. "The sheer numbers of the prisoner class and their terms of existence make them a mighty reservoir of revolutionary potential," wrote George Jackson, the most well known of the prison activists.

Jackson had advocated Black prisoners' right to self-defense and was the author of *Soledad Brother*; he was killed in a shoot-out at San Quentin prison in 1971.[20] Hoping to halt the spread of such radicalism, the Bureau of Prisons adopted a policy of transferring prison activists from various sites across the US to Marion, where, administrators hoped, the new behavior modification techniques would prove effective.

Then, after a Marion prison guard racially abused Jesse López, a Chicano inmate, provoking a violent altercation, hundreds of prisoners who had been organizing there went on strike. A series of violent confrontations ensued. The prison authorities responded by placing over a hundred prisoners in segregation units. This was the beginning of what would become a new "long-term control unit" at Marion, where officials could separate large numbers of disruptive prisoners from the rest of the prison population and subject them to round-the-clock solitary confinement. A team of guards would place inmates in handcuffs and leg chains every time they left their cell. Exercise was limited and personal property removed from cells, except for a few family photos and letters. Only four non-contact visits, each one hour long, were allowed each month, always preceded and followed by strip searches, including rectal examinations called "finger waves." Prisoners were only allowed to speak with chaplains, case workers, or psychologists through the bars of their cells.[21] The warden of Marion, Ralph Aron, was clear about the purpose of these methods; they exist "to control revolutionary attitudes in the prison system and in the society at large," he stated. For those placed in the control unit, the effects were devastating: one survivor wrote that, after a few days, "there is no longer intercommunication between sense organs and the brain. The nervous system has carried so many pain impulses to the brain until the brain refuses to accept any more signals. Feelings become indistinct, emotions unpredictable. The monotony makes thought hard to separate and capsulate."[22]

In 1973, other federal penitentiaries and thirty-six states began sending prisoners to the new unit.[23] The Marion model soon began to spread across the US. Throughout the 1980s and 1990s, as mass incarceration took off, whole prisons were built on the new principle of total isolation—they came to be known as supermax prisons. By 1999, forty-four states and the federal government had constructed supermaxes; together these housed approximately 25,000 people. Apart from the supermaxes, almost every prison and jail in the US had some kind of solitary confinement unit. Prison officials had initially presented solitary confinement as an occasional tool to uphold prison discipline. But it became a normal part of incarceration for many thousands of people. By 2005, more than 80,000 men, women, and children were held in a solitary confinement unit or supermax prison.[24] Black people are even more over-represented in solitary confinement than they are in the prison system in general: about 9 percent of Black men in the US have been held in solitary for more than fifteen consecutive days, and nearly one in a hundred have experienced solitary for a year or longer by the age of thirty-two.[25]

These kinds of regimes target what makes us most human: our relationships to others. As Five Mualimm-Ak, who spent five years in solitary confinement in the New York State prison system, puts it. "The very essence of life is human contact, and the affirmation of existence that comes with it. Losing the contact, you lose your sense of identity. You become nothing . . . I became invisible even to myself."[26] This destruction of the self is exactly what prison regimes of isolation are intended to achieve. With solitary confinement, writes the law scholar Colin Dayan, the US has "invented a new form of death—a death-in-life that needs no judicial decision and is not open to scrutiny." Because basic human needs—food, clothing, shelter—are met, liberal conceptions of law consider the practices acceptable; the destruction is mental rather than physical.[27] Solitary confinement is costly and does not reduce violence and hostility in prisons. Its purpose is the control of the troublesome, to render them mentally dead even as they are physically alive. Imposing near-complete forms of isolation is a way of disappearing the problems that prisoners seem to embody—a process that is lubricated by racist assumptions about the people vanished in this way. In this sense, solitary confinement functions as a concentrated form of incarceration in general, which, as the formerly incarcerated philosopher Angela Davis writes, "relieves us of the responsibility of seriously engaging with the problems of our society."[28] Prisons exist so that we can ignore inconvenient truths about how our society is organized. This is why solitary confinement not only destroys the humanity of those subjected to it but also reduces the capacity of us all to be fully human.

In the first decade of the twenty-first century, the US supermax prison was globalized. The carceral sites that emerged during the global War on Terror—at Guantánamo, Abu Ghraib, Bagram, and countless other places—followed the supermax model. Techniques that US government agencies had earlier developed in response to what they called Black extremism were now deployed against what they called Islamic extremism. Observers usually regard Guantánamo as an aberration from the way the US normally runs prisons. But the regimes at Guantánamo and other War on Terror prisons are the same as at US civilian supermax prisons: they all involve practices such as prolonged and indefinite solitary confinement, sensory deprivation, permanent monitoring, force-feeding of hunger strikers, and systematic secrecy.[29] Today's practices at Vught can only be understood in this context. Vught is part of the global infrastructure of counterterrorism supermax incarceration that imprisons so-called Muslim extremists around the world.[30] The Netherlands has a reputation for its liberal criminal justice system: in 2017, newspapers reported that its problem—unusual in the prison field—was that it had too few prisoners to fill its facilities.[31] But, Vught, a site built by the Nazis to carry out the genocide of Jews, now serves as a "Muslim detention center" where people are, in effect, tortured. The visitors to the memorial at Vught are literally bystanders to racist oppression taking place on another part of the site.

Extremism

What happened at Vught in 1943 and 1944 and what happens there today are, of course, not equivalent. Yet neither are the uses to which the camp has been put in these two periods entirely separable. With their "final solution," the Nazis sought the complete elimination of European Jewry. Incarceration was a means to this end. The European and US governments that have implemented a global War on Terror have a different aim. Their goal is the integration of Muslims into what they call "liberal" society. At the ideological center of their project is a distinction between the moderate Muslim and the extremist Muslim. The moderate is offered a form of inclusion; the extremist is subjected to state violence. But since the perception of the moderate is that they are always at risk of becoming an extremist, all Muslims are continually suspect. As the liberal columnist Timothy Garton Ash wrote in the *Guardian* newspaper in 2007: "All over our continent, and around its edges, there are hundreds of thousands of young Muslim men who could go either way. They could become tomorrow's bombers; or they could become good citizens, funders of our faltering state pension schemes, tomorrow's Europeans."[32]

War on Terror administrators talk about "radicalization" as the process by which moderates are gripped by extremist Islam, transforming them, the theory goes, into violent fanatics. Governments have established vast systems of surveillance to try to identify the would-be extremist Muslims hidden among the moderates. In practice, the classifying of Muslims into these two categories is not a matter of consistent and explicit criteria. Moderate Muslims are defined as those who restrict their religion to the private sphere. But they are also expected to publicly condemn interpretations of Islam that Western governments consider dangerous. Moderate Muslims are supposed to value freedom of speech. But they are considered extremists if they use their freedom of speech to criticize the West. Moderate Muslims are required to publicly condemn the use of violence to achieve political ends. But when the US government uses violence to achieve its political ends, condemnation must give way to consent. Western governments define Muslim extremism as a rejection of liberal values but, in practice, they almost always use the term to label Muslims who oppose their own power.

What is regarded as the cultural identity of moderate Muslims is celebrated within a framework of diversity and inclusion. Extremist Muslims, on the other hand, have their mosques and community organizations closed down, their speech criminalized, their bank accounts frozen, their clothing regulated (as with the Dutch ban on wearing a niqab or burka in certain public spaces, introduced in 2019), even their citizenship canceled.[33] If they live in certain parts of the Middle East, Africa, or South Asia, they are subject to execution from the air by missile-bearing drones, or capture and transport to secret locations to face torture and indefinite imprisonment. In the cases of Afghanistan and Iraq, entire countries were invaded, occupied, and destroyed. Researchers at the Watson Institute for International and Public Affairs at Brown University have documented the deaths of around half a million people in Iraq, Afghanistan, and Pakistan as a direct result of the War on Terror from October 2001 to October 2019. Around half of the deaths are thought to be of civilians. This is a highly conservative estimate because it only counts deaths that are directly the result of war. The actual death toll of the War on Terror is much higher: many of those killed have not been counted, and many more have died indirectly from the destruction of the infrastructure that people depend upon for food, water, and health. Deaths resulting from war-induced malnutrition and environmental damage are likely to far outnumber deaths from combat.[34] We do not know how many men, women, and children have been needlessly killed by the US and its junior partners, such as the UK, in the War on Terror. But the number is definitely over a million. At the same time, war forced over 14 million Iraqis and Afghans to flee their homes in fear of their lives while the US and the other wealthy countries who share responsibility for their displacement violently prevented the overwhelming majority from seeking sanctuary.[35]

The mass violence of the War on Terror has not required a Nazi party to take over the US or UK governments and transform them in its image. There has been no creation of an SS to do the dirty work that the normal agencies of state power would have been unwilling to carry out. The regular militaries, intelligence agencies, law enforcement agencies, border agencies, private contractors, and courts are sufficient. To understand how the ordinary processes of nominally liberal states can administer violence on this scale requires that we understand the particular form of racism that is bound up with it. Former UK prime minister Tony Blair, a key architect of the War on Terror's destruction of Iraq, described this violence as being aimed not at regime change but at "values change." Influenced by neoconservative scholars such as Bernard Lewis, Blair had come to believe that Iraqi cultural values were so antagonistic to his idea of liberal modernity that only a war to tear apart Iraq's social fabric would make possible the new kind of Iraq he envisioned. This was part of "an elemental struggle about the values that will shape our future . . . a war, but not just against terrorism but about how the world should govern itself in the early 21st century."[36] Such was the logic of the War on Terror in a nutshell: violence is deemed necessary, not primarily to prevent terrorism, but to bring about a cultural change among Muslims around the world. Though rarely made explicit by the War on Terror's political leaders, this argument carries a terrifying implication: that the cultural problems in Islam are so deeply embedded that they can only be resolved through the kind of industrial violence that destroys over a million lives. Anti-Muslim racism is therefore indispensable to the War on Terror. Only by imagining barbarism as somehow a *natural* feature of Islam can government agencies present war, torture, assassination, and arbitrary imprisonment as necessary. Anti-Muslim racism functions by setting aside all the contingent social and political factors that create the conditions in which some Muslims do indeed commit terrifying acts of violence and, instead, seeing their actions as simply the automatic expression of an Islamic culture of fanaticism. We can then tell ourselves that their violence reflects the deep flaws of their culture while our much greater violence is a rational, even liberal, response, aimed at modifying their barbaric behavior. Genocidal violence does not always announce itself in the rhetoric of overt hatred; it can also be hidden by the managerial language of cultural reform.

The AIVD, the Dutch agency that encouraged the opening of the high-security unit at Vught, played an important role in developing the idea of the Muslim extremist. Before other countries' national security agencies took up the concept of Muslim "radicalization," the AIVD had pioneered it as a way to refer to a process through which moderates are turned into extremists by religious ideology, rather than by social or political factors.[37] Vught's high-security unit is a response to the "radicalization" that the AIVD believed it had identified among Muslim inmates. Echoing the logic of US efforts to stem prisoner radicalism during the 1970s, the purpose of extreme isolation at Vught is to break down the personalities of extremist Muslims and remold them as moderate Muslims—part of a broader program of violently imposed cultural change.

Vught is thus a place haunted by the presence of multiple forms of oppression. Nazi anti-Semitism instigated the construction of the original site of incarceration. Dutch colonialism led to the imprisonment of one of its detainees, Black revolutionary Anton de Kom. The War on Terror shaped a new logic of confinement decades later, influenced by US practices that were responses to Black-led prison rebellion. All of these different oppressions can be described using the term "racism"—as we shall see, the term's power lies precisely in its enmeshing of different histories of oppression. Yet most of these racisms remain invisible. The usual assumption is that what happened in the past at Vught is the defining example of racism while what happens there now has nothing to do with racism. Thus, at a site to commemorate Nazi racism, we become bystanders to the other racisms that surround us.

To make fully visible the different forms of racism at Vught requires that we move beyond the liberal theory of racism that the Vught memorial implies. On this theory, racism is a matter of prejudices and biases that shape personal relationships. It is a mental disposition, an attitude, or a set of beliefs. With Nazism, emotionally manipulative propaganda exploited these prejudices to mount a totalitarian assault on liberal government. The lesson of Nazism, on this view, is that racist prejudices, left unchecked, can be exploited by political extremists and become a threat to liberal values of individualism, rationality, and progressive reform. Antiracism, therefore, employs education to tackle prejudices, promote tolerance of diversity, and cultivate a more rational public discourse. But there is another way of telling the story of racism, which we find not at the Vught memorial but in the writing of Vught prisoner Anton de Kom—which the memorial ignores. De Kom wrote about racism in terms of the everyday colonial hierarchies through which labor is categorized and differentiated as part of nominally liberal ways of organizing society—backed by the routine administrative powers of the state. His was a structural theory of racism. For him, racism, of course, expresses itself in individual attitudes but these attitudes are themselves expressions of deeper social and economic forces. On his account, racism is also protean; in the face of resistance, it could reconstitute itself in new forms, from plantation slavery to the racially segmented labor systems of European colonialism in the early twentieth century. He understood that, when this happened, the espousal of liberal values could mask new systems of oppression.

Today's dominant and most harmful racisms are hard to recognize if one starts from the idea that racism is a form of extremism that threatens liberal values—with Nazism as a paradigm. Associating racism with extremism makes anti-Muslim racism particularly hard to see. This is because the War on Terror hides its anti-Muslim racism by projecting onto its victims the accusation of extremism. When this happens, anti-Muslim mass violence does not appear as extremism, but as the fight *against* extremism. This is what is happening when War on Terror ideologues claim their program is analogous to the fight against the Nazis or talk about "Islamo-fascism." Anti-Muslim racism will also be invisible if antiracism is defined as tolerance of diversity, because the War on Terror's rhetoric of the liberal inclusion of moderate Muslims cannot then be understood as itself part of a racist project. Indeed, starting from these flawed definitions of racism in terms of extremism and intolerance can easily lead to the thought that the problem is not the West's liberal values, but those from elsewhere who do not share them. That is why the Dutch government tests would-be immigrants for signs of intolerance, showing them images of topless women sunbathing on Dutch beaches and of two men kissing in a meadow, and denying them entry if they respond negatively. The assumption is that the Netherlands is so tolerant it needs to be protected from the intolerance of foreigners—the irony of this reasoning is lost on its advocates.[38]

To properly see the racisms of our age, we need to follow De Kom in understanding them not primarily as extremist outbursts that endanger liberal society, but as routine sets of practices, bound up with global structures of power, often articulated in terms of liberal values. What is significant about the racist regimes at prisons, from Vught in the Netherlands to the practices of extreme isolation across the US prison system, is that they are concentrated expressions of broader structures of racial hierarchy. Indeed, they are places where the contradictions of our societies are deliberately rendered invisible. As we have noted, liberal institutions, such as the law and the academy, are part of this process.

To develop this argument, we need to understand how we inherited two quite different concepts of racism: the more commonly held one rooted in a liberal theory, the other deriving from structural theories, such as De Kom's. One way to approach this is to examine the surprisingly short history of the word "racism" itself.

2

The Liberal Theory of Antiracism

In 1933, Magnus Hirschfeld wrote a letter to his friend George Sylvester Viereck trying to persuade him to be less racist. Hirschfeld was Jewish and gay. He was known for his advocacy of gay rights, for establishing the Institute of Sexual Science in Berlin in 1919, and for his studies of transvestism—a term he coined. The year after his Institute opened, Hirschfeld was beaten by a right-wing mob after he gave a lecture in Munich. The attack was so close to being fatal that the *New York Times* published his obituary.[1] A Bavarian newspaper columnist described Hirschfeld as the "apostle of sodomy" and praised the beating for its message that, if the "old bastard swine" returned, "his skull might be crushed."[2] When the Nazis came to power in 1933, they closed down the institute and burned 10,000 of the books in its library. In their denunciations of Hirschfeld, they fused his sexuality and his Jewishness into a single image of degeneracy.[3]

His friend Viereck, on the other hand, was one of the leading campaigners for Nazism in the United States. In 1934, with Hitler in power in Germany, Viereck gave a pro-Nazi speech at a fascist rally of 20,000 "friends of the new Germany" in Madison Square Garden. Swastikas and posters of Hitler hung from the walls, interspersed with American flags and pictures of George Washington.[4] Yet Viereck was an admirer of Hirschfeld. Four years earlier, he had organized publicity for Hirschfeld's tour of the United States and dubbed him "the Einstein of sex." (Einstein was another Jewish friend.)

In his 1933 letter to Viereck, Hirschfeld wrote: "I will not reject you; for I know your mentality all too well, and foresaw

Magnus Hirschfeld

that you would not be able to resist Hitler's mass suggestion." Hirschfeld was trying to do something that others had done before him: engage with an individual to challenge their prejudices. What was different on this occasion was that Hirschfeld was able to give a name to the system of beliefs he was opposing. With his letter to Viereck, he included a book he had written in German on Nazi ideology, entitled *Rassismus*, adding, "I hope it will convince you."[5] Written in the early 1930s, the book was published in English in 1938, three years after Hirschfeld died in exile in France. The book's title, *Racism*, was the first time the word had appeared in an English-language scholarly text. Hirschfeld appears to have adopted the word "racism" from France, where anti-fascist activists used the term *racisme* in the early 1930s.[6] It is striking that a word so widely used today entered regular use less than a century ago.

Hirschfeld hoped his book would systematically demonstrate the falsehoods at the core of Nazi propaganda. By doing so, he thought he could weaken the hold of Nazism on the German people, including his own friends—although of course the Nazi censors would not allow the book to appear in Germany. It was the first act of antiracism to understand itself as such. With the appearance of the word "racism" in English, a concept began to coalesce of what racism is and how it functions. "Race war instead of class war," wrote Hirschfeld, is the "momentous watchword" of the Third Reich.[7] In other words, its race ideology was a way to weaken socialist movements among the working classes by emphasizing an imagined shared racial interest between workers and capitalists. It therefore depended, at least by implication, on a theory of what that shared racial interest was and which racial enemies threatened it. Hirschfeld thought this racial theory was a vulnerability in Nazi politics that should be attacked.

Racial theory, he wrote, was "universally derided" when first proposed but, within a few decades, won "a multitude of zealous adherents." He recalled that in school he had been taught that humanity is divided into five distinct races—black, white, yellow, red, and brown. This color-coded taxonomy, he noted, was devised earlier by the German naturalist Johann Friedrich Blumenbach in 1775, who claimed these racial types could be identified by skull measurements. The theory was flawed yet teachers were still deeming it valid a century later, Hirschfeld complained. Exposing the follies of racial theory was crucial because "paroxysms of racism" similar to Nazism were occurring in almost every country of Europe as well as the US.[8] Thus, in language at once accessible and scientific, Hirschfeld embarked on a survey of writers who advocated racial theories, from the Enlightenment to the twentieth century, and set out the flaws in their reasoning. There is no record of what Viereck's reaction was to Hirschfeld's letter and book. But he continued to be a Nazi. In 1941, he was arrested in the US and convicted of working as a Nazi secret agent. He served four years in federal prison.

Hirschfeld made a number of assumptions in his analysis—which continue to shape how most white people think about racism today. The book's starting point was Nazi anti-Semitism—which is not a color-based form of racism. Yet almost all its pages lay out his criticisms of the idea that skin color is an indicator of a natural hierarchy among human beings. He thus tied together anti-Semitism and color-based forms of racism with what he assumed to be a shared intellectual lineage—a set of false scientific claims about the division of the human species into superior and inferior races. Though these claims are false, he noted, large numbers of people nevertheless believe them. And they adhere to these false beliefs with a fervor. Rationality, he suggested, is subjugated by more visceral forces of fear and hatred. Emotional manipulation by charismatic leaders triumphs over the social cultivation of truth. Racism is a failure of public reason. These racist beliefs, in turn, lead governments to implement racist policies. Because the beliefs are irrational, so too are the policies that flow from them. They result in senseless and unnecessary violence and conflict. Because racism involves the irrational denial of other peoples' rights and freedoms, to be a racist is an individual moral failure as much as it is an intellectual failure. A racist is a bad person. And racists can be identified by their individual attitudes and biases.

Implicit in this view of racism is an idea of the normal functioning of modern, liberal societies, from which racism marks an exceptional descent into extremism. This liberal theory of racism should be familiar. In its essentials, it is the story many of us told ourselves in 2016 when Donald Trump was elected to the White House. The only difference in this case is that the failure of public reason was traced to the algorithmic flow of racist memes on Facebook rather than to the distribution of race science books a century before. If this is what racism is, then the answer to it is the defense of rationality: fact checking, myth busting, antiracist education workshops. In this view, racists and antiracists are adversaries in a battle over what people believe. This is what Hirschfeld thought too. Reason was the remedy, education the way to deliver it. Racists needed to have their rationality restored to them. That is what he hoped his *Racism* book would do for people like his Nazi friend Viereck.

Trying to dissuade someone from their racist beliefs is a worthy endeavor. Hirschfeld's mistake was to think those beliefs constituted the core of the problem of racism. As we shall see, in the last half century, in countries like the US, racism has come to exist as a societal force independently of whether the majority of people subscribe to it. But for Hirschfeld, racism was nothing but a doctrine to be believed or not believed. Moreover, he did not attempt to incorporate the question of European colonialism into his analysis of racism. He used the word "racism" to connect anti-Semitism to color-based racist ideology, but he did not see the latter as bound up with the routine political and economic violence of colonialism.

In fact, Hirschfeld was well aware of the brutality of colonial rule: he had carried out psychological examinations of troubled German perpetrators of colonial violence in Africa. These men had served under General Lothar von Trotha, whom the Kaiser appointed to suppress the anticolonial resistance of the Herero and Nama peoples in present-day Namibia, in the first decade of the twentieth century. Trotha's strategy was to use German artillery to drive the Herero into the Kalahari Desert; 80 percent of them perished. "My intimate knowledge of many central African tribes," he stated, "has everywhere convinced me of the necessity that the Negro does not respect treaties but only brute force." This was the first genocide of the twentieth century. Those Africans who survived the desert were placed in labor camps, where the German geneticist Eugene Fischer conducted "race science" experiments; his work was an influence on Hitler, and one of his prominent students was Josef Mengele, who ran the gas chambers at Auschwitz.[9] Yet none of this was part of Hirschfeld's analysis of racism. There were other ways, too, that his antiracism was limited: he supported eugenics and thought that gay liberation was good for a country's "racial hygiene" because it meant that "mentally deficient" children would be less likely to be born.[10]

Had Hirschfeld thought more structurally about German colonialism in Africa, the first systematic use of the word "racism" might have given the word a very different set of associations. He might have followed Anton de Kom in understanding racism as an unexceptional and ordinary feature of colonizing capitalism. Instead of attributing racism to extremist propaganda and calling liberal reason its remedy, he might have come to see racisms that were themselves closely bound up with the liberal forms of reason he valorized.

Cultural relativism

The first systematic analysis of "color prejudice" in the United States was produced by W. E. B. Du Bois in 1899. His *The Philadelphia Negro* was an empirical study of the lives of Black people in the city, surveying their employment, housing, education, community organizations, and social lives. He hoped further use of the "methods of sociological research" would lead to "practical reform" and thus "to realize the ideals of the republic and make this truly a land of equal opportunity for all men."[11] The book was generally ignored by academia and his plan for a larger research program never received the funding needed to carry it out.[12] In 1909, he shifted to more of a campaigning approach, helping to found the National Association for the Advancement of Colored People (NAACP). Du Bois edited its monthly journal *The Crisis* and proclaimed in its introductory editorial that the journal intended to set forth "those facts and arguments which show the danger of race prejudice." What he called "the Negro problem" could be solved, Du Bois thought, by scientific knowledge.[13] "The world was thinking wrong about race because it did not know," he reflected. "The ultimate evil was stupidity. The cure for it was knowledge based on scientific investigation."[14]

Only with the rise of Nazism in Germany and the onset of World War II did liberal funders in the US begin to share the enthusiasm for research-driven advocacy that Du Bois had felt. Then, liberals in the US began to use the term "racism"—which appeared with the publication of Hirschfeld's book in 1938—to name the intellectual disease that scientists could cure. In 1939, for example, the word appeared in the program of the World's Fair in Queens, New York, where hundreds of people attended lectures on "How Scientists Can Help Combat Racism."[15] Among the lecturers was the anthropologist Franz Boas, whose work was pivotal to the development of antiracism among liberals in the US. Through events like the World's Fair, and later with more systematic methods of mass communication, Boas and his colleagues introduced to the public a new way of thinking about race and culture.

Prior to 1900, the word "culture" in both English- and German-speaking contexts did not have the main meaning it has today, of a distinct set of traditions and norms that define a particular group. Rather, "culture" referred to art, science, knowledge, and refinement, and these were understood to spring from a human capacity to distance oneself from the natural world of animal instincts and biological needs. In this sense, it was meaningless to talk about cultures; there was only "culture" in the singular, present in all persons to a higher or lesser degree. For many, "culture" in this sense was the organizing term in a racial evolutionary scale of civilization, with whites at the summit and Blacks at the bottom. In this scheme, the white races had advanced further, freeing themselves from bodily passions through a rational ordering of society. Therefore, colonial governments could legitimately impose these techniques of civilization on less developed races.[16]

But how could one explain the assumed racial differences in cultural attainment? For some, the explanation for the claimed superiority of white civilization was straightforwardly physiological. In his 1850 book *The Races of Men*, the English anatomist Robert Knox held that race was a physical difference in the body that determined behavior, character, and mental capacity. "Race is everything: literature, science, art—in a word, civilization, depends on it," he wrote.[17] Others took a different but no less racist view: they supposed racial differences to have their origins in history, not the body. Rather than try to explain patterns of history in terms of race, they tried to explain patterns of race in terms of history. The popular English social theorist Herbert Spencer, for instance, wrote in his 1851 book *Social Statics* that races behave differently not because of unchanging biological differences, but because of different patterns of adaptation to the circumstances they find themselves in. What he considered the more advanced races had had the good fortune of encountering social and natural environments that provided more opportunities for adaptation to a higher form of life. Once established, these adaptations became hereditary through habit and formed into a kind of racial instinct. Races were like organisms, adapting to their environment, each generation passing on its acquired habits to the next; culture was what the higher of these competing organisms gradually acquired, while the lesser were by nature eliminated. The "perfect economy of Nature," Spencer wrote, arranged for superior races to serve "civilization by clearing the earth of inferior races of men." The theory provided an origin story for white domination and, through the idea of racial competition, made genocide seem natural. "Civilization" apparently did not condemn mass racist violence but demanded it.[18]

Writing in the early twentieth century, Boas rejected the idea of a single evolutionary scale of civilization and began for the first time to write about cultures in the plural.[19] He gave the word "culture" a new meaning—as the specific traditions, customs, habits, and norms that shape a group's behavior, acquired "less by instruction than imitation."[20] There was no single principle that could explain why one culture differed from another, he claimed. And it was "impossible for us to appreciate [another group's] values without having grown up under their influence," he wrote. Likewise, "the value which we attribute to our own civilization" was "due to the fact that we participate in this civilization, and that it has been controlling all our actions since the time of our birth."[21] Each culture was its own whole way of life and could only be understood and evaluated on its own terms, not seen as a stage in a grand evolutionary journey. This implied that the forms of life Europeans had referred to as "primitive" were in their own way as sophisticated as the cultures of Europe. Just as each individual held equal value, even as their personalities and capacities differed, so too did each culture.

This cultural relativism offered a new way to think about human variation. It differed radically from how nineteenth-century intellectuals in Europe and the US had thought about the matter. For them, differences in norms and behaviors across humanity were explained by race, which referred to physiological differences or traits originally produced through environmental factors. Race explained culture or the lack of it. Boas instead argued differences in norms and behaviors across humanity could be explained in terms of the plurality of cultures, which he maintained had a reality independent of race. The older view was either that the varying nature of bodies from one race to the next explained the varying nature of societies, or that the different circumstances in which societies developed explained the different racial characteristics of bodies. But Boas's thinking pointed toward a separation between bodies and societies, and between race and culture. Race, now detached from culture, referred to inherited physical variations such as skin color that were largely irrelevant to explaining social and cultural phenomena. On the older view, race did not necessarily correspond to color; Knox, for example, wrote about Celts and Saxons as distinct races despite their having the same skin colors. On the new view, race became much more about visible physical differences. Before, the idea of culture as refinement suggested that to be cultured was to possess a kind of freedom from the weight of inherited tradition. The new idea of culture was the opposite: it proposed that traditions, habits, and norms determined behavior. This cultural determinism meant that culture, in this new sense, could substitute for the older idea of race and claim to explain all the same phenomena, but without having to refer to biological ideas about inherited racial characteristics.

Tolerance education

As World War II began in Europe, liberals in the US believed these new ideas about race and culture had a role to play in the ideological war against Nazism.[22] If scientists like Boas had determined that race was irrelevant to explaining anything important in human affairs, if there was no validity to the Nazi claim that race was the most important predictor of human character, then Hitler's entire political ideology could be discredited. With this in mind, Boas and his supporters set out to educate the US public in their new ideas so that Nazi-like arguments would be less persuasive. The anthropologist Ruth Benedict—Boas's most well-known and influential collaborator took up the charge. She decided to write a book of popular science that she hoped would serve as a "handbook" for "tolerance education" in schools, churches, and clubs throughout the United States.[23] Published in 1940 with the title *Race: Science and Politics*, the book stressed the principle of cultural relativism as a way of countering the racist idea of an evolutionary hierarchy of cultures, from primitive to civilized. Achievements in art and invention were evenly distributed across cultures, Benedict argued. She defined racism as "the dogma that one ethnic group is condemned by nature to congenital inferiority and another group is destined to congenital superiority."

Ruth Benedict
Archives and Special Collections, Vassar College Library

European colonialism, she wrote, which involved the enslavement of Africans and the elimination of Indigenous people, "set the stage" for the emergence of modern doctrines of racism at the beginning of the nineteenth century.[24]

Significantly, the book linked three issues that, before then, would have typically been seen as distinct from one another: the treatment of Jews in Europe, the treatment of Black descendants of slaves in the US, and the treatment of the colonized under European rule in Africa, Asia, the Americas, and the Caribbean.[25] Benedict's book introduced the term "racism" to the US public as, above all, a way to connect these three issues and analyze each in terms of the others. This is what the word "racism" added to the existing vocabulary of "white supremacy," "anti-Semitism," and "colonialism." Joining these issues together made sense, Benedict thought, because of the similar arguments with which their respective doctrines claimed to legitimize oppression. The word "racism" referred precisely to the commonality in those doctrines: an irrational belief in the superiority of one race over another.[26]

Three years after the publication of Benedict's *Race: Science and Politics*, the Public Affairs Committee, a nonprofit organization in New York, funded a more accessible version. This thirty-one-page, illustrated pamphlet, costing only ten cents, was "designed to fit a serviceman's pocket and to fight Nazi racial doctrine," according to *Time* magazine. The War Department ordered 50,000 copies of the pamphlet to help "counteract the Nazi theory of a super-race," but stipulated that they would only be distributed to officers. By the end of the war, the pamphlet had sold three-quarters of a million copies. In 1946, the United Auto Workers created an animated film based on the pamphlet.[27]

What motivated these initiatives of the 1940s was the sense that racism threatened liberal government and could, as had happened in Germany, completely overwhelm it. This fear led normally cloistered biologists, anthropologists, and social psychologists to become the public faces of a new antiracism, mobilizing the authority of their academic credentials to counter the scientific pretensions of racism. Dogma was the problem, and antiracist expertise the solution.[28] At the same time, antiracism could be presented as one of the values for which the US was waging war against Nazi Germany. The US began to officially describe itself as an antiracist, diversity-celebrating nation, a conception popularized in films like *The House I Live In*, released in 1945, in which Frank Sinatra sang, "all races and religions, that's America to me."[29] There was, of course, the problem that the US, while claiming to be defending democracy from Nazi racism, was itself a racist society. This issue only intensified after the end of World War II as the US emerged as the dominant world power and found that its ability to claim an international leadership role depended on asserting an official form of liberal antiracism that was inconsistent with the realities of US apartheid.

WHAT IS ANTIRACISM?

Gunnar Myrdal's book *An American Dilemma*, published in 1944, provided the blueprint for how the new, liberal antiracists in the US would try to solve this issue in the decades after the war. Myrdal, a Swedish economist, was lavishly funded by the Carnegie Corporation to conduct "a comprehensive study of the Negro in the United States." With a level of research resources that Du Bois had always been denied, Myrdal was able, in effect, to scale up the empirical work of *The Philadelphia Negro* published decades earlier; to do so, he recruited many of the Black social scientists whom Du Bois had trained.[30] In his framing of the research, Myrdal accepted the liberal premise that racism is fundamentally a matter of misguided beliefs and values in the minds of individual white Americans. "There the decisive struggle goes on. It is there that the changes occur," he wrote. He distinguished between what he called the general "American creed" of equal rights and the specific beliefs of white supremacism. The inconsistency between the two, he argued, had in recent decades been sharpened as science, thanks to Boas and his colleagues, had refuted the racist theories behind prejudice and discrimination. This gave rise to a moral dilemma for white Americans, as the beliefs and values by which they lived could no longer maintain coherence. "The white man is thus in the process of losing confidence in the theory which gave reason and meaning to his way of life. And since he has not changed his life much, he is in a dilemma." Whereas Benedict suggested there were doctrinal similarities between white supremacy in the US and European imperialism, Myrdal disconnected racial prejudice in the US from the global color line that imperialism had produced. "World politics and the color issue are, in the final analysis, of secondary importance to American Negroes," he wrote. "The American Negro is thoroughly Americanized; his complaint is merely that he is not accepted."[31]

Fortunately, by fully embracing equality, the "upper class of white people" had made good progress in resolving this dilemma, argued Myrdal. The "racialist" theory was "almost destroyed for upper class and educated people." On the other hand, the poor and the uneducated, especially in the South, still subscribed to dogmas of racial superiority. Among them, a mixture of emotional impulses and prejudices had won out over reason. The strength of prejudice seemed "everywhere to stand in a close inverse relation to the individual white's level of education." Over time, though, education would eradicate prejudices among the lower classes too: "There is a considerable time-lag between what is thought in the higher and in the lower social classes. But as time passes the lower social strata also will change their beliefs. These ideas are spread by the advance of education."[32]

Myrdal thus believed there was every reason to be optimistic that the egalitarian values of the American Creed would progressively triumph over racism. Yes, white people did not want to be made uncomfortable by having their racial prejudices pointed out to them: Myrdal referred to the "sense of uneasiness and awkwardness" that arises when the subject of race comes up and the "mental strain" they feel when they encounter a threat to their moral integrity—what the educator Robin DiAngelo has more recently described as "white fragility." Nevertheless, progress was possible if upper-class, liberal antiracists organized themselves effectively. The US government ought to lead a process of liberal reform, supported by institutions like schools, universities, and churches. This would begin with detailed studies to observe and record racist beliefs "in a systematic way" so that levels of prejudice could be measured in different regions and classes. These studies could then be benchmarks for an organized campaign in which "a constant pressure is brought to bear on race prejudice" by pointing to the inconsistency between racial prejudice and American norms—a process of "social self-healing."[33] For white America, Myrdal added, the moral dilemma it faced was also an opportunity. If it could heroically achieve its moral conversion and self-healing, by assenting to the equality of African Americans, it would be able to demonstrate to the world the superiority of its values.[34] As it was "America's turn" to "take world leadership," its "prestige and power abroad would rise immensely," especially among the nonwhite majority of the world population. "America would have a spiritual power many times stronger than all her financial and military resources."[35]

This was the liberal antiracism that became dominant among progressive whites in the US. Its elements were: a focus on individual racial attitudes, feelings, and beliefs, to the exclusion of social and economic structures; a narrowing of the question of racism to the white-Black relationship; a faith in education and other forms of public rationality as remedies to racism; a belief that economic hardship makes racist prejudice more likely; an assumption that moral progress is guaranteed by the excellence of the US's core values; a claim that US liberalism offers a universal ethos for the world; a separation of domestic antiracism from international struggles against racism, colonialism, and imperialism; and, above all, a view of liberal government institutions and ruling elites as leading the way in antiracist progress.

While this liberal antiracism was forming in Europe and the United States, a radically different way of thinking about racism was taking shape in the places that Europe had colonized.

3

Imperialism and the Uses of Diversity

While my Dutch grandfather was imprisoned at the Vught concentration camp, my Indian father was growing up in the province of Sindh in northwestern colonial India. Sindh had been colonized by the British from 1843, following a military operation led by Sir Charles Napier. His method was to deliberately provoke local rulers until they resisted his demands, and then use their resistance as a pretext to conquer the territory for the British Empire and imprison the former rulers. Sindh was valuable to the British for two reasons: it could serve as a frontier to block incursions into British-controlled India from central Asia (the empire feared Russia's designs on the region); and its port of Karachi and the river Indus made it commercially valuable. During the conquest, Napier's artillery took four hours to massacre 6,000 local fighters; a month later, another 5,000 suffered the same fate.[1]

In the British Parliament, MP John Arthur Roebuck described the subjection of Sindh "to the dominion of England" as "a series of inconceivably brilliant actions, displaying at once the bravery of our troops and the consummate skill of their commander."[2] The East India Company—the corporation that drove British colonization of India and, through the might of its private army, the de facto ruler of the country—increased its already vast profits as a result of the conquest. This was in large part because Napier ended the traffic in "Malwa opium" that passed through Karachi on its way from inland cultivators to China, and which was the only competitor to the company's own exports of opium. The company's opium came from the eastern Indian province of Bengal, where the corporation had previously enforced the exclusive right to control production and sale of the drug.³ The opium exports to China brought addiction to unprecedented levels but also solved a balance of payments problem for Britain, which, opium apart, imported far more from China than it was able to sell. When the Chinese emperor banned the company's opium trade, the British responded with gunboats to secure the essential traffic. For his military occupation of Sindh, the company rewarded Napier with a payment of £70,000, close to a million dollars in today's money. "We have no right to seize Sind, yet we shall do so and a very advantageous piece of rascality it will be," wrote Napier before the campaign.⁴

According to British colonial legend, after the capture of Sindh, Napier sent a message to his superior that consisted of a

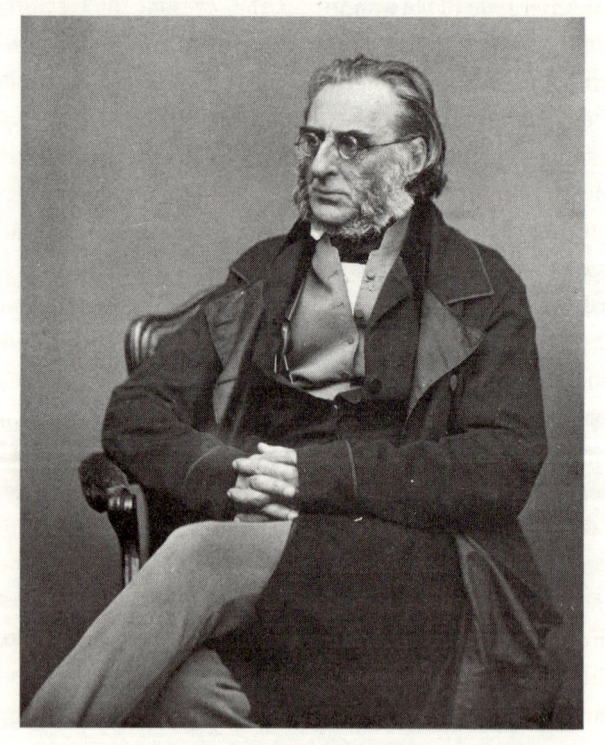

Charles Napier, 1849
William Edward Kilburn, Royal Collection Trust

single word in Latin, *peccavi*, which means, "I have sinned." A colonizer's pun, delivered in a language the English upper classes had been schooled in, suggested that, wrapped in the confirmation of a successful conquest ("I have Sindh"), there lay a confession of guilt. But Napier did not dispatch any such message. It was a story invented afterward by the journal *Punch*. And Napier's conscience did not keep him up at night; he wrote of the Sindh campaign: "I may be wrong, but I cannot see it, and my conscience will not be troubled. I sleep well while trying to do this, and shall sleep sound when it is done."[5]

In a book about the conquest of Sindh, Napier's brother William wrote that colonialism was justified on the grounds that the British were "more civilized, more knowing in science and arts, more energetic of spirit, more strong of body, more warlike, more enterprising" than the Sindhis, and "must necessarily extend their power until checked by natural barriers, or by a counter-civilisation."[6] Charles Napier himself legitimized his role in imperialism in the language of liberal progress, especially the liberation of women. He claimed his goal was the freedom of the "slave-girls of the harems" and the abolition of sati—the practice, largely obsolete at the time, of widow immolation. When a priest complained that sati was a custom of the Hindu minority in Sindh that ought to be respected, Napier reportedly replied: "Be it so. This burning of widows is your custom; prepare the funeral pile. But my nation has also a custom. When men burn women alive we hang them, and confiscate all their property. My carpenters shall therefore erect gibbets on which to hang all concerned when the widow is consumed. Let us all act according to national customs."[7] He sardonically granted the priest his claim to his own cultural identity only to then override that identity with an imagined version of his own, backed by the authority of a greater capacity for violence and an assumed universality.

The appropriate response to Napier is not to defend the rights of Hinduism—that would mean reinforcing gender and caste oppression, and ultimately lead to the Hindu-fascist politics of

India's current government, under Narendra Modi. No doubt the women of Sindh were subject to a system of oppression, of which sati was perhaps the most violent, if rare, expression. But the unpunished murder of women by English men was, and is, also all too common. The circumstances of Sindhi women were not improved by their being colonized, just as Afghan women were not liberated by US military occupation after US political leaders made arguments similar to Napier's in 2001.[8] In both cases, imperialists justified their actions with the false argument that the native culture was so static and intractable that the emancipation of women could only occur through armed domination by the ostensibly liberal West. Today, a statue of Charles Napier stands at one corner of Trafalgar Square in London; it has not attracted the youthful protests that have elsewhere in England toppled the likenesses of slave traders.

When he was barely a teenager, my father became involved in the political movements of the mid-1940s to end British rule. Leaders of the underground resistance were his inspiration, especially the socialists Jayaprakash Narayan, Ram Manohar Lohia, and Hemu Kalani, who hailed from my father's hometown and was hanged by the British at the age of nineteen after he was caught sabotaging railroad tracks that a British troop train was set to pass over. Younger teenagers took on the task of clandestinely distributing anticolonial newspapers that the British had censored. Sindhis were no strangers to radical politics: their national poet, Shah Abdul Latif, sang tributes to Shah Inayat, the leader of a seventeenth-century guerrilla campaign that, aiming to redistribute land to propertyless peasants, was socialist in all but name.[9]

At stake in the Indian freedom struggle was control over India's wealth and resources. From 1400 to 1700, and perhaps later, China and India were the two richest countries in the world and dominated the global economy on the strength of their higher manufacturing productivity.[10] Through this period, Sindh had been known for its weavers and dyers, and exported high-quality cloth to Arabian and Portuguese traders.[11] In the early eighteenth century, Bengal's textile industry employed a million workers and was the leading supplier to the world market. Domination of textiles meant domination of the world economy—cotton was the most important manufacturing industry in the world between 1000 and 1900.[12] The problem for Europeans was they had no products that could compete in Asia. Their opening came, though, as a result of the genocidal colonization of the Americas and the transatlantic trade in Africans. Europeans accumulated an unprecedented amount of wealth from the trade, from the production of sugar and tobacco on slave plantations in Brazil, the Caribbean, and the North American colonies, and from the gold and silver extracted after invaders captured South and Central American land from Indigenous peoples.[13] This wealth enabled Europeans to place themselves into the Asian trading system and eventually to use military means to assert political control over much of Asia.

In India, this process began in 1757, when the East India Company used its private army to occupy Bengal. Within a few years, it had obtained the sovereign right of tax collection and a monopoly on trade. Company rule expanded by force across India over the following decades. Peasants found they could only pay their taxes by selling their produce—such as rice, indigo, jute, raw cotton, and grain—to the company for export. Since Indians in effect paid for the company's purchase costs with their taxes, the company was able to obtain India's produce for free.[14] This form of plunder was accompanied by deindustrialization. Contrary to the myth that colonialism brought modernity to a preindustrial society, Britain's Industrial Revolution depended on India's industrial decline. Existing Indian industries, such as textiles and metalworking, had to be destroyed to create export markets for Lancashire cotton and Sheffield steel.[15] In the nineteenth century, the Indian textile industry was effectively replaced by force with a new system that involved the cultivation of raw cotton on slave plantations in the Caribbean and the US, its shipment to factories in the north of England to be manufactured into cloth, and then its sale around the world, especially in India.[16] English colonialism "inundated the very mother country of cotton with cottons," wrote Karl Marx.[17] And the "veiled slavery of the wage labourers in Europe needed the unqualified slavery of the New World as its pedestal."[18] A new set of international economic linkages thus tied Mississippi to Manchester to Madras in a circuit of enslavement, exploitation, and expropriation.

British rule, draped in liberal doctrines of "free trade," introduced new private property rules for land ownership and a system of courts to enforce it; at the same time, it subjected agriculture to competition with world markets. The traditional elites of Indian society became landowners and money lenders whose only incentive was to maximize rent and interest. Neither they nor the colonial administrators allied with them had much interest in investing in the development of agricultural production by, for example, constructing systems of irrigation. As such, food production stagnated while cash crops like opium and tea were cultivated solely for export. Even where harvests were abundant, starvation resulted because colonialism had displaced earlier practices of subsistence farming in favor of exporting grain to England, which profited landowners and merchants but left the masses vulnerable to international price fluctuations.[19] In all these ways, colonialism fostered an uneven and unbalanced capitalism in which the potential for development was distorted to meet the needs of Britain's growth. The extraction of raw materials and foodstuffs supported the industrialization and enriching of Britain while Indigenous growth was quashed.[20]

Define and rule

The organized destruction of India inevitably sparked opposition. Resistance grew, culminating in 1857 with a mass uprising in northern India against the rule of the East India Company.

What began as a revolt among Indian recruits to the company's army ended up with wide swathes of the civilian population joining the insurrection, from peasants to princes, bridging their religious differences. The insurrectionists slew hundreds of British officers and civilians. The immediate British response in India was a public display of violent retaliation, in the hope of restoring the "spell of inviolability" of colonial power. The British shot and hanged thousands of Indians, or blasted them from the mouths of cannons—the latter method of killing intended to fragment bodies into so many pieces that funeral rites could not be performed.[21]

Thereafter, the British government removed the East India Company from its role in administering India and took direct control. Official London, thrown into shock by the insurrection, launched a "what went wrong" discourse of the sort that empires engage in when confronted with uprisings. The conclusion was that the problem lay in the character of the "native mind"—local customs and traditions, in short, "culture." The idea of ranking civilizations in a racial and cultural hierarchy had long been a rationale for colonialism. Herbert Spencer, for example, had published his version of this idea a few years before the 1857 uprising. But the question for colonial administrators was whether, through suitable tutelage, Indians could gradually be raised up the civilizational scale toward the level of Europeans. The 1857 uprising was interpreted as a signal that this was impossible. The attempt to export liberal values, especially that of free trade, from Britain to India had apparently foundered on the rocks of intractable cultural differences: the native was irredeemably irrational. Reflecting elite opinion, Queen Victoria wrote to Lady Canning, wife of the governor-general of India, that Indians were "a fanatical people" and "the greatest care ought to be taken not to interfere" with their traditions.[22] Cultural reform was too difficult. To effectively rule India, British officials argued, the empire would have to ease off on its civilizing mission. The assumption that liberal government would be universally accepted was abandoned and replaced with a new method of governing through the careful investigation, preservation, and manipulation of cultural differences—what came to be known as "indirect rule."[23]

The new method employed what we would today call the recognition of "diversity." The colonial government divided the population into a series of cultural groups, defined by caste (such as brahmin, outcaste, or aborigine) and religious affiliation (Hindu, Muslim, Sikh, Christian, and so on). It then assigned each group its own intermediaries to act as community representatives and gave each group a set of "customary laws" to observe, reflecting assumed traditional rules on marriage, divorce, inheritance, adoption, civil disputes, and so on. British colonial rulers dealt with Hindus and Muslims according to separate "personal codes" for each sect. All of this was intended to stabilize the colonial structure so that it could continue to perform its economic functions for Britain. An 1858 proclamation by Queen Victoria announced that Britain would "disclaim alike the Right and the Desire to impose our Convictions on any of Our Subjects."[24] And this was true in a way: the colonial government did not wish to erase native cultures; instead it sought to mobilize them to its own ends. It defined what India's cultural traditions were, set the boundaries of when they applied, and decided who could authentically represent them. As the political scientist Mahmood Mamdani puts it, it was not so much divide and rule as "define and rule." The same approach would be used in new ways during the War on Terror, when Western powers would mobilize an idea of moderate Islam with its own officially sanctioned representatives.[25]

For the new method of ruling India to work, the colonial administration had to create an expanded bureaucracy tasked with managing and monitoring the peoples belonging to each officially recognized cultural group. For this reason, carrying out a regular census became essential to governing India. By 1881, colonial administrators were collecting the names of every person in India, along with their age, occupation, caste, religion, literacy, place of birth, and current residence. Amassing this information required half a million people to be engaged as census workers. Manuals guided them in the standardized recording of caste and subcaste identity with entries like "Sutihar, Bihar—a low caste who spin cotton thread." The census not only counted how many people were affiliated to various social categories; it also hardened and objectified those categories, intensifying their political salience.[26] This was one of the ways in which indirect rule reshaped how Indians saw themselves. Eventually, caste and religious identification became the basis of quotas governing people's access to educational institutions, government jobs, and electoral representation.[27] A middle class of salaried Indian bureaucrats came into being and grew steadily as the colonial state expanded. The colonial administration no longer proclaimed the imposition of a "universal" European culture. Instead, native cultures were superficially respected through a complex and shifting regime of diversity management. Colonialism, it turned out, did not only work through the rhetoric of European cultural superiority; it could also, if pushed, work through the rhetoric of cultural relativism and respect for non-European cultures.[28]

The colonial plunder continued through indirect rule. The East India Company monopoly ended, but a new trading and taxation system established by the British government ensured that up to a third of the total tax and other revenues raised in India were set aside for Britain to spend on its own account instead of being spent in the country in the normal way. Much of this capital was then invested in the industrialization of Europe and the white settler states of North America and Australasia.[29] The growth in the wealth of the US, culminating in its becoming the richest nation in the world by the end of the nineteenth century, depended on British imperialism in two ways. First, the vast wealth amassed from the US cotton plantations derived from their integration with an international trading system controlled by Britain. Cotton picked by slaves in the US South was manufactured into cloth in the textile mills of northern England and then sold across the British Empire; the whole system depended on colonial violence to suppress non-Western manufacturing while monopolizing non-Western markets. Second, a good deal of the capital generated from British imperialism was re-invested in the development of manufacturing industries in the US. When the Empire's poet Rudyard Kipling called on the US in 1899 to take up the "white man's burden," he was asking the ruling class of the US to not only be beneficiaries of imperialism but to share in the responsibility of directly ruling over the "half devil and half child" peoples of Asia, Africa, and the Caribbean. The US was already part of the globally integrated economic system of imperialism; the question was whether it would take on an explicit role in its governance outside of the North American territories it had colonized in the nineteenth century.

At the end of the nineteenth century, the Indian nationalist Dadabhai Naoroji studied the economic data that Britain had itself collected on India's economy and demonstrated that colonialism functioned economically as a "wealth drain," robbing India of its resources to enrich Britain. "What then must be or can be the effect of the unceasing drain which has now grown to the enormous amount of some £30,000,000 a year?" he asked (£30 million amounts to around $4 billion in today's money). His answer: "Famines and plagues, destruction and impoverishment!"[30] The capitalist development of England, made possible by colonialism, meant famines were a rare occurrence in England, while in India their frequency and intensity increased.

Over 10 million Indians died in the last quarter of the nineteenth century as a result of famines induced by the British colonial government. Amid the devastating famines of the 1870s, the British official responsible for famine relief, Sir Richard Temple, set up a system requiring starving Indians to walk to camps at least ten miles away, where they were conscripted as coolie labor on railroad and canal projects in exchange for food.

The writer Mike Davis points out that the amount of food provided, known as the "Temple wage," constituted less sustenance than the diet inside the Buchenwald concentration camp. This paltry ration, along with the heavy physical labor and poor sanitation, "turned the work camps into extermination camps." For Temple, those who perished were undeserving of rescue. "Nor will many be inclined to grieve much for the fate which they brought upon themselves," he wrote, "and which terminated lives of idleness and too often of crime."[31]

Seventy years later, famine struck in Bengal. A colonial government inquiry estimated it to have led to the deaths of one and a half million people.[32] Most experts think that double that number died of starvation in 1943 and 1944. The immediate cause was British prime minister Winston Churchill's policy of plundering India's resources during World War II.[33] Real incomes among India's poor declined as a result of deliberately engineered price inflation in India, designed to assist Britain in financing its war budget.[34] Throughout the famine, the British exported food from India. Churchill's policy was informed by his belief that progress demanded the elimination of inferior races. Herbert Spencer had written that the forces of civilization "exterminate such sections of mankind as stand in their way."[35] Churchill shared this view. "I do not admit," he said, "that a great wrong has been done to the Red Indians of America or the black people of Australia," when a "stronger race, a higher-grade race, a more worldly wise race to put it that way, has come in and taken their place."[36] He described the people of India as a "foul race" protected "from the doom that is their due" by their "pullulation"—that is, their rapid breeding. Today, a widely accepted mythology holds Churchill to be the greatest of Englishmen, in large part because he is credited with the defeat of Nazism. Yet even his own cabinet colleague, secretary of state for India Leopold S. Amery, observed to Churchill that he did not "see much difference between his outlook and Hitler's."[37] At the same time, Churchill's racism expressed in a more concentrated form the imperatives that structured British imperialism. As the writer George Orwell asked on the eve of World War II: "What meaning would there be, even if it were successful, in bringing down Hitler's system in order to stabilize something that is far bigger and in its different way just as bad?" He was referring to the British Empire. "It is not in Hitler's power," he wrote, "to make a penny an hour a normal industrial wage; it is perfectly normal in India, and we are at great pains to keep it so."[38]

In 1947, two dynamics finally converged in the ambiguous creation of India and Pakistan as independent nations: the mass mobilization of the anticolonial freedom movement made continuing British rule impossible; at the same time, the decades of pursuing define-and-rule policies culminated in a partition along religious lines, creating two separate nations: one, India, with a Hindu majority, the other, Pakistan, with a Muslim majority. Sindh became part of Pakistan. My father was one of the 12 million people made refugees by the partition; a million died in the violence that resulted from the religious bordering of the subcontinent. Around 75,000 women are thought to have been abducted and raped in the great convulsion that partition gave rise to.[39] The wealth that Britain had drained from India by this time, according to economist Utsa Patnaik, amounts in today's money to at least £9 trillion.[40]

Such was European colonialism: a vast system of legalized pillaging, enshrined by racism, and upheld by cannon and cavalry. India was the largest colonial territory of the largest European empire, but the pattern implemented there was common to the other places Europe occupied. The economic, political, and cultural structures that the European colonial system produced defined the geography of the modern world, generating, on one side, ever greater levels of wealth and industry and, on the other, mass hunger and rule by spectacular violence. But from colonialism's subjugated peoples also came revolutionary ideas and organization. Among those ideas were new ways of thinking about how to overthrow the colonial structures that imbricated economic exploitation with racist oppression. This was the question that preoccupied Anton de Kom, as well as a multitude of other anticolonial activists from the Caribbean to East Asia. And it is from answers to this question that a different conception of racism derives—that of racism as a structural phenomenon. To understand how this happened, we first need to understand the Marxist debate on racism and colonialism that these writers were in part responding to.

4

Marxists Confront Colonialism

The strength of Marxism was that it did not idealistically claim social conditions could be transformed by any people at any time simply through wishing it so; it proposed a theory to predict when such transformations were likely to succeed. But the version of that theory taken up in the formative years of the European Marxist tradition, influenced above all by the 1848 *Communist Manifesto*, was Eurocentric. It held that successful socialist movements could occur only where capitalism had given rise to industrial workforces concentrated together in modern towns and cities, made ready to act as a self-conscious political force by the organization of modern industry itself. The possibility of socialism therefore depended on industrialization to produce a modern, industrial working class that was able to lead a revolution. Capitalism produced "its own grave-diggers," as Karl Marx and Frederick Engels put it in the *Manifesto*.[1]

For the colonized world, where the mass of the population was not an industrial workforce but a peasantry, two possibilities flowed from this assumption. Either European colonialism was introducing to Asia, Africa, and the Caribbean the industrialization necessary to make socialism possible, in which case it was a progressive force to be supported by socialists; or colonialism blocked the development of industry and so the colonized would not be able to reach the level of modernity necessary for them to self-consciously transform their lives—they would have to wait for European workers to make a socialist revolution on their behalf. In either case, colonized peasants were fated to be carried along by European historical tides rather than navigate their own destiny.

Marx himself did not always remain consistent with this Marxist position. His later writing, especially, accords to colonized workers the possibility of their pursuing their own paths to emancipation.[2] The 1857 uprising in India may have prompted Marx to focus more seriously on revolutionary upsurges from colonized peoples.[3] Earlier in his political writing, he did on occasion refer to anticolonial agitation, but presented it as a distant possibility alongside the progressive influence of colonialism. "The Indians will not reap the fruits of the new elements of society scattered among them by the British bourgeoisie," he wrote in 1853, "till in Great Britain itself the now ruling classes shall have been supplanted by the industrial proletariat, or till the Hindoos themselves shall have grown strong enough to throw off the English yoke altogether."[4]

In any case, by the beginning of the twentieth century, simmering disagreements among European Marxists on how class struggle related to colonialism were coming to a head. And, at the same time, revolutionaries from the colonized regions were beginning to confront the white Left in Europe. At the Second International congress of socialists held in Stuttgart, Germany, in 1907, for example, Bhikaji Cama spoke of the catastrophic famines British colonialism spawned in India. Cama was an Indian socialist who had worked with Dadabhai Naoroji in London but had grown dissatisfied with the reformist approach of Indian nationalist leaders like him and now favored an armed struggle against British colonialism. In Stuttgart, she unfurled for the first time the "flag of Indian independence," one of the templates from which India's national flag was later created, and called for the congress to support a resolution to "assist in freeing one-fifth of the world's population." The congress audience, made up mainly of representatives of European socialist and labor parties, enthusiastically cheered her speech. But when it came to voting on her Indian independence resolution, organizers found a technicality to avoid a vote after the delegation from Britain made it clear they opposed independence for India.[5]

Another resolution was proposed that condemned colonialism on principle, but this was voted down by most of the European contingent, who constituted the entirety of the congress's committee on colonialism; their reasoning was that "under a socialist régime, colonization can be a work of civilization." Leading German social democrat Eduard Bernstein supported the procolonialist position, declaring that "a certain tutelage of the civilized peoples over the uncivilized peoples is a necessity"; Karl Kautsky, another prominent German social democrat, opposed on the grounds that colonialism meant having to adopt a "theory according to which there are two groups of people, one which is destined to dominate and the other to be dominated." The Dutch social democrat Hendrik van Kol, speaking for the congress's committee on colonialism, responded with a racist speech that apparently delighted much of the audience:

> If we send a machine to the Negroes of central Africa, do you know what they will do? Very probably they will execute a war dance around our European product (*hilarity*) and it is also probable that the number of their innumerable gods will be increased by one (*further hilarity*) . . . It could even be possible that they skin us alive or else that they eat us and then . . . (*rubbing his stomach*) I strongly fear, as my corporal development somewhat exceeds that of Kautsky, that I would be given the preference by my Negro friends. (*Hilarity.*) If we Europeans went to Africa with our European machines, we would be the victims of our expedition. We must, on the contrary, have arms in our hand in order eventually to defend ourselves, even if Kautsky calls this imperialism. (*"Very good" from some of the benches.*)

When the issue was put to a vote of the congress's 886 delegates, they rejected the pro-colonialist position and resolved instead that "the civilising mission claimed by capitalist society is only used as a pretext to cover its thirst for exploitation and conquest."

But the vote was close. A resolution opposing any restrictions on the free movement of workers from one country to another passed more easily.[6]

From pre-revolutionary Russia, Vladimir Lenin attended the Stuttgart congress. He was disturbed by the way that the pro-colonialist faction was able to exploit the "chauvinism" of European workers. Upon his return, he developed his argument. He wrote that

> as a result of the extensive colonial policy, the European proletarian *partly* finds himself in a position when it is *not* his labour, but the labour of the practically enslaved natives in the colonies, that maintains the whole of society. The British bourgeoisie, for example, derives more profit from the many millions of the population of India and other colonies than from the British workers. In certain countries this provides the material and economic basis for infecting the proletariat with colonial chauvinism. Of course, this may be only a temporary phenomenon, but the evil must nonetheless be clearly realised and its causes understood in order to be able to rally the proletariat of all countries for the struggle against such opportunism.[7]

What Lenin had identified was a deep problem for any socialist movement trying to organize in imperialist countries: the ruling class could win over white workers to a conservative politics, not just through ideological appeals to nationalism or racism but by grounding those appeals in material privileges paid for by the greater exploitation of workers of color in the colonies.

But the problem ran deeper than Lenin allowed. If Indians were effectively the largest section of "British" labor, were they not better placed to lead a socialist transformation than the workers of Britain itself? In which case, ought not socialists concentrate their efforts on organizing the people of the colonized world? In his *Imperialism: The Highest Stage of Capitalism*, written in 1916, Lenin tried to develop the theoretical basis for an answer. "Imperialism," he wrote, "is capitalism at that stage of development at which the dominance of monopolies and finance capital is established; in which the export of capital has acquired pronounced importance; in which the division of the world among the international trusts has begun, in which the division of all territories of the globe among the biggest capitalist powers has been completed." Imperialism becomes a stabilizing force for capitalism in the short term because, argued Lenin, the "superprofits" it generates make "it economically possible for [capitalists] to bribe certain sections of the workers, and for a time a fairly considerable minority of them, and win them to the side of the bourgeoisie of a given industry or given nation against all the others."[8] Du Bois made a similar argument in his 1915 essay "The African Roots of War," pointing out that European nations saw imperialist exploitation in Africa as a way to reduce class conflict at home: "the white workingman has been asked to share the spoil of exploiting 'chinks and niggers.'"[9]

Fearing the tsar's censors, Lenin did not include in his published text the political implications of his analysis. But after the October Revolution of 1917, which brought the Bolsheviks to power in Russia, Lenin's analysis of colonialism became central to Soviet policy-making. Lenin held that since colonialism took the form of national oppression, the struggle against it was bound to take on a nationalist form as well. But nationalist struggles against colonialism typically aimed at no more than the creation of an independent nation-state, and civil and political rights for its citizens, not at building socialist societies. Despite its lack of a socialist agenda, Lenin argued, anticolonial nationalism nevertheless had some justification, because any attack on imperialism weakened capitalism. Anticolonial nationalisms ought therefore to be temporarily supported by socialists as a necessary intermediary stage; at the same time, socialists should help the growth of independent workers' movements among the colonized.

Lenin applied this argument not only to European imperialism but also to the issues of white supremacy in the US and the treatment of national and religious minorities within Europe. These were similar problems to the problem of imperialism, he held: they were all instances of national oppression. For Lenin, national oppression, including anti-Semitism and white supremacy, was an arena of struggle that was separate from but related to class exploitation. National oppression was not simply a reflection of class struggle—it had its own autonomous dynamic. But it was also bound up with class struggles in various ways. What Lenin was doing, however tentatively, was opening up Marxism to multiple axes of struggle beyond class struggle narrowly understood. He was addressing the same problem of the relationship between race and class that, more recently, has given rise to ideas of intersectionality and allyship. In standard histories of the Left, "1917" is about a narrow class politics and "1968" is about opening that orientation up to new forms of identity politics, especially on matters of race and ethnicity. But the question of how class exploitation relates to racial oppression was already a feature of debates among the Left in Europe in the first decades of the twentieth century.

It followed from Lenin's argument that socialists had to fight not only for the emancipation of European workers but also for the national liberation of the colonized and the overthrow of white supremacy. But how could these different struggles be linked together? On what basis could solidarity be established? Those questions were addressed in 1920, after the Bolsheviks established the Comintern, or Third International, to coordinate communist revolutionary activity around the world. Its meetings in Petrograd and Moscow adopted a set of "Theses on the National and Colonial Questions" that were supposed to guide how communists worked with and in the colonized nations.[10] The Theses were shaped by two overlapping but distinct approaches to anti-imperialism: Lenin's and that of the Indian communist Manabendra Nath Roy.

"Complete liberation of all dominated peoples"

Roy had been a revolutionary since his teenage recruitment to Bengal's radical underground. He spent over a year in jail around 1910, when he was twenty-three years old, charged with waging war against the British government in India.[11] During World War I, he was active on the West and East Coasts of the US, looking for opportunities to mobilize for Indian freedom. He helped organize a plot to sail a ship carrying armed revolutionaries from the US to Calcutta, picking up Indian radicals from East Asia along the way, before joining local fighters in an uprising against British rule. The plot was funded and assisted by German diplomats who hoped to weaken the British during the war. But the elaborate plan failed to come together.[12] In Palo Alto, Roy fell in love with a Stanford University graduate student, Evelyn Trent, who became his intellectual and political collaborator over the next decade.[13] In 1917, they fled to Mexico after US authorities charged Roy with violating neutrality laws by supplying weapons to the resistance against British colonialism.[14] He joined Mexico City's revolutionary circles, where he was described as "a black Quixote who lectured on the evils of British and Yankee imperialism." With Mexican peasants engaged in armed insurrections since the 1910 revolution, he came to believe their political movements were at a more advanced stage than the labor movements of Europe. In an essay criticizing President Woodrow Wilson's promises to establish peace after World War

M. N. Roy

I, he wrote that the war had been caused by the "imperialist greed of the European nations," and only "the complete liberation of all dominated peoples and countries, not only in Europe, but also in Asia and Africa" would "prepare the way for humanity towards its goal of peace and fraternity."[15] After the October Revolution in Russia, Roy cofounded a socialist party, which later became the Partido Comunista Mexicano. With this history of revolutionary activity behind him, Roy left Mexico in 1919 for Moscow, accredited as a Mexican delegate to the upcoming congress of the Comintern.[16]

At the Comintern meeting, Roy disagreed with Lenin on the key questions of what kinds of struggles by colonized peoples would be possible and what their relationship would be to the working classes in the colonizing nations. For Lenin, there were limits to what the national liberation struggles against colonialism could achieve in the near future. Perhaps they could end European rule of the colonies but, because they were essentially bourgeois movements, they would leave in place much of the structure of exploitation. Achieving a socialist society in the colonies was therefore a two-stage process: first, an anticolonial stage to overthrow European rule and establish an independent nation with civil and political rights; second, an anticapitalist stage in which the industrial working class leads the nation to socialism. The second stage would naturally only be possible after a period of national independence, during which time the industrial development that colonialism had blocked could be advanced, creating the conditions for a revolutionary working class. In the short term, though, anticolonial movements could have indirect—though potentially revolutionary—effects within Europe. If their empires were defeated, he thought, European capitalists would be more vulnerable to socialist revolutions involving industrial workers within Europe. The anticolonial revolt of the East was a spark that could ignite a revolutionary fire in the West.

Roy, on the other hand, was more consistently internationalist. Rather than the East performing a supporting role for revolution in the West, he thought East and West would be joint leading actors on the world stage. Revolutionary workers in the colonizing nations needed to act in concert with revolutionary workers and peasants in the colonized nations. "These two forces must be coordinated if the final success of the world revolution is to be guaranteed," he stated.[17] Roy's scandalous argument was that white workers by themselves could not overthrow capitalism; their emancipation depended on their entering into a shared struggle with people of color. In India, for example, Roy argued, there was, in fact, a "revolutionary proletariat," though it was ignored by the European Left. Lenin was therefore mistaken in advocating support for anticolonial nationalists, such as the Indian National Congress, led by Mohandas K. Gandhi and Jawaharlal Nehru. There was no need to rely on its bourgeois leadership in the struggle against imperialism, said Roy; their project did not represent the masses of workers and peasants, and aimed only at getting rid of the colonizers in order to place themselves at the helm of Indian capitalism. Instead of two stages, Roy argued, colonized workers and peasants could move straight from colonialism to a socialist revolution. The lesson of his involvement in political movements in India and Mexico was that the struggles against colonialism and for socialism had to be waged simultaneously. As a result of Roy's criticisms, Lenin modified his draft of the Theses so that instead of supporting "bourgeois-democratic liberation movements" in the colonies, communists were called upon to only support "revolutionary movements of liberation." The Comintern also adopted Roy's own supplementary theses along with Lenin's draft.[18]

By opening the question of how class struggles connected to struggles against racism and colonialism, the 1920 Theses decentered Soviet communism from its European origins and forced a reassessment of the place of colonized peoples in the course of history. Lenin and Roy both agreed that anticolonialism and anticapitalism were struggles that intersected. Moreover, the Theses referred to "the Negroes in America" as also involved in a struggle to liberate a Black nation within the US nation.[19] White supremacy in the US, according to Lenin and his coauthors, was a sort of internal colonialism in the Black Belt states of the South where African Americans were a majority but suppressed through political violence. An independent Black struggle for civil rights, the Theses implied, was a communist goal. This Black Belt thesis encouraged an alignment with Soviet communism among some Black organizations in the US, such as the African Blood Brotherhood, militant Black-nationalist socialists who had come together in Harlem in 1919 and claimed 2,500 members by 1921.[20] Meanwhile, after reading the Theses in a Paris newspaper, Ho Chi Minh became convinced they laid out the path to Vietnamese liberation from French rule; he became a founding member of the French Communist Party. In South Africa, the Theses helped turn the then whites-only Communist Party toward a program of organizing the African masses.[21] Still, white communists in the US, Europe, and South Africa remained reluctant to take self-organized Black and anticolonial struggles seriously, even if the Comintern had recommended they do so.

The bigger problem was that, for all their opening up of Marxist orthodoxy, the Theses still assumed there were only two classes capable of self-conscious social change: the bourgeoisie, as in the US in 1776 and in France in 1789, and industrial workers, as in 1917. Only by matching one of these paradigms could anticolonial struggles meet the criteria of being capable of social transformation. The debate between Roy and Lenin therefore coalesced around the question whether movements of the colonized resembled the one or the other of these two paradigms; the answer to that question determined whether they were progressive—but only temporarily, if at all—or genuinely revolutionary; whether they were ultimately to be struggled with or struggled against. For Lenin, the key factor was that countries like India were quite unlike Russia in 1917. Based on his experience of leading the 1917 Russian Revolution, Lenin believed that working classes could only be revolutionary under the leadership of parties of professional socialist agitators. A workers' revolution in India was therefore a distant possibility because no communist party existed there, and it would take a long time for one to assume a leadership role; the more modest goal for the time being would have to be that the Indian bourgeoisie win national independence and democratic rights. Roy, on the other hand, to support his case that a 1917-style revolution in India was possible, emphasized the proportion of its workers in industrial sectors and the number of strikes they had carried out. His sense that socialist revolution was as likely to happen in Asia as in Europe was an improvement on Lenin's analysis. But, in making his case in Moscow, Roy exaggerated the significance of India's small industrial workforce.[22]

Later in 1920, Roy was one of the seven men and women who gathered in Tashkent, capital of Soviet Turkestan, to found the Communist Party of India.[23] He turned out to be right about the immediate potential for revolutionary activity in India: in the 1920s and 1930s, there was an upsurge of mobilization, with demands not just for national independence but for radical social change. But much of the energy in this period of agitation came from peasant struggles, women's struggles, and struggles against the caste system, not just from the small Indian industrial working class. For decades, anti-caste movements had been describing the Indian National Congress as an organization of Hindu upper-caste interests seeking the end of the wealth drain from India to Britain but the *preservation* of the wealth drain from Indian peasants to Indian landlords.[24] These kinds of social movement did not fit either of the two accepted historical paradigms of revolution and were neglected by the nascent communist movement in India, although in 1927 Roy himself proposed the formation of a "people's party" to unite the peasant majority with industrial workers.[25]

A Black revolution

In 1938, the same year the term "racism" first appeared in a scholarly text in English with the publication of Hirschfeld's book, the writer C. L. R. James authored a newspaper column on European "racism in Africa." Born in 1901 in Trinidad to a lower-middle-class family, James had received a classical European education at the elite Queen's Royal College after winning a rare scholarship. Aspiring to be a writer, he sailed to England in 1932 to pursue his literary ambitions. But, after settling in Lancashire, he was swept up in local working-class political movements and soon became active in Trotskyist and anticolonial organizing work. By 1938, he had emerged as a somewhat prominent Marxist intellectual, and the Socialist Workers Party in the United States invited him to conduct a lecture tour. The planned six-month visit turned into a permanent stay in New York.[26] In his 1938 column, James understood racism not, following the liberal theory, as a set of ideas propagated by extremist propaganda and emotional manipulation, but as a matter of how land and labor were structurally organized. In British-occupied Kenya, wrote James, the "accepted policy is to take the best land for the whites and to segregate the Africans in areas too small for them. This is one of the means by which black labor is assured. Unable to earn a living and money for the Government tax in the restricted areas assigned to him, the African must go to the settler and seek employment at whatever terms the settler offers." Racism, in James's description, was not a set of beliefs or attitudes but a structure of generally observed social rules and policies that enabled economic exploitation. Individual racist attitudes no doubt existed but were not fundamental. This economic arrangement, James argued, could only be maintained "by a regime approximating to Fascism." Though the British pretended otherwise, colonialism was akin to Nazism in the kinds of political terror it used to maintain its power and in its racist effects. "There is no form of racial discrimination practiced by the Nazis against the Jews, that is not practiced by the Europeans in Kenya against the Africans."[27]

James was one of a number of Black Caribbean writers, including Aimé Césaire and Frantz Fanon, both of Martinique, who took the new word "racism" and recast it to focus on social structures rather than mental attitudes. To the idea of racism as something located in individual mindsets, they added the idea of racism as a routine and pervasive set of social rules that were bound up with the functioning of colonialism. As with some of the liberal theorists of racism, their use of the term made connections between different histories of oppression. In contrast to the liberals, what tied those different oppressions together was not the similarity in their legitimizing attitudes and beliefs but the fact that each was grounded in the same social system. Through the work of these writers, the word "racism" came to be associated for the first time with a structural analysis.

In developing their ideas, James, Césaire, and Fanon were each shaped by the aftermaths of plantation slavery in the Caribbean. From the plantations came an unprecedented accumulation of capital that enabled Europe to place itself at the center of the modern world. But rebellions punctuated the colonial era in the Caribbean, most significantly with the slave revolution in Saint-Domingue, which, from 1791 to 1803, overthrew the plantation system and created the Black-led republic of Haiti. Through the late nineteenth century, slavery was formally abolished in the rest of the Caribbean, only for the former slaves to be enslaved in new ways, as De Kom had highlighted. People of color continued to be governed by white minorities on behalf of European nations. With the genocide of Indigenous populations and the violence of the transatlantic traffic diminishing organic connections with the past for the mass of the population, people of color could observe capitalist modernity in the Caribbean in a brutally pure and undisguised form. As Jamaica Kincaid put it in her book *A Small Place*: "We, for as long as we have known you, *were* capital, like bales of cotton and sacks of sugar, and you were the commanding, cruel capitalists, and the memory of this is so strong, the experience so recent, that we can't quite bring ourselves to embrace this idea that you think so much of."[28] At the same time, the insurrectionaries of Caribbean history—from Toussaint L'Ouverture, leader of the Saint-Domingue revolution, to Marcus Garvey, the Jamaican Black nationalist who built a mass movement across the African diaspora—demonstrated the political possibilities upon which a radical analysis could rest.

For James, a structural analysis involved focusing on the relationships between economic interests, cultural attitudes, and political organization. His thinking about those relationships was built from Marxist components. But he had to "blacken" the orthodox European version of Marxism, just as African slaves in the Caribbean, deprived of their ancestral languages, creolized Dutch, English, French, and Spanish to create languages of their own. His work, like Roy's, thus represents a pivotal moment in the history of Marxism's nexus to Third World peoples.

James began with Marx's account of the relationship between a society's economic base and its cultural superstructure. In Marx's *Eighteenth Brumaire of Louis Bonaparte*, his account of the 1851 coup in France, he had written: "Upon the different forms of property, upon the social conditions of existence, rises an entire superstructure of different and distinctly formed sentiments, illusions, modes of thought and views of life. The entire class creates and forms them out of its material foundations and out of the corresponding social relations."[29] Marx meant that, in general, the opinions and beliefs of bourgeois individuals do not spring from their own individual reasoning. Nor do they rest on the universal principles they claim to uphold. Their real driving force is the specific property interests of their class section. Landowners, factory-owners, slave-owners, shop-owners, ship-owners, and bank-owners each generate their own ideological superstructure that simultaneously expresses, conceals, and ratifies a corresponding economic base.

In his *The Black Jacobins*, a history of the Saint-Domingue revolution, also written in 1938, James adapted Marx's base/superstructure formulation and developed it into a structural analysis of racism. He argued that ideological racism was sustained by the economic interests in the transatlantic trade of Africans and the plantation system, irrespective of the racial prejudices of the individual decision-makers upholding these systems. Of course, prejudices permeated pre-revolutionary Saint-Domingue, an island entirely organized around its slave plantations. Whites despised Mulattoes and Blacks; Mulattoes, in turn, despised Blacks. But these "matters of social prestige" were themselves the products of "Government policy, enforced by bullets and bayonets" and motivated by "the justification of plunder by any obvious differentiation from those holding power." The planter class in the Caribbean needed to control the slave population, which was the source of its huge profits: "Apart from physical terror, the slaves were to be kept in subjection by associating inferiority and degradation with the most obvious distinguishing mark of the slave—the black skin." Furthermore, the structural racism of the plantations was supported by the bourgeois legislators in Paris, who had become the dominant political force after the French Revolution. These, James wrote, harbored "no color prejudice." They were, though, "sober men of business" and they understood that the wealth of their class, and therefore its political power, was based on the continued existence of slave labor in the colonies. "Though the bourgeoisie traded in other things than slaves, upon the success or failure of the traffic everything else depended." Racist prejudice was a dependent variable, not the primary cause; the stronger historical force, in James's account, was the social and economic structure that bound the accumulation of wealth to the oppression of Africans. When political upheaval weakened this structure, the associated prejudices disappeared too. Prejudice, where it existed, was an effect of the structure, not its cause.[30]

If racism is structural and essentially operates at a deeper level than individual prejudices, then antiracism must involve radical collective action to transform societies, rather than liberal education to transform personalities. How could a collective force be constituted? What kind of action should it take? Who could lead it and who could support it? For an antiracism that thinks in structural terms, these are the key questions. *The Black Jacobins* was James's answer. In 1920, Roy and Lenin had debated revolutionary strategy with two paradigms in mind: the eighteenth-century revolutions in France and the US, led by the bourgeoisie, and the 1917 revolution in Russia, led by the industrial working class. In *The Black Jacobins*, James proposed a third revolutionary paradigm: the Saint-Domingue revolution, led by enslaved Africans. The enslaved who carried out the revolution were, he wrote, in some respects similar to modern factory workers: "Working and living together in gangs of hundreds on the huge sugar-factories . . . they were closer to a modern proletariat than any group of workers in existence at the time." This implied that they were as able as European factory workers in organizing "a thoroughly prepared and organised mass movement." In other respects, they resembled revolutionary peasants, because they "worked on the land" and, as such, "aimed at the extermination of their oppressors." But crucially, the slave revolutionaries were not organized on the Leninist model of a vanguard party of professional revolutionaries; their instruction in revolutionary technique came from the collective experience of insurrection accumulated and stored in the cultural life of the people. Thus, for James, the cultural traditions denigrated by European colonialism actually bore the seeds of resistance and revolt.[31] And the Saint-Domingue revolution was an African revolution organized by workers in the colonies more than a century before 1917. This history utterly refuted the white Left's dismissal of Black agency.

At the same time, for James, the Saint-Domingue revolution had to be understood in terms of its symbiotic relationship to the class struggles in France. The 1789 French Revolution, which had begun as a conflict between the royalty and the rising bourgeoisie, instigated two parallel political processes. In France, it opened a breach through which the urban masses entered as a political force. In Saint-Domingue, it did the same for the enslaved Africans. The fate of each was tied to the other. By fighting for abolition, the slaves were weakening bourgeois power in Europe, while workers and peasants in France saw abolitionism as their cause too. For a brief moment, Black and white acted in solidarity:

> The workers and peasants of France could not have been expected to take any interest in the colonial question in normal times, any more than one can expect similar interest from British or French workers to-day. But now they were roused. They were striking at royalty, tyranny, reaction and oppression of all types, and with these they included slavery ... Henceforth the Paris masses were for abolition, and their black brothers in San Domingo, for the first time, had passionate allies in France. The National Convention would be elected and would deliberate under the influence of these masses. The slaves in San Domingo by their insurrection had shown revolutionary France that they could fight and die for freedom; and the logical development of the revolution in France had brought to the front of the stage masses who, when they said abolition, meant it in theory and in practice.

In the end, the white Jacobins in France were unable to consolidate a democratic republic as counterrevolution set in; the Black Jacobins in Saint-Domingue were forced to continue alone, and triumphed. The ideals of the French Revolution were realized more fully by Africans in the Caribbean than by Europeans in Europe.[32]

Recognizing Saint-Domingue as a third paradigm of revolution meant rewiring the international circuits of agency and solidarity. In the conventional Western historical narrative, Europeans move heroically forward to modernity, from Plato to NATO, while the Third World, by nature static, waits for opportunities to benefit from Europe's progress. James's interpretation implied this narrative had to be thrown out. Instead, revolutionary ideals were likely to be realized not in Europe but in its colonies. And the composition of the working class that would lead the world to socialist progress had to extend far beyond the waged workers of Europe. If the enslaved had led a revolution, then so could other kinds of unwaged workers, such as peasants. Rather than rely solely on the methods of industrial militancy that were central to European socialist history, socialism could just as likely root itself in the struggles of the Third World's peasant masses.[33] An autonomous African struggle for socialism was possible and necessary. From the vantage point of the 1930s, the Saint-Domingue revolution appeared to James a precursor to the coming African revolts that he thought (accurately, as it turned out) were about to emancipate the continent from direct European domination. When appropriate, these African revolts would seek unity with Western socialists, but never dependency on them.

In the United States, James's analysis resonated with Du Bois's evolving position. Disillusioned with the capacity of scientific knowledge and liberal reform to bring about social change, Du Bois resigned from the NAACP in 1934. The following year, his book *Black Reconstruction in America* argued that the history of the Black struggle for freedom in the US needed to be interpreted in terms of the history of workers' struggle under capitalism. Applied to the Civil War era, this premise implied that "the black worker won the war by a general strike which transferred his labor from the Confederate planter to the Northern invader." Du Bois, like James, widened the conception of class struggle beyond the white, industrial workforces of Europe and the US to include the Black enslaved peasantry of the plantations. There was an invisible "dark proletariat," he wrote, that "vast sea of human labor in China and India, the South Seas and all Africa; in the West Indies and Central America and in the United States—that great majority of mankind, on whose bent and broken backs rest today the founding stones of modern industry." Even though this proletariat had "practically identical interests" to white workers, the prospect of interracial unity among the working classes was, for Du Bois, not foreseeable. Modern US capitalism, he argued, was shaped by white workers' refusal of such unity. Even when their wages were low, white workers clung to the "psychological wage" of having civil rights that were denied to Black people; that meant racism, though "founded and retained by capitalism," was "adopted, forwarded and approved by white labor." Drawing on the conception of a "nation within a nation," Du Bois supported Blacks' upholding a capacity for autonomous struggle, even as that struggle ultimately pointed to a socialism that would benefit white workers too.[34]

In the struggle against white supremacy in the US, James likewise affirmed the necessity of an independent Black movement not subservient to a white-led socialist party—a position his own Socialist Workers Party adopted in 1939.[35] It would not do, argued James, to assimilate Blacks to a labor movement that understood exploitation through the experiences of white workers. The Black struggle in the US "has a vitality and a validity of its own . . . deep historic roots in the past of America and in present struggles . . . an organic political perspective [and] is able to intervene with terrific force upon the general social and political life of the nation." It is "in itself a constituent part of the struggle for socialism." Black freedom movements, then, are implicitly socialist but not reducible or assimilable to white working-class struggle. This was not the conventional "black and white unite and fight" position of asserting the need for class unity over racial difference. Nor was it a Black nationalist argument for separatism under capitalism. Instead of asking whether race or class issues should be given primacy, James saw the struggle for socialism and the struggle against racism as each passing through the other. Moreover, there was no need for a vanguard party of professional revolutionaries to lead Black people. "Every cook can govern," James was fond of saying—ordinary people have the capacity, creativity, and desire to be self-governing. Leadership emerges organically, schooled in the conditions of life of the people, not party doctrine. Through the 1940s, James grew increasingly distant from the Trotskyist position, frustrated with its continuing belief in a vanguard party.[36]

The upsurge of Black revolt in the US, James argued in the 1940s, needed the support of organized labor, but, rather than leading or assimilating Black movements, labor organizations needed to use their strength to help shield Blacks from the retaliatory violence of the state. Without that support, "there will fall upon the Negro people in the US such a repression, such persecution, comparable to nothing that they have seen in the past. We have seen in Germany and elsewhere the barbarism that capitalism is capable of in its death agony. The Negro people in the US offer a similar opportunity to the American bourgeoisie."[37] Within a few years of writing these words, the repressive powers of the US state were directed at James himself: the US government imprisoned him at Ellis Island and deported him to Britain in 1953, as part of a broader targeting of left-wing activists.

By the late 1960s, James celebrated the newly emerging Black Power movement as the organically produced, independent Black American socialism he had first anticipated in the 1930s.[38] Of Black Power leader Kwame Ture (then known as Stokely Carmichael), James commented: "No clearer or stronger voice for socialism has ever been raised in the US."[39] The repression that James feared did indeed fall upon Black America as the revolts of the 1960s were defeated and the era of mass incarceration began.

James's analysis of racism was sculpted from Marxist clay. But his understanding of Caribbean history gave him a sense of class struggle no longer centered upon England and France. For him, antiracism meant organizing among Black workers from Alabama to Africa, building autonomous, grassroots collective power, rooted in the dynamic cultural life of a people, and aiming at the revolutionary dismantling of structural racism and the building of a socialist society.

5

Racism Is a Structure

C. L. R. James had argued in 1938 that white liberals who condemned fascism tended to ignore the violent methods of European colonialism, which hardly differed from those the fascists used. Liberal antiracism of the 1940s did occasionally make connections between fascism and colonialism, but it did so by identifying similarities in the kinds of racist beliefs used to justify each. It stopped short of examining the deeper analogies and linkages between the two. In his *Discourse on Colonialism*, written shortly after World War II and published in France in 1950, the Martinican poet Aimé Césaire proposed a different way of understanding the structural relationships between colonialism, racism, and fascism—one which continues to be crucial to understanding the far Right today. Indeed, for Césaire, European fascism actually began with European colonialism.

Césaire started his argument by describing how, in order to impose their rule, colonizers had to inflict terrible violence on the colonized. Then, "in order to ease his conscience," the colonizer "gets into the habit of seeing the other man as *an animal*, accustoms himself to treating him like an

C. L. R. James, 1938

animal, and tends objectively to transform *himself* into an animal." The psychological effect of the colonial system was to brutalize not just the colonized but the colonizer, "to degrade him, to awaken him to buried instincts, to covetousness, to violence, race hatred, and moral relativism." The system made the racist, not the other way around. This moral degradation then flowed back from the colonies to Europe itself: "A poison has been distilled into the veins of Europe and, slowly but surely, the continent proceeds to savagery. And then one fine day the bourgeoisie is awakened by a terrific boomerang effect: the gestapos are busy, the prisons fill up, the torturers standing around the racks invent, refine, discuss." Nazism for Césaire was nothing but colonialism coming home to Europe. Hitler's crimes were unique, he wrote, but only because "he applied to Europe colonialist procedures which until then had been reserved exclusively for the Arabs of Algeria, the 'coolies' of India, and the 'niggers' of Africa." And so long as those crimes "had been applied only to non-European peoples," Europeans "absolved it, shut their eyes to it, legitimized it." As such, the European expression of liberal values was "narrow and fragmentary, incomplete and biased and, all things considered, sordidly racist," because "capitalist society, at its present stage, is incapable of establishing a concept of the rights of all men."[1]

This way of thinking about racism was quite different from the liberal theories of Hirschfeld, Boas, and Benedict. Racism became a structural aspect of colonial systems—a matter of organized political and economic practices—hidden behind the colonizers' rhetoric of spreading modern, liberal values to less developed peoples. This structural racism, and the mass political violence inevitably bound up with it, occurred out of view in the hidden zones of colonial administration. But European society was nevertheless dependent upon the continuation of these practices, economically, socially, and culturally; as such, the vaunted liberalism of the modern state was necessarily bound up with a disavowed colonial violence.

Césaire thus interpreted European fascism as the process by which the racism and political violence of colonialism boomeranged back to Europe. What had been hidden in the peripheries of the European empires made its appearance in Europe itself. But its origins were disguised and so its arrival felt like a mysterious and sudden upheaval. The liberal theory that Nazism originated in a set of ideas about racial superiority was an attempt to explain this mystery. It presented fascism as an attack on European liberal government from the outside. But fascism was a pathology internal to liberalism. Self-proclaimed liberal governments first introduced the political practices of Nazism—censorship, stripping civil rights, conducting mass expulsions, martial law, concentrating populations in camps, and perpetrating genocides, all organized through racist categories—in the colonies. What was exceptional about Nazism was not the extremism of its racist ideas but the application of such practices to Europeans. Liberal theories presented Nazism as the paradigm of racism and understood other racisms by analogy with it; Césaire instead analyzed Nazism as no more than a particular case of racist colonialism. Nazi anti-Semitism, he implied, was simply the form that German settler colonialism took in eastern Europe. This mode of analysis enabled him to trace the line from genocide in Africa to genocide in Europe, which Hirschfeld was unable to see. And it explained why Nazi policy-makers borrowed so heavily from the history of US settler colonialism.[2]

As Western intellectuals tried to make sense of Nazism in the years after World War II, there was a growing awareness that the genocide of European Jews was the central crime of Hitler's regime. This raised the question of how the people of one of the most modern societies in the world could carry out acts so barbaric. Indeed, the way that the genocide was rationally planned and bureaucratically organized indicated that it was an expression of, not a lapse from, modernity. On the other hand, many insisted that the genocide could only be understood as a singularity, a unique evil not to be analytically related to other historical processes. Césaire's analysis rejected the latter proposition and pointed out that the coupling of modern rationality with deliberate mass murder was an ordinary feature of colonialism.

In the 1930s in Paris, where Césaire had been a student, he helped launch the Négritude movement, a collaboration of poets celebrating Black cultural heritage in French-colonized Africa and the Caribbean. Négritude was a way of overcoming the white supremacist histories that Caribbean schools had inculcated into their students. As De Kom had highlighted, official Caribbean culture only celebrated "the sons of another people," which had the consequence of projecting an image of negativity and shame onto Africa.[3] The first stage of antiracism was the attempt to invert this image and assert the beauty and power of African cultures. Césaire nevertheless was opposed to Martinique becoming independent of France; instead, he argued for its full integration into the French system of government with its people receiving the same civil, political, and social rights as the French.

In the years after World War II, Césaire was also a member of the French Communist Party and successfully campaigned to be elected to the French National Assembly as its candidate.[4] He hoped for a communist revolution that would, as he wrote in *Discourse on Colonialism*, end "the narrow tyranny of a dehumanized bourgeoisie" and bring the "preponderance of the only class that still has a universal mission, because it suffers in its flesh from all the wrongs of history, from all the universal wrongs: the proletariat."[5] Who made up this proletariat was left unclear. But the French Communist Party consistently supported French colonial policy in Algeria, despite the party's nominal acceptance of the 1920 Theses on anticolonialism. In 1956, Césaire's mounting frustration with the Communist Party led him to resign. Explaining his decision, he wrote that "our struggle—the struggle of colonial peoples against colonialism, the struggle of peoples of color against racism—is . . . of a completely different nature than the fight of the French worker against French capitalism, and it cannot in any way be considered a part, a fragment, of that struggle." He remained a Marxist and a communist but wanted "Marxism and communism [to] be placed in the service of black peoples."[6]

Stretching Marxism

Six years after the publication of *Discourse on Colonialism*, Césaire's former student Frantz Fanon delivered a lecture on "racism and culture" at the First International Congress of Black Writers and Artists, held at the Sorbonne University in Paris in September 1956. The Congress's 600 participants included the writers James Baldwin, Chester Himes, George Lamming, Léopold Senghor, Richard Wright, and Césaire. Though he did not refer to it in his lecture, Fanon was privately preparing to resign as head of the psychiatric department at Blida-Joinville Hospital in French-occupied Algeria. There, as the French colonizers escalated the brutality of their regime in the face of Algerian opposition, Fanon treated men and women who had been tortured as well as others tormented by the torture they had carried out on behalf of the colonial system. The experience transformed him. He came to understand that colonial racism destroyed the minds of both the dominated and the dominator. There was no way out except through the complete struggle for decolonization being waged by the Algerian National Liberation Front, and he began to provide its fighters with medical assistance.[7] In his letter of resignation, submitted a few months after his lecture, he wrote that psychiatry, "the medical technique that aims to enable man no longer to be a stranger to his environment," is impossible in Algeria where the colonial "social structure" systematically dehumanizes and is "hostile to any attempt to put the individual back where he belonged."[8] Fanon then became fully active in the Algerian struggle for liberation and, in the following years, was its most eloquent spokesperson.

His lecture in Paris was, in effect, a devastating assault on the liberal theory of racism. We should abandon the habit, he said, "of regarding racism as a disposition of the mind, a psychological flaw." A "colonial country is a racist country" even if a majority of its citizens do not have racist mindsets. If it is only a minority of whites who express racist beliefs, this minority is at least upholding an ideology that is consistent with the economic structures of their society. The more liberal majority are simply in denial about the true nature of how the wealth of their country has been obtained. Racist ideology "is not fundamentally determining." Rather, "military and economic oppression most frequently precedes, makes possible and legitimates" racist beliefs. "It is not possible to enslave men," Fanon argued, "without logically inferiorising them through and through." And racist attitudes are "merely the emotional, affective and sometimes intellectual unfolding of this inferiorisation." It "is only one element in a larger whole: namely the systematic oppression of a people." Oppression, for Fanon, did not mean simply discrimination exercised by prejudiced individuals in positions of relative privilege. He meant a deeper structure of inequality that pervades the "social constellation, the cultural whole."[9] That structure had been established in the nineteenth century, when French troops occupied Algeria and handed most of its productive land to European settlers. The cheaply obtained land was then used for food production for France while the settlers were a new export market for industrial capitalists in the French mainland. Most Algerians, expelled from the land they once cultivated, became destitute.

This implied, furthermore, that the structures of racism in a society shift over time, as society itself changes. Racism "has to renew itself, to take on shades, to change its physiognomy" in line with the broader structure it is a part of. The abolition of plantation slavery in the nineteenth century, for example, gave rise to new forms of enslavement. Now, in the mid-twentieth century, as the colonized overthrew direct European colonialism, there was a danger again that racism would be reconstructed, both in the colonized regions and in Europe and the US. In the 1950s, Fanon could already see that "vulgar, primitive and simplified" beliefs in biological differences between the races were giving way, owing to the developing "complexity of the means of production, the development of economic relations." More "subtle arguments" that amounted to a "cultural racism," targeting "a certain way of life" were the future. Racism "dares no longer show itself without disguise." Some think that racism has disappeared. Others think that racist prejudices have "become unconscious." But an entire country "cannot be racist unconsciously." What is actually happening is that racist domination is able to hide itself in abstract economic processes, such as systems of land ownership and international trade rules. "The truth is that the rigour of the system makes it superfluous to make a daily assertion of superiority." At the same time, with the growing strength of movements of the colonized and racialized, there is a need for a "less brutal, more subtle" mode of conducting day-to-day social interactions that preserves domination without that domination having to be constantly vocalized.[10]

Indeed, Fanon says, in this new moment, the celebration of cultural diversity can be part of the way that structural racism maintains itself. There is a "respect for the traditions, the cultural peculiarities, the personality, of the enslaved peoples," so long as these cultures are represented in a "mummified" way. The aim is to "objectivate, encapsulate, imprison and encyst" these cultures, render them inert and incapable of living and breathing, so that they cannot pose a political threat. Cultures that were "formerly full of life, and open to the future" become "fossilised" in a "sustained death agony" rather than suffer "complete disappearance." With these words, Fanon was thinking of Algeria, where French colonialists closed the existing Islamic schools and courts, and then established a Muslim council of appointed loyalists to superficially recognize Algeria's Islamic tradition. But he could equally have been describing Britain's cultural policies of indirect rule in

India after Queen Victoria's 1858 proclamation. In either case, his argument implied that, while movements such as Négritude, which celebrated Black culture, were part of the process by which antiracist struggles might emerge, by themselves they were insufficient and not necessarily radical—the system already knew very well how to perform a celebration of Black or Asian cultures in its own interests. Transformation will come not from cultivating an authentic relationship to a fixed idea of African or Asian cultures but from a "total and absolute" struggle to build new political structures enabling an entirely new cultural life.[11] As he put it in his final and most influential book, *The Damned of the Earth* (usually translated as *The Wretched of the Earth*), "We must start again, develop new thinking, and attempt to set afoot a new humanity."[12] Fanon was not calling for Africans to have their culture recognized among the great civilizations of the world. His was not a politics of diversity of the kind implied by Boas's and Benedict's idea of cultural relativism. The African revolution he fought for was about developing a new universal paradigm of how to live; its contribution to humanity lay not in preserving pre-colonial African cultural traditions but in the energy and creativity of Black mass struggle.

Fanon is such a powerful analyst of racism because virtually no one is more attuned to the destruction that it wreaks on the souls of those caught up in it, while simultaneously understanding how it operates through political and economic forces beyond the individual psyche. Fanon's earlier book *Black Skin, White Masks* analyzed the "massive psychoexistential complex" produced by structural racism. "The analysis that I am undertaking is psychological," he wrote. But the psychological effects of racism are "the outcome of a double process: primarily, economic; subsequently, the internalization—or, better, the epidermalization—of this inferiority." In other words, racism is a projection onto the skin ("epidermalization") of structures of inequality that were initiated for economic reasons, from slavery to colonialism. The psychological processes Fanon was examining were mediated through individual personalities but were tied to economic structures. If racism is structural, it cannot be dismantled by setting out to change individual mindsets. It is no use trying to use the power of reason "to show the white man that he is at once the perpetrator and the victim of a delusion." A delusion that derives its power from property cannot be undone by persuasion. At the same time, there can be no effective transformation without engaging the psychological processes through which structures are lived.[13]

But recognizing an economic basis to colonial racism does not mean that its structures can be grasped simply by transposing Marxist orthodoxy from Europe. "Marxist analysis," he writes, "should always be slightly stretched every time we have to deal with the colonial problem." The metaphor of "stretching" is significant: it implies the need for an adjustment but not a wholesale rejection. What did he mean? First, in the colonial context, Fanon says, Marx's claim that the ideological superstructure is determined by an economic base does not completely hold. Rather, the ideological racism of the colonial superstructure shapes the economic base, as much as the other way around. Racism in the ideological superstructure not only legitimizes an underlying economic infrastructure but also determines the form it takes. The economic cause is itself an ideological effect: "You are rich because you are white, you are white because you are rich." In other words, racism is not just an illusion masking class inequality but becomes a material reality of its own. Second, the relationship between classes in the colonial setting is not mediated by the whole host of educational and cultural institutions that in Europe allow ruling classes to be less reliant on state violence. European Marxist thinking on the role of ideology in stabilizing capitalism cannot therefore be applied to colonial societies. In the colonies, the governing class defines itself by its being racially separate, which means its power depends much more on direct force. The "police and the military have an immediate presence, intervening frequently and directly with the colonized to advise them, by means of rifle butts or napalm, not to stir." Third, Fanon, like James, rejected the presumption that opposition would come most effectively from waged industrial workers. In the colonies, that workforce was small in size, "pampered by the colonial regime," and "relatively privileged," Fanon pointed out. There would be no 1917-style revolution led by industrial workers in Africa.[14]

Nor would there be a 1789-style revolution led by the bourgeoisie. The bourgeoisies of the Third World would be able to lead a process of national liberation to achieve formal independence from colonial rule. But upon coming to power, they would probably be unable to carry out the modernizing economic tasks that their class carried out in Europe after the French Revolution. "The bourgeois phase in the underdeveloped countries would only be justified," Fanon wrote, "to the extent that the national bourgeoisie is sufficiently strong economically and technically to construct a bourgeois society, to create the conditions for the development of a sizeable proletariat, to industrialize agriculture, and finally to make possible an authentic national culture." But instead, because of the underdevelopment that colonialism imposes, the Third World bourgeoisie tends not to be entrepreneurial, and aims mainly at establishing itself as an intermediary between the former colonizing power and the exploited masses. It would thus proceed to enrich itself through taking its cut on exports of raw materials, rather than investing in production, leaving the majority in rural poverty. Colonial economic structures would remain in place, presided over by new governing elites holding power through single-party political systems, narrow appeals to ethnic identity, and cozy relationships with the former colonial powers. In these circumstances, Lenin's prescribed two-stage path to socialism was a dead end.[15]

How then could the structures deposited by colonialism be overthrown? In *The Damned of the Earth*, Fanon looked to the revolutionary potential of the peasantry, especially the landless peasants who were forced to leave the rural districts and "rush toward the towns, crowd into the slums, and try to infiltrate the ports and cities born of colonial domination." This urban "lumpenproletariat"—peddlers, day workers, sex workers, hustlers, all the shack-dwellers of the cities without access to a regular wage—together with the peasant masses constituted the social forces that might lead the African revolution. Whereas in the European socialist tradition, these groups are typically regarded as easy recruits to conservatism, in Fanon's rendering they "participate decisively in the great procession of the awakened nation" in its struggles against colonialism. In doing so, they undergo a political transformation that can lead "from a total, undifferentiated nationalism to a social and economic consciousness."[16]

Instead of calm handovers of power from erstwhile colonizers to Indigenous elites, Fanon laid out the possibility of collectively organized mass struggles to destroy colonial structures. Such mass struggles would inevitably be met with violence. "The colonizer derives his truth, that is to say his property, from the colonial system." He would fight to preserve that system at all costs. The colonized masses were in turn clear that they would have to be "ready for violence at all times" if they were to free themselves. Fanon was all too familiar with the consequences of this "murderous and decisive confrontation between the two protagonists" from his psychiatric treatment of the mentally scarred on both sides. But this absolute confrontation was, Fanon held, the only means by which racism could be fought at the levels of both individual psyche and social structure. For the individual participant, the struggle is "detoxifying"; it "rids the colonized of their inferiority complex, their passive and despairing attitude. It makes them bold and restores their self-respect." Victory in this struggle would also free the colonizer from the soul-destroying effects of perpetrating oppression which Fanon had encountered as a psychiatrist. This process of total political struggle, he thought, would have profound effects: new kinds of human beings would be made, relating to each other in new ways, and making possible a revolutionary restructuring of the world.[17]

Psyches and structures

By the 1950s, the word "racism" had acquired two distinct and opposed personalities, one liberal and one radical. The great innovation of the liberal version of the word was its combining together separate forms of oppression on the basis of the similarities in the doctrines that legitimized them. The word "racism" connected the anti-Semitic beliefs central to Nazism, the belief systems that justified European colonialism, and the white supremacist beliefs bound up with the treatment of Black people in the post-slavery societies of the Americas. Central to liberal antiracism were the analogies between these doctrines. But the method of analogy was not applied equally. Because liberal uses of the word "racism" derived from the attempt to understand Nazism, there was a tendency for liberal thinkers to make sense of the other racisms through the lens of this paradigm, rather than the other way around. Moreover, Nazism itself was understood in a particular way: as a matter of propaganda-fueled hatred corrupting liberal reason by exploiting preexisting irrational prejudices, perhaps exacerbated by economic distress, as liberals assumed had happened in Germany in the years before the Nazis seized power.

Other ways of thinking about racism that derived from different starting points tended to be marginalized by liberal antiracism. The experiences of the US system of apartheid or of European colonialism only made sense to liberals if they were squeezed and reshaped to fit a preexisting mold of what racism was assumed to be. Those aspects that could not fit the mold were cast off so that the liberal theory of antiracism could preserve its intellectual authority.[18] Thus, liberals understood white supremacy in the US not as a political and economic structure but as, at root, a problem of racial beliefs, attitudes, and feelings among ordinary individuals. As the Trinidadian American sociologist Oliver Cromwell Cox wrote in 1948, the problem with the liberal version of the word "racism" was that most people who use the term conceive of it as a racial ideology or philosophy of racial superiority; but, in addition, they usually make the implied or expressed assumption that racism is the substance of modern race antagonism. This almost always leads to confusion because it ordinarily resolves itself into a study of the origin and development of an idea rather than the study of social facts and situations.

In this way, analysts like Myrdal and Benedict close their "eyes to the material interests which support and maintain race prejudice."[19] And liberal antiracism had next to nothing to say about the economic inequalities between nations that imperialism had generated—it would have been hard to see them as resulting from individual prejudices.

Above all, liberal antiracists clung to their belief that racist attitudes could be gradually eliminated by well-meaning elites cultivating attitudes of rationality, tolerance, and the celebration of diversity, as Boas, Benedict, and Myrdal had proposed. They were, as Cox put it, "not concerned with problems of power but rather with problems of 'regenerating individual' by idealistic preachments."[20] With the exceptions of extremist states such as in the US Deep South and apartheid South Africa, governments were, for liberals, not the problem but the solution to racism; their institutions were to act as mediators between groups victimized by racism, on the one hand, and those whose attitudes led to these harms, on the other. On this view, political and cultural elites had a heroic role to play in challenging racist prejudices and thereby saving liberal democracy from the threat of extremism.

The subsequent history of liberal antiracism is the history of the various techniques deployed to carry out this moralistic, top-down program of unmasking false ideas and rooting out improper attitudes. Its relentless attention to using the correct racial vocabulary, for example, rests on the hope that to abolish a word is to abolish the attitude it expresses—ignoring how the attitude is sustained by social structures that consist of more than vocabularies. Its calamitous training programs for tackling "unconscious bias" rest on the reasoning that the only way to explain why the decline in the expression of racist beliefs has not reduced racial disparity is that biases have hidden themselves in the unconscious—ignoring how, as Fanon argued, a society cannot be unconsciously racist, but it can function in a racist way without a large number of people holding racist beliefs, consciously or otherwise. And liberal antiracism's development of the terminology of "hate speech" and "hate crimes," culminating in the ubiquitous, vapid slogan "love trumps hate," rests on the assumption that oppressive cruelty is the behavioral expression of a hateful disposition—ignoring the corporate executives, asset managers, lawmakers, government officials, judges, police officers, corrections officers, military personnel, and immigration officers who, in the name of security and profit, calmly and routinely operate infrastructures of racist violence. By relocating racism to the unconscious mind, to the use of inappropriate words, and to the extremist fringes, liberal antiracism ends up absolving the institutions most responsible for racist practices.

From the moment Donald Trump emerged as the Republican candidate in the 2016 presidential elections, liberal antiracists were everywhere. They explained his appeal by saying that the propaganda of the Trump campaign was manipulating the irrational racist prejudices of voters whose attitudes had perhaps been made more extreme by growing economic inequality. As a result, liberals argued, the values and norms of liberal government faced an existential threat from Trumpian fascism. The proposed remedy was, in effect, to relaunch Myrdal's 1940s version of antiracism: credentialed elites once again leading a top-down process of educating the white, working classes out of their incorrect attitudes, this time with a focus on the flow of disinformation on social media. This was the argument of former president Bill Clinton's secretary of state Madeleine Albright, who wrote a simpleminded book comparing Trump to the fascists of the twentieth century. Fascists, she argued, established "an emotional link to the crowd and, like the central figure in a cult, brought deep and often ugly feelings to the surface." In the twenty-first century, she saw "fascism's early stirrings" in leaders such as Recep Tayyip Erdoğan, Vladimir Putin, Rodrigo Duterte, Viktor Orbán, Hugo Chávez, Kim Jong-un, and Donald Trump— a list of politicians so lacking in common attributes that to label them all "fascist" virtually empties the term of any meaning. Since the return of fascism is driven by "media and information bubbles that reinforce our grievances," a key part of her proposed remedy is "putting a saddle on the bucking bronco we call the Internet."[21] Likewise, the neoconservative Robert Kagan warned that "popular passions" were being manipulated by a tough-guy leader (neoconservatives would never, of course, manipulate the public).[22] And historian Timothy Snyder predicted that Trump would take advantage of a sudden emergency to suspend constitutional rights, as European fascists had done in the first half of the twentieth century.[23] These accounts seemed to make sense because they were stories we had been told before. Albright, Kagan, and Snyder were rehashing the standard liberal theory of racism, rooted in an account of how Nazism came to power by manipulating widely held prejudices. By that standard, Trump turned out to be a highly incompetent fascist. When a global pandemic presented the opportunity to declare a state of emergency, he instead went on television to recommend drinking disinfectant. While Trump was in office, he was content to work within the US political system rather than try to overthrow it. There is indeed a fascist threat to the normal functioning of governing institutions in the US, as the Capitol attack on January 6, 2021, demonstrated. But to understand this threat requires paying attention to the ways that ostensibly liberal government creates the space for fascism to emerge.

We can see more clearly what Trump represents if we think of fascism in the way that radical antiracists proposed. For Césaire and James, fascism was not only about a moment of collapse, when the nation descends into authoritarianism, but, more fundamentally, about the racist violence that governing agencies routinely administered. Historically, fascist-like forms of state violence were present in colonial contexts for long periods of time, working through nominally liberal institutions, before this conjunction unraveled, thereby opening the way for the destruction of liberal governments within Europe itself. Similarly, in the US case, the rise of fascism in recent years is strongly connected to the US's neocolonial wars abroad. After the Vietnam War, a white power movement came together among veterans, uniting the Ku Klux Klan, neo-Nazis, skinheads, and other activists. Since then, the movement has thrived in the backwash of the US's endless but unsuccessful wars. To its participants, this movement offers an explanation for US military defeats: it says the US has been weakened by succumbing to hidden global forces and through demographic change—what it calls the "great replacement" of whites by other groups. It also proposes a course of action for anyone who knows how to use a weapon: bring the war home to fight the domestic enemies responsible for undermining the US.[24]

The War on Terror has supercharged this process. It has renewed official approval of the notion that racial enemies need to be surveilled, tracked, and dominated through violence. By declaring the whole world a global battlefield, it has further blurred the boundaries between war abroad and policing at home, encouraging the idea of a war to be fought within the US. Above all, the War on Terror reactivated settler-colonial furies of American exceptionalism and expansionism. When those furies met military defeat abroad, they had nowhere to go except inward to find new enemies within the US and at its borders.[25] Trump was, quite simply, the War on Terror coming home—Césaire's boomerang effect of violence inflicted abroad returning to corrupt the homeland. Trump was bringing fascism to the US, but not as something alien to its institutions; he was making explicit in his rhetoric what was already implicit in the War on Terror, the War on Drugs, and the longer history of US warfare and policing—that certain racially defined populations were dangerous threats to be met by an overwhelming coercive force. The main effect of Trump's presidency was to bring to the fore and publicly celebrate the racisms already embedded in counter-terrorism policy, immigration policy, and crime policy. No wonder such a large proportion of Trump's active support comes from police officers, border agents, and military personnel. Albright, Kagan, and Snyder interpreted the danger of Trump in terms of his polarizing effects on US politics. They bemoaned the emptying of the bipartisan space where liberals and conservatives found common ground. What they missed were the ways that Trump had expanded the routine racism of the state by working through the infrastructures created in that same bipartisan space.

But liberal antiracists ignore state racism. Of course, that is to be expected of Albright. As secretary of state, she told an interviewer in 1998 that, even if her sanctions policy against Iraq were causing the death of half a million Iraqi children, "the price is worth it."[26] And Kagan was one of the most effective cheerleaders for the 2003 military occupation of Iraq, promoting the falsehood that the Saddam Hussein government was linked to al-Qaeda.[27] The US's policies that led to so many Iraqi deaths were tightly bound up with racism. But because Albright's and Kagan's hearts never seemed full of hatred, they did not resemble the liberal portrayal of racism—though more death flowed from their desks than from any neo-Nazi gang. Having done so much to help create the ideological conditions for fascist movements to flourish, their sudden discovery of anti-fascism in 2016 was absurd. But the larger problem was the liberal framing that allowed prominent advocates of racist state violence to plausibly claim antiracist credentials.

The radical alternative to liberal antiracism has its origins in James's, Césaire's, and Fanon's attempts to link the term "racism" to the structures of colonialism. From them derive our contemporary ideas of structural racism. Of course, they understood that racism could be seen in the individual attitudes, prejudices, and dogmas of some members of the societies they were writing about. But more significant to them were the ways that land, labor, and rights were socially and politically organized through racist structures that had an independent coherence and necessity. For this argument to make sense, radical antiracists had to explain what exactly the "structure" was in structural racism. The word "structure" suggested an assembly of connected elements organized according to a single design or purpose. Or perhaps a set of laws shaping human behavior that operate at a deeper, hidden level than the statute-book laws human beings consciously make. For most conservatives, "structural racism" was a meaningless term because racism must be intentional for it to count as racism, and social structures do not have intentions.[28] Without a more precise account, it was hard to know what the term "structural racism" really meant—especially as, from the 1940s to the 1970s, racist structures were themselves reshaped by the struggles for decolonization and Black freedom that James, Césaire, and Fanon were a part of.

6

Internationalists

In the three decades after World War II, anticolonial movements in Africa, Asia, and the Caribbean liberated the majority of the world's population from direct rule by Europe. Decolonization was one of the great epochal transformations of the twentieth century, generating a gigantic shift in the tectonic plates of world politics. In 1957, Ghana, led by Kwame Nkrumah, became the first African colony south of the Sahara to free itself from British colonialism. Within a few years, most of Africa was liberated. As Nkrumah noted: "In 1945 Africa largely comprised the colonial territories of European powers, and the idea that the greater part of the continent would be independent within twenty years would have seemed impossible to any political observer in the immediate post-war period."[1] Key to this change was the mobilization of ordinary people by the leaders of the anticolonial movements. At the Pan-African Congress held in Manchester, England, in 1945, with Du Bois chairing most of the sessions, there was a new emphasis on mass participation in the movement for African liberation. A declaration issued by the Congress, written by Nkrumah, called on "the workers and farmers of the colonies to organize effectively" and "be in the front lines of the battle against imperialism."[2] In this way, anticolonialism unleashed new political forces—organized workers and peasants—who sought a broad transformation of the societies they lived in, not just a change of guard at the top. For Nkrumah, this meant decolonization had to involve more than wresting control of national governments; it had to also involve canceling the international relations of dependence and domination that he called "neocolonialism." In analyzing neocolonialism, he developed new layers to the structural account of racism.

"In place of colonialism as the main instrument of imperialism," he wrote, "we have today neo-colonialism. The essence of neo-colonialism is that the State which is Subject to it is, in theory, independent and has all the outward trappings of international sovereignty. In reality its economic system and thus its political policy is directed from outside."[3] In his book *Neo-Colonialism: The Last Stage of Imperialism*, published in 1965 while he was president of Ghana in the years after its independence, Nkrumah set out the processes by which neocolonialism emerged and sustained itself. To grasp it required first understanding the problem that neocolonialism aimed to solve. Faced with the growing strength of European and US labor movements in the decades before World War II, capitalism had survived, wrote Nkrumah, through creating welfare rights and raising living standards among a core working-class population.[4] This built "a protective armour around the inner workings of its system."[5] And this protective armor was racially organized.

Franklin D. Roosevelt's New Deal was the US's version of this capitalist survival strategy. It involved federal policies that deliberately aimed at institutionalizing a racial boundary, granting privileges for white people, subordinating African Americans, and excluding and deporting Mexicans. The national labor market, recently transformed by the New Deal's regulations, set lower wages for Black workers for the same work in the South; in the North, it created a new kind of urban ghetto, resulting not only from the old methods of coordinated realtor and lender discrimination, and whites-only restrictive covenants on land ownership, but also from a mix of city, state, and federal policies that enshrined racial segregation in slum clearance, redevelopment, public housing projects, and the underwriting of mortgage loans.[6] The Federal Housing Administration, created in 1934 to insure and stabilize the home finance industry, subsidized suburban home ownership, helping drive the abandonment of inner city areas. But, with a policy that warned "if a neighborhood is to retain stability, it is necessary that properties shall continue to be occupied by the same social and racial classes," the beneficiaries were predominantly white.[7] At the heart of the New Deal's labor policies was a division between those entitled to a "family wage"—sufficient to support children and a dependent, unwaged wife at home—and those who were not. Women employed outside the home were placed outside of the New Deal's protections and expected to receive a lower wage for the same work. And areas of work in which Black people and Mexicans were heavily employed—agricultural work and domestic service—were placed in a separate sphere where the legal definition of a "worker" in federal labor and social welfare legislation did not apply; these groups were thereby excluded from the New Deal's benefits.[8] Unemployment insurance, for example, did not cover work in these two areas and, as a result, the majority of Black workers were not entitled to one of the chief benefits of the New Deal; 87 percent of wage-earning Black women were ineligible.[9]

In Europe, the protective armor of the welfare state was economically possible because of the superprofits obtained by imperialist methods, as Lenin had indicated. The policy of funding social provisions with the proceeds of empire found support in Britain from capitalists such as Cecil Rhodes and prominent figures of the Left, such as the Fabian leaders George Bernard Shaw, Sidney and Beatrice Webb, and Clifford Sharp, editor of the *New Statesman*.[10] For Sidney Webb, policies to provide adequate healthcare, education, and housing for British workers "must necessarily form the principal plank in any Imperial programme" in part because, without such measures, British families had too few children and risked "this country gradually falling to the Irish and the Jews," which was "race deterioration, if not race suicide."[11] Along these lines, the majority of workers within the protected core were invited into accepting the system through increased living standards, expanded social security packages, and, for trade union leaders, a new junior role in policy-making. Meanwhile, peoples colonized by Europe had no say in the running of the imperial system they subsidized. Democracy meant white democracy. This welfare-state capitalism began to present itself as an economic system that could generate abundance for all, but this required making invisible the masses of impoverished peoples in the colonies.[12] When workers in the colonies made demands for welfare, they faced suppression from the very governments that were introducing advanced systems of welfare at home. The same Labour government ministers who established a cradle-to-grave welfare state for workers in Britain after 1945 also sent gunboats and marines to crush striking workers in the Caribbean colony of Grenada and imprisoned trade union leaders without trial in Malaya and Kenya.[13] Racism served to make the boundary between these different categories of entitlement seem natural.

This arrangement worked for a time because it was still possible for capitalists to turn a profit, even with a relatively generous welfare state and high wages, so long as those entitlements were only provided to a small section of capitalism's international workforce. These reforms "helped to blur fundamental contradictions" between labor and capital, Nkrumah wrote, but they also had the effect of "transferring the conflict between rich and poor from the national to the international stage."[14] There was therefore pressure on each imperialist power to find ever new colonial markets and sources of raw materials to sustain the growth of welfare capitalism at home. In the first half of the twentieth century, that meant intensifying rivalry between imperialists, culminating in the huge destruction of two world wars.

Decolonization was, in effect, a demand to desegregate world capitalism by removing the racial boundary between those inside and outside the protective core of welfare. Anticolonial leaders like Nkrumah proposed that, after independence, their countries could begin the process of industrialization that colonialism had blocked. And with industrialization would come the wealth necessary to lift the Third World's peoples out of poverty. But this was a danger to European capitalists. Third World industrialization would have meant the loss of export markets for European manufacturing and rising prices for the raw materials and foodstuffs that Europe extracted cheaply from the Third World. Obtaining these "by one means or another, by hook or by crook" was "a life and death matter for the economy of this country" noted John Strachey, the minister of food in Britain's postwar Labour government.[15]

"Collective imperialism"

The neocolonial response to this problem was to develop a new relationship in which economic domination coexisted with formal political independence. The aim was to preserve colonial economic relations even after direct colonialism was over, so that welfare capitalism in the West would continue to be viable. The new system of neocolonialism, wrote Nkrumah, typically involved not direct military occupation by an imperialist power but domination by "a consortium of financial interests" not attached to a particular country.[16] These financial interests floated free of specific national economies. The domination they established was not about international competition for colonial territories; rather, it involved all the major powers integrated into a single system, under US leadership. Nkrumah called it "collective imperialism."[17] Along with maintaining colonial economic relations, it was a way of restraining the inter-imperialist rivalry that had led to two world wars, each of which generated the conditions for communist revolutions, the first in Russia, the second in China. With the erstwhile imperialist powers of Europe weakened by the end of World War II, the US took on the responsibility of managing Western imperialism on behalf of the capitalist system as a whole. Maintaining a stable and cheap supply of Middle Eastern oil, for example, became a key US objective.

Debt was among the deadliest weapons in the neocolonial armory, Nkrumah argued. Domestic markets in Third World countries were not large enough to generate the capital needed to develop industrial production. And Western markets were typically only open to exports of cheap raw materials from the Third World; industrial exports tended to be blocked in order to protect Western manufacturing industries. Because Western interests controlled the markets where raw materials from the Third World were sold, they could ensure that prices were kept low, so that Third World countries faced declining revenues even when they increased their exports. All of this meant the only way to industrialize was to borrow capital from Western banks or development agencies. Third World leaders were driven toward being dependent on Western lenders, who were, in turn, able to assert control over the governments of the Third World. The lenders, wrote Nkrumah, "have the habit of forcing would-be borrowers to submit to various offensive conditions, such as supplying information about their economies, submitting their policy and plans to review by the World Bank and accepting agency supervision of their use of loans."[18] Central to neocolonialism were the international financial institutions created by the major industrial powers at Bretton Woods, New Hampshire, during a historic conference in 1944—what would become the International Monetary Fund and the World Bank. As the New Deal sought to stabilize capitalism by pacifying labor movements at home, these institutions sought to stabilize capitalism by regulating international finance in order to avoid a repetition of the economic chaos of the 1930s.[19] And as the New Deal implanted racial oppression in its policy-making, the Bretton Woods institutions implanted neocolonial oppression in their policy-making. "The principle of mutual inter-imperialist assistance whereby American, British, French, and West German monopoly control extends joint control over the wealth of the non-liberated zones of Africa, Latin America and Asia," wrote Nkrumah, "finds concrete expression in the formation of interlocked international financial institutions and bodies of credit."[20] As with loans, Western development aid was also conditional on meeting neocolonial requirements, such as "the conclusion of commerce and navigation treaties; agreements for economic co-operation; the right to meddle in internal finances, including currency and foreign exchange, to lower trade barriers in favor of the donor country's goods and capital; to protect the interests of private investments; determination of how the funds are to be used; forcing the recipient to set up counterpart funds; to supply raw materials to the donor; and use of such funds—a majority of it, in fact—to buy goods from the donor nation." Pressured by these mechanisms, Third World governments tended to be more beholden to their neocolonialist masters than to the interests of their own people; meanwhile, the potentially explosive conflicts between capitalists and workers in the West were channeled outward to destructive effect in the Third World.[21]

What Nkrumah called neocolonialism, US policy-makers called "modernization." They claimed the Third World could achieve its goals within a Western capitalist framework. A group of US academic economists and political scientists—funded by the Rockefeller Foundation, the Ford Foundation, and the CIA—developed a body of scholarship called "modernization theory" to explain how this would happen. Its most important exponent was Walt Whitman Rostow, a national security adviser to Presidents Kennedy and Johnson. He argued there was an "inner logic" to political and economic development, as every nation passed through essentially the same five stages, from tradition-bound poverty to high mass-consumption prosperity. In this framework, the Third World existed at an earlier stage of development; the US was at the last stage, which everyone else was heading toward. This positioned the US's development experts as intellectual authorities. Their advice to the Third World was that prosperity could be reached by following the natural pathway through the various stages, without unnaturally trying to jump stages to catch up with the West. The first step was to create what

Rostow called the "pre-conditions for take-off," which centered upon the emergence of "new types of enterprising men" able to lead a process of science-based industrialization and expanding commerce—in short, the coming together of a bourgeois class.[22]

In the hands of liberal policy-makers in the 1950s and early 1960s, modernization theory led to US support and funding for development policies in the Third World that were the counterpart to New Deal policies at home: land reforms, public education programs, housing programs, and tariffs on imports to support domestic industrialization.[23] Government officials who had worked on Roosevelt's New Deal fanned out to implement these modernization policies in Latin America, Southeast Asia, and Africa.[24] The long-term goal of US-led neocolonialism was to free the movement of investments and profits around the world from tariffs, from the protected trade zones that European imperialism had created, and from the risks of nationalization under the leadership of left-wing governments. In the short term, though, US policy-makers believed in taming capital flows somewhat in order to create stable capitalist economies in the Third World.[25] In their view, stability depended on a bourgeois civil society, which could only emerge if US development policy enabled more people to privately own land; if it funded the circulation of a scientific worldview through schools and universities; if it encouraged urbanization; and if it fostered a proper level of industrial development. The Pakistani political analyst Eqbal Ahmad called it "welfare imperialism."[26]

What modernization theory ignored was that Western development was itself dependent on Third World underdevelopment; therefore, Third World development could not be modeled on Western development. The theory promised US-style prosperity for everyone but did so within a system of imperialism that, as Nkrumah described, was structured to prevent that promise from ever being realized. By the late 1960s, the failure of modernization policies was apparent. Rather than the promised "take-off" of Third World development, there was an ever-increasing wealth gap between rich and poor countries. The pattern of growing inequality between the West and the Third World that had been set by European colonialism in the nineteenth century continued through the 1950s and 1960s, despite formal independence. In 1970, Americans enjoyed a GDP per capita twenty times higher than Indians; a century earlier, the ratio had been 4 to 1.[27]

Moreover, Third World countries were not all developing into stable subordinate participants in the capitalist system but, in some cases, seeking to alter the system itself. The Third World masses whom independence movements had mobilized were now demanding their governments deliver on the promise of liberation. Despite the powerful forces arrayed against them, some Third World leaders were seeking to obtain better control of their terms of trade. Indeed, it appeared the modernization policies intended to peacefully incorporate Third World countries into Western capitalism were having the opposite effect by holding out a promise of prosperity that the system could not deliver.

In response, Western powers were increasingly having to rely on violence to impose neocolonial policies. US and European intelligence agencies organized coups to ensure that oil, in particular, remained in the hands of Western multinationals, which paid minuscule rents to Third World governments for control of the most valuable commodity in world trade.[28] After the Iranian parliament voted to nationalize the country's oil production in 1951, Western corporations responded with trade blockades, causing an economic crisis, which then made the government an easy target for a US- and UK-orchestrated military coup in 1953 that restored the pro-Western shah to power. In Iraq, after nationalist army officers in 1958 overthrew the puppet monarchy created by British colonialists, they began efforts to gain greater control over oil production and use the revenue from oil exports to industrialize and introduce social reforms to alleviate poverty; these advances in Iraq were short-lived, however, as the government was overthrown in a CIA-backed military coup in 1963.[29] Nkrumah noted that "Africa, Asia and Latin America have begun to experience a round of coups d'état or would-be coups, together with a series of political assassinations which have destroyed in their political primes some of the newly emerging nations' best leaders."[30] In fact, between 1947 and 1970, the US intervened against local revolutions and nationalist regimes on average once every sixteen months.[31] This aspect of US leadership of the capitalist system was an expression of the new national security agencies created after World War II and the expanding military-industrial complex.

Shortly after the publication of Nkrumah's *Neo-Colonialism* in 1965, the deputy director of the CIA was sent an internal memo on the book.[32] Four months later, Nkrumah's government was ousted in a military coup, victim to exactly the methods of covert action his book described. The CIA station in Ghana played a major role in the coup, funding and advising the dissidents in the Ghanaian army who carried it out.[33] Nkrumah's removal set in motion a realignment of Ghana's politics that suited the interests of Western multinational corporations. Harvard University economist Gustav Papanek arrived in Ghana, fresh from a similar assignment in Indonesia, to advise the new government to privatize its publicly owned businesses and reorient the country toward the West.[34] A subsequent US national security memo to President Lyndon B. Johnson described the overthrow of Nkrumah and the Indonesia coup of the previous year as a "fortuitous windfall." Whereas Nkrumah was "doing more to undermine our interests than any other black African," Ghana's "new military regime is almost pathetically pro-Western." The memo recommended that a small amount of aid granted to Indonesia and Ghana would whet "their appetites, and enables us to use the prospect of more as leverage."[35]

Like James, Nkrumah understood capitalism as a globe-spanning structure in which there were hidden but fundamental dependencies between the industrialized core and the colonial periphery. Western labor struggles and Third World struggles could each be played off against the other. But they could also be mutually reinforcing. Solidarity for Nkrumah was not a matter of European expressions of sympathy for the suffering masses of Africa, Asia, or the Caribbean; nor was it ultimately a question of calling for Western politicians to make better moral choices in their policy decisions. His analysis of neocolonialism implied an internationalist politics, in which the radicalization of class struggles in the West and the radicalization of Third World national liberation movements were symbiotic. If Third World movements were able to weaken neocolonialism, then capitalists would have less leeway to pacify working classes in the West; if working-class movements in the West were able to weaken big business, Wall Street, and the national security state, they would be curtailing the forces arrayed against not only themselves but also the Third World. Nkrumah also recognized, though, that by the 1950s there was little chance of a Western labor movement successfully overturning the capitalist structures that gave rise to neocolonialism, in no small part because of the success of the welfare policies of the protective core and their associated notions of racial privilege. But there was another arena of struggle in which an internationalist politics of solidarity between movements in the West and Third World liberation could emerge—the US Black freedom movement.

"The triply-oppressed status of Negro women"

While Nkrumah argued that the class struggle in the West was inseparable from the struggle against neocolonialism in Africa, Black women in the US argued that class struggle was inseparable from gender and racial liberation. In both cases, they exposed how New Deal–style welfare states in the US and Europe rested on racial divisions: between the colonizing and colonized worlds, and between workers in the West deemed entitled to a family wage and those cast as undeserving or dependent. An idea of antiracism was emerging that encompassed international struggles against imperialism as well as domestic opposition to the racial and gendered divisions of welfare-state capitalism.

In 1940, for example, Black communist activist Esther Cooper Jackson studied the experiences of Black women domestic workers in the US and described how their exploitation had to be understood as shaped simultaneously by race, gender, and class. The trade union movement was wrong to think them necessarily unresponsive to organizing efforts. Black women, the group most excluded from the provisions of the New Deal and most ignored by the mainstream Left, had, she suggested, the potential to be a vanguard for radical social change.[36]

Similarly, Vicki Garvin, another Black communist, wrote in 1950 that Black women were at the "very bottom of the nation's economic ladder" and therefore their struggle for betterment was an "acid test for democracy" in the US. As she was growing up in early twentieth-century Harlem, Garvin had seen her mother work as a domestic in white households, sometimes paid in leftover food and discarded clothing. "My mother stood on the streets of the Bronx," she recalled, in "what was then known as the slave line hoping that she would be selected by one of the white women who walked up and down this line bargaining for pickings of an hourly rate, usually twenty-five cents."[37] In the 1930s, Garvin emerged as a powerful organizer and strategist in New York City's Black Left.[38] Her movement work in Harlem was a major influence on Malcolm X, and she helped him to see the Black struggle in the US as part of an international struggle for self-determination.[39]

It was in the work of Cooper Jackson's and Garvin's comrade Claudia Jones that these ideas coalesced into an analysis that dramatically expanded Marxist thinking on the relationships between race, gender, and class struggles, laying down positions that were later picked up by Black feminist organizers in the 1970s.[40] In the mid-1930s, while barely out of high school, Jones heard Black communists in Harlem talk about the Scottsboro Boys case, in which nine Black teenagers were falsely accused of raping two white women aboard a train near Scottsboro, Alabama, in 1931. What struck her was the way the speakers connected the case to international struggles against colonialism and fascism. "I was impressed by the communist speakers who explained the reasons for this brutal crime against young Negro boys; and who related the Scottsboro case to the struggle of the Ethiopian people against fascism, and Mussolini's invasion," she wrote. Jones had arrived in the US aged eight years old, traveling with her family from Trinidad. By the late 1940s, she had become a leading organizer and theoretician in the Communist Party.[41]

In the early years of the Cold War, Jones recognized the growing strength of women's groups around the world in opposing the buildup of arms and tensions. In the US, she felt, working-class women could play leading roles in new movements to call for the abolition of nuclear weapons and of the draft.[42] Women were also joining the US labor movement in record numbers and challenging the family wage concept central to the New Deal.[43] Jones saw, in particular, a growing militancy of Black women, thousands of whom had joined the Communist Party in the 1930s and 1940s.[44] "From the days of the slave traders down to the present, the Negro woman has had the responsibility of caring for the needs of the family, of militantly shielding it from the blows of Jim Crow insults, of rearing children in an atmosphere of lynch terror, segregation and police brutality and of fighting for an education for their children," she wrote. "The bourgeoisie is fearful of the militancy of the Negro woman and for good reason. The capitalists know, far better than many progressives seem to know, that once Negro women undertake action, the militancy of the whole Negro people and thus of the anti-imperialist coalition, is greatly enhanced."[45]

To the existing notion, derived from the debate between Lenin and Roy, of understanding national and racial oppression as a second axis of struggle alongside class struggle, Jones added gender as a third axis. "Negro women—as workers, as Negroes, and as women—are the most oppressed stratum of the whole population," she wrote. The "triply-oppressed status of Negro women is a barometer of the status of all women."[46] Jones was developing arguments that were echoed in the famous 1977 statement of the Black feminist socialist Combahee River Collective and later with theories of intersectionality. In her version of this argument, though, it was not that "the major systems of oppression are interlocking," as the Combahee statement put it, in "the conditions of our lives."[47] Rather race, class, and gender were all different aspects of a single system, capitalism. The measure of race and gender oppression was the extent to which it enabled capitalists to usurp greater profits from the labor of Black and women workers. "The superexploitation of the Negro woman worker is thus revealed not only in that she receives, as woman, less than equal pay for equal work with men, but also in that the majority of Negro women get less than half the pay of white women," Jones wrote. The labor movement, she pointed out, ignored domestic service and agricultural work, the two main areas of employment of Black women, and had not challenged the exclusion of these sectors from the social insurance provisions of the New Deal. In Jones's analysis, the working class was not homogenous but materially segmented by race and gender. Consequently, the labor movement had to "have a special approach to Negro women workers." And women's groups could not think of Black, working-class women as being involved in the same struggles as middle-class, white women: ruling class ideologists, after all, cannot "with equanimity or credibility . . . speak of the Negro woman's 'place' as in the home, for Negro women are in other peoples' kitchens."[48]

Central to Jones's antiracism was a linking of struggles against structural racism at home to struggles of African and Asian peoples elsewhere against imperialism. For her, the victories that anticolonial movements were winning from the late 1940s fed into the Black freedom movement in the US, suggesting new

Claudia Jones
London Borough of Lambeth, Archives Department

modes of analysis and new methods of struggle. Indeed, racism in the US was actually a form of imperialism, Jones believed. Black people constituted "a nation oppressed by American imperialism, in the ultimate sense as India is oppressed by British imperialism and Indonesia by Dutch imperialism." The Black struggle in the US was therefore fundamentally a national liberation movement against an internal form of colonialism. In the Black Belt Southern states, a Black peasant class formed a majority; methods of overthrowing white minority rule in Africa could equally be applied in Alabama. This implied not only sympathy for anticolonial struggles elsewhere but a transformation in how Black people saw themselves, no longer minorities in the US but part of an international movement that had already proven it could defeat white power structures.[49]

It was important, wrote Jones, that "Negro and white workers form strong bonds of unity with each other." But this could not be done on the basis of an abstract idea of class unity that ignored the differences in how Black and white workers related to the capitalist system. Black people experienced a "double oppression," she wrote, "as wage slaves and as Negroes." Like the situation colonial workers faced elsewhere, their racial oppression enabled capitalists to pay less for the same work. Whereas all waged workers were exploited "wage slaves" in the sense that capitalists were able to extract a surplus value from their employment, Black workers were exploited at a systematically higher rate, enabling superprofits tied to racial oppression. "Scarcely less than before the Civil War," Jones wrote, "is the Black Belt a prison-house of the Negroes, the chains which hold them now are the invisible chains of poverty, the legal chains of debt-slavery and when the landlords deem it necessary, the iron shackles of the chain gang."[50]

Formally, the argument had its origins in the 1920 Lenin-Roy debate on national oppression but, by the 1940s, US communists had moved away from the Black Belt thesis and tended to take the view that racial integration was becoming possible. Jones believed otherwise, anticipating the frustration with the limits of integration policies that would later emerge in the mid-1960s.

For Jones, the internal colonialism of US racial oppression mapped onto the US's militarist foreign policies at the start of the Cold War. "The cost of a single battleship could provide 325 family-sized dwelling units," she wrote. "Shall this money be used for a false national emergency in which 70 billion is being spent for bombs or shall the money be spent for housing projects and homes?"[51] The burgeoning war economy had to be defunded and resources diverted to meet the social needs of working people, Jones emphasized. To this end, she enthusiastically supported the campaign of Henry Wallace's Progressive Party in the 1948 general election. Speaking at the opening session of the party's convention in Philadelphia, Jones's friend and fellow Black Left activist Shirley Graham, later to marry Du Bois, laid out a program of untethering the New Deal from its militarist, sexist, and racist moorings, mirroring Jones's analysis. The adopted program advocated peaceful coexistence with the Soviet Union, ending Jim Crow segregation, and social programs to tackle poverty, including universal public healthcare.[52] Among the 150 African American delegates at the convention was a young Coretta Scott King.[53]

With the war in Korea that began in 1950, Black people in the US, Jones wrote, "see in the bloody massacre of the people of Korea an extension of the foul white supremacy oppression and contempt for the Negro people and the coloured people of all of Asia." There was a continuum in the horrors of racist police violence against Black people within the US and the racist violence of military "police" actions against Asians: "Children at play, women washing on the riverbanks, and peasants working in the fields have been the targets of bombing and strafing by the American armed forces whose so-called 'police action' was to bring 'freedom' to the 'unhappy' Korean people!"[54] Over a million civilians were killed by US bombing in the war.[55] Whatever the official justifications, Jones wrote, at root the war was driven by "Wall Street imperialism." She drew attention to the ways the US was displacing and surpassing European imperialism by introducing new forms of indirect control through economic dependency, backed by the US's military power. In the Caribbean, she saw US neocolonialism complementing British power in a "family arrangement" that enabled US corporations to control Trinidadian oil, Jamaican bauxite, and Guyanese aluminum. Likewise, the US supported French imperialism in Vietnam with Marshall Plan funding, she wrote.[56]

Like Césaire, Jones focused her thinking upon the hidden connections between fascism and imperialism. She thought it was wrong to think there was a fundamental antagonism between

US liberal democracy and European fascism. Rather, the "main danger of fascism to the world," she argued after World War II, "comes from the most colossal imperialist forces which are concentrated within the United States."[57] The oppression of Black people in the US, she held, was a reservoir from which fascism could be channeled to the rest of the US system. Increases in the frequency of lynching, white racist riots, and police murders of Black people were the warning signs of a fascist upsurge. The agencies of national security that had been expanded in the US after World War II and granted new powers of surveillance, criminalization, and deportation were, for Jones, ways that fascist impulses acquired an institutional presence in the existing structures of government.[58] Jones conceived of fascism not as a sudden coup that appears from the extremist fringes, but as a gradual process in which law enforcement, immigration control, military, and intelligence agencies acquire steadily more capacities for repression and violence, in an ideological atmosphere of racism and sexism. To Jones, European fascism was a cousin to the structural racism she experienced in the US.

A further development of the analogy between European fascism and US racism was the Civil Rights Congress's 1951 petition to the United Nations, charging the US with committing genocide against Black people. Jones was one of the petitioners who worked on the document, Du Bois one of the signatories. The Convention on the Prevention and Punishment of the Crime of Genocide had been approved by the UN General Assembly three years earlier. It defined genocide as the crime of killing, causing serious bodily or mental harm, deliberately inflicting conditions of life calculated to bring about physical destruction, or preventing births within a group, with the intent to "destroy, in whole or in part, a national, ethnical, racial or religious group, as such."[59] In the document that outlined the petitioners' argument, edited by William L. Patterson and titled *We Charge Genocide*, the authors systematically laid bare the extent of the physical and economic violence directed at Black people across the US. Significantly, they used the term "racism," which had recently entered the vocabulary of US liberalism, to draw a comparison between the treatment of Jews by the Nazi government in Germany, the paradigm case of genocide, and the treatment of Black people by the US government. Segregation in the US was "based on the Hitler-like theory" of white supremacy, stated the petitioners. "There is infinite variety in the cruelty we will catalogue, but each case has the common denominator of racism." In suggesting that the oppression of Black people in the US derived from the widespread acceptance of racist theories, the petitioners deployed a major plank of the liberal account of racism. But the petitioners also marshaled the more radical, structural concept of racism derived from anticolonial thinking. Black people in the US, the petitioners wrote, were experiencing a "colonial-type oppression" that was propelled by capitalist profit-making. The "foundation of this genocide of which we complain is economic. It is genocide for profit. The intricate superstructure of 'law and order' and extra-legal terror enforces an oppression that guarantees profit." The oppression of Black people was "the original base of Wall Street superprofits," and the government maintains an edifice of racist violence strictly in order to defend this source of profits. For the same reason, this oppression was also a threat to other peoples:

> We solemnly warn that a nation which practices genocide against its own nationals may not be long deterred, if it has the power, from genocide elsewhere. White supremacy at home makes for colored massacres abroad. Both reveal contempt for human life in a colored skin. Jellied gasoline in Korea and the lynchers' faggot at home are connected in more ways than that both result in death by fire. The lyncher and the atom bomber are related. The first cannot murder unpunished and unrebuked without so encouraging the latter that the peace of the world and the lives of millions are endangered. The tie binding both is economic profit and political control.[60]

The United Nations, dominated by Western powers, ignored the petition. At its founding meeting in San Francisco in 1945, the UN had already rejected efforts by Indian and Haitian delegates to pass a resolution using the new term "racism." The delegates argued that, as World War II had demonstrated, doctrines of racial supremacy endangered world peace.[61] In a similar vein, the major powers rebuffed efforts by Third World activists to secure a commitment to colonial independence in the UN Charter.[62]

In 1948, the national security and immigration control agencies that Jones had identified as vectors of a nascent fascism began an attempt to deport her to Trinidad. She was arrested and briefly imprisoned at Ellis Island before being released on bail. She was arrested again two years later, under the new McCarran Act, which empowered the government to deport or deny admission to individuals deemed subversive.[63] The "overt act" justifying her arrest was her speech that year on International Women's Day, in which she presented her ideas on the role of women in the struggles against imperialism, capitalism, and fascism.[64] Upon her sentencing to a year and a day in federal prison, she told the court that she had been convicted for no other reason than "holding Communist ideas," fighting for the "peaceful coexistence of nations," trying "to repel the fascist drive on free speech and thought in our country" represented by the new national security apparatus, and opposing "racist ideas, so integral a part of the desperate drive by the men of Wall Street to war and fascism."[65]

Jones was deported from the US in 1955 after nine months of imprisonment at the Federal Prison for Women in Alderson, West Virginia. She settled in London, where she became a leader of the African Caribbean community, founding and editing one of the first Black newspapers in Britain, the *West Indian Gazette*, which served as a promotional tool for her antiracist campaigning. The newspaper also helped publicize a series of annual indoor Caribbean carnival events, which Jones initiated from the late 1950s; these grew into the city's annual Notting Hill carnival.[66]

WHAT IS ANTIRACISM?

For the Black Left of the 1940s, antiracism in the US was part of an international movement against fascism and imperialism. But, by the end of the decade, that framing was running up against the imperatives of the Cold War. As former European colonies in Africa and Asia became formally independent, the US government sought to win them over to its side. It was harder to do this as evidence mounted of the oppressive treatment of Black people in the US, especially because this was now understood in terms of "racism," and therefore was comparable to Nazism. In this new political terrain, the federal government began to gently embrace the kind of liberal antiracism that Myrdal had proposed, with the State Department eager to encourage the perception that the US was progressively addressing the "American dilemma" of racial prejudice.[67] If the granting of civil rights was tied to the US government's management of its reputation abroad, then there could be little room for the radical idea that Black freedom in the US was part of an international struggle against imperialism, including US imperialism. To say that the US had a problem of structural racism in housing, education, policing, or employment was now widely perceived as siding with the Soviets. The agencies of national security surveillance and criminalization that targeted Claudia Jones were employed to hound a long list of other Black radicals through the 1950s.[68] Even Du Bois was indicted as an unregistered foreign agent. The case against him collapsed at trial but the affair destroyed his reputation: newspapers no longer ran his columns, commercial publishers rejected his book manuscripts, and for eight years the State Department prevented him from traveling abroad by denying him a passport.[69] Yet in spite of these efforts, the antiracism of the 1940s Black Left survived and reemerged in new forms in subsequent decades.

7

Antiracism Means Anticapitalism

In March 1957, just months after the successful conclusion of the Montgomery bus boycott, Martin Luther King Jr. and Coretta Scott King traveled to Africa to celebrate another antiracist victory: Ghana's independence after having won, under Nkrumah's leadership, freedom from British colonialism.[1] In his speeches that year, Martin Luther King used the word "racism" to refer not to the situation in the US, but to the struggle against colonialism in Asia and Africa. He talked of the "colored" majority of the world, who "for years lived under the bondage of colonialism and imperialism" but have "decided to rise up." Their message was, "Racism and colonialism must go."[2] Like the radicals of the 1940s, the Kings placed the US Black struggle in this international context. "The two struggles, against colonialism in Africa and racial oppression in America, were tributaries of the same river," Coretta Scott King wrote.[3]

Anticolonial struggles in Asia and Africa were, for the Kings, directly relevant to the Black struggles for freedom in the US. Martin Luther King repeatedly described the Black ghettoes of US cities as the result of "internal colonialism" or "domestic colonialism," a terminology that harked back to the communist Black Belt thesis that Claudia Jones had espoused. The implication was that the kinds of structural racism that shaped colonial settings also applied to cities like New York, Los Angeles, and Chicago. In early 1966, the Kings arrived in Chicago to lead a new civil rights campaign tackling school segregation, job discrimination, housing discrimination, and police brutality. Renting a home in the impoverished West Side, Coretta Scott King wrote: "In all my life, I had rarely seen anything like the conditions we faced in Chicago. The level of poverty called to mind our travels through Bombay a few years before."[4] Martin Luther King wrote of a "total pattern of economic exploitation under which Negroes suffer in Chicago and other northern cities."[5] He broke down this "pattern" into a number of components within an overall structure. With fewer resources in ghetto schools, "slum education is designed to perpetuate the inferior status of slum children and prepare them only for menial jobs in much the same way that the South African apartheid educational philosophy does for the African," he wrote. Discrimination by federal housing agencies, real estate agents, landlords, and banks trapped Black people in slum housing with higher rents than equivalent properties in white neighborhoods. As for the criminal legal system: "The courts are organized as a tool of the economic structure and political machine," and the "police are little more than 'enforcers' of the present system of exploitation."[6] "No Negro escapes this cycle of modern slavery," he wrote.[7]

Coretta Scott King at the Democratic National Convention,
New York City, 1976
Warren K. Leffler—NYWT&S/Library of Congress, Washington, DC

There was little sense here of civil rights as a matter of formal equality under the law. Rather, antiracists had to confront what he called the "white power structure."[8] Against the liberal suggestion that segregation was based on attitudes of hatred, fueled by doctrines of superiority, he argued the origin of structural racism lay in the economics of inequality, not the psychology of animosity. In the ghettoes, he wrote, "every condition exists because someone profits from its existence." Providing Black people inferior schooling, for example, "continued the availability of cheap labor as the basis of economic expansion. This is but a sophistication of slavery." The liberal progressive vision of a redemption that flows inexorably from America's founding values here runs up against a King who is attuned to the ways that oppression reconfigured itself through the centuries, from the plantation to the ghetto. And he was a critic of the liberal idea that progress would come from diversifying those in positions of power; in the Northern cities, this was what he called "plantation politics," in which elites recruited pliant Black leaders to shore up an appearance of change while the underlying structures that oppress the Black masses remained unaltered.[9]

In the struggle against the internal colonialism of the ghettoes, King advocated that students boycott inadequate schools, that protestors block highways to draw attention to poverty, and that tenants use rent strikes to campaign for better housing.[10] Such actions, he argued, connected Black people in the US to a world movement against colonialism. Indeed, the "hope of the people of color in the world may well rest on the American Negro and his ability to reform the structure of racist imperialism from within." In Latin America, for instance, US corporations control the "life and destiny" of the region. "Here we see racism in its more sophisticated form: neocolonialism," King wrote in 1967, using Nkrumah's term. Racism was for King tightly bound up with structures of economic exploitation, both within the US and between the West and the Third World.[11] When he called for an end to the "three major evils—the evil of racism, the evil of poverty, and the evil of war," he was trying to get Americans to be part of an organized and disciplined international movement to radically transform the economic and political structures with which "these three evils are tied together." Only such a movement could bring about the vast redistribution of wealth he envisaged.[12]

Martin Luther King is nowadays remembered and celebrated as the greatest symbol of liberal antiracism. The historian Jeanne Theoharis notes that today's mainstream liberal story of the civil rights movement dresses its participants "in the cloak of sanctified, not-angry nobility, who struggled respectably and were destined to win" because of the decency of American values and "the disenfranchised's ability to use the levers of democracy and of the willingness of the powerful to change."[13] Because the fundamental values and institutions of the US were sound, on this account, it was possible for civil rights protestors to successfully challenge the violations of their rights by pointing out the gap between the nation's professed moral principles and the practice of racial segregation—the Myrdal formula for antiracism. When these appeals by civil rights leaders won the sympathy of decent politicians, they worked together to change white attitudes and pass the Civil Rights Act of 1964 and the Voting Rights Act of 1965. The injustices of the past were thus redeemed through a renewed commitment to the nation's founding principles. Reassuringly, antiracism meant creating an America that was more fully American.

This was possible, according to the mainstream story, because there were heroic individuals on both sides. The victims of injustice who spoke out needed to be capable of persistence and determination, able through their self-expression to move others to empathize with their plight, and they needed to believe in the capacity of the American system to tend toward justice. Martin Luther King Jr., at the center of the mainstream story, is thus feted for his fortitude, the persuasive power of his voice, and his belief in American values. In this way, one charismatic male leader is substituted for the messy energies of the actual movement he was a part of, and his allotted role becomes to discipline Black people into adopting supposedly dignified and respectable methods of protest while granting white people a collective forgiveness, as if any one person could reasonably do either. At the same time, the powerful white politicians who heard King's message needed to be able to rise above partisan interests to honor a moral principle and able to inspire ordinary people to overcome their prejudices. Finally, once racist laws were gone, and equal opportunity and diversity officially proclaimed, the only remaining barriers to freedom were individual acts of discrimination and fringe perpetrators of extremist hate, both of which were now condemned by law and mainstream morality.

But none of that represents what King stood for or the contemporary reaction to his activism. The beating heart of his politics was more the radical antiracism of the 1940s than the US liberal tradition with which he is typically associated. Racism in the US was, for him, a structural form of oppression that he repeatedly compared to European colonialism elsewhere. It was connected to capitalist profit-making, and ending it meant also ending war and poverty. This conception had its roots in the Black Left of the 1940s; it aligned closely with Shirley Graham Du Bois's 1948 program that had influenced Coretta Scott King as a student. Coretta Scott had tended to have views that were "more global and more pacifist" than Martin's, as she put it, and her public opposition to the Vietnam War came earlier. In 1962, she had visited Geneva as a delegate to the international Women Strike for Peace movement, which sought to bring about nuclear disarmament. But her longstanding belief in the need to defund the military and create a peace economy based on meeting human needs for education, housing, and healthcare was always shared by Martin.[14] The way Martin Luther King is usually remembered also airbrushes out the widespread hostility to his activism. From the moment he emerged as a leader, liberal as well as conservative opinion column writers admonished him, and FBI agents spied on him. There was no American public figure who was more disliked in the 1960s, according to repeated Gallup polling through the decade; only Nikita Khrushchev and Fidel Castro scored more negatively in surveys.[15]

It is true that Martin Luther King sometimes drew on less radical framings of antiracism. He was not averse to presenting the civil rights movement as an expression of American values. It was "standing up for the best in the American dream and carrying the whole nation back to those great wells of democracy which were dug deep by the founding fathers in the formulation of the Constitution and the Declaration of Independence," as he put it in 1967.[16] In his book *Where Do We Go from Here: Chaos or Community?*, he repeated Myrdal's argument that the work of healing racism presented an opportunity for the US to demonstrate its morality, and he quoted Benedict's definition of racism as an irrational doctrine. But a closer look at how King used the word "racism" indicates that liberal-sounding arguments jostled uneasily in his thinking next to ideas that were closer to those of radical antiracists like Kwame Nkrumah and Claudia Jones. King's understanding of racism was certainly more multifaceted than the liberal analysis usually ascribed to him.[17]

The distortion of King's life into a false icon of liberal antiracism erases the anticapitalism that was essential to his worldview, not just toward the end of his life, but throughout. To commemorate King properly means seeing the relevance to our own times of his campaigns against the structural racisms of Northern cities; it means taking seriously his denunciations of liberals who oppose racism in the narrow sense of individual beliefs and attitudes while living in comfort within broader racist structures they do nothing to challenge; and it means making anticapitalism and anti-imperialism central parts of our politics.

"Resistance is not enough"

On August 31, 1967, several thousand delegates gathered at the Palmer House Hotel in Chicago for the opening rally of the National Conference for New Politics (NCNP) convention. The weekend-long event was an ambitious attempt to forge a broad coalition of the white New Left and the Black freedom movement; 200 different organizations participated, including King's Southern Christian Leadership Conference (SCLC), Students for a Democratic Society, the Socialist Workers Party, and the National Committee for a Sane Nuclear Policy.[18] On the opening night, King told the audience: "Capitalism was built on the exploitation and suffering of black slaves and continues to thrive on the exploitation of the poor—both black and white, both here and abroad." The only solution: "a radical redistribution of political and economic power."[19] There was talk at the convention of running King as an independent candidate of the Left in the following year's presidential elections. Despite the prominent role of King and his SCLC, the leading Black organization at the NCNP convention was the Student Nonviolent Coordinating Committee (SNCC), chaired by Jamil Al-Amin, then known as H. Rap Brown.

Born in Baton Rouge, Louisiana, Al-Amin worked with the civil rights movement in Alabama and Mississippi in the mid-1960s. He was only twenty-three years old when he was elected SNCC's national chair, four months before the NCNP convention. As he traveled the US that summer, federal agents and informants constantly tailed him. In the month and a half before arriving in Chicago, he had been shot in the face with buckshot by a deputy sheriff and arrested twice, on incitement to arson and riot in Maryland (a state attorney later admitted to fabricating the charges) and on firearms charges in Louisiana (these were voided on appeal when it emerged that the judge had announced at the state's Bar Association convention before the trial that "I'm going to get that nigger").[20] A few days before the NCNP convention, FBI director J. Edgar Hoover sent a memo to all the bureau's field offices, instructing them to establish a new, secret "counterintelligence endeavor," known as Cointelpro, to "expose, disrupt, misdirect, discredit, or otherwise neutralize the activities of black nationalist, hate-type organizations and groupings." Among the groups targeted were King's Southern Christian Leadership Conference. Al-Amin was one of the four "extremists" mentioned by name in the memo.[21] Over the following three months, the FBI sent the White House an average of two memos a week describing Al-Amin's activities.[22]

With his down-to-earth way of speaking about Black liberation, Al-Amin was a new Malcolm X in the eyes of many.[23] He was an agitator and an instigator; in his speeches, he rhymed, joked, and provoked. After the Detroit uprising in the summer of 1967, he said: "They used to call it Motown; now it ain't no town. They used to call it Detroit; now they call it destroyed."[24] But behind the "rap," there was also a substantial political analysis. At his speech to the NCNP convention's Black Caucus, Al-Amin drew a grim picture of the situation facing Black America. "America is . . . putting into effect the genocide of Black people," he announced. That was happening in four ways: Black people made up one in three of the US deaths in the war in Vietnam, though they represented only one in ten of the US population; huge numbers of Black children in the Deep South were dying each year of poverty; Black people were being sent to prisons in the name of law and order; and they were being targeted for birth control. Al-Amin rejected the liberal narrative that the US was on the verge of overcoming past legacies of racism. The racial advances that liberals celebrated in the 1960s were superficial, he argued; in fact, there was regress, not progress. The only way to stop this impending violence was by force. "If you choose to play Nazis, we ain't gonna play Jews," Al-Amin said.

Though he referred to the concept of genocide, Al-Amin did not draw on any of the liberal theories of racism that emerged from the analysis of Nazism. Violence against Black people, perpetuated by both political parties and enabled by the repressive powers granted to national security agencies, was, he argued, escalating because of economic changes: "We were brought here as slaves to work. There is no more work. We are a problem to America." Now the US has "a surplus of niggers . . . We have outlived our usefulness."[25] As he told a French journalist in an interview a few weeks later, "the capitalistic system, as it is set up, cannot accommodate forty or fifty million Black people . . . We believe that that structure can't be reformed."[26] Thus, for Al-Amin, racism in the US was a system of carceral, economic, police, and military violence tied, at this historical moment, to a coming contraction of capitalism's need for Black waged labor. To be deemed surplus to capitalism was, he suggested, to be vulnerable to mass expulsion or elimination.

"We have to begin to talk about revolution," Al-Amin told the NCNP's Black Caucus in Chicago. That meant connecting to "other oppressed groups across the world," in Puerto Rico, Vietnam, Africa, and Latin America. "We are a colony inside of America. Black people constitute a colony. An internal colony." Al-Amin's predecessor as SNCC's chair, Kwame Ture (then known as Stokely Carmichael), wrote that the slogan of "Black Power," which SNCC had adopted the previous year, meant "that black people see themselves as part of a new force, sometimes called the 'Third World.'" And "Black and colored peoples are saying in a clear voice that they intend to determine for themselves the kinds of political, social and economic systems they will live under." To clarify the distinction between anticolonial and liberal accounts of racism, Ture (and his coauthor Charles V. Hamilton) introduced the term "institutional racism" to refer to the "less overt, far more subtle" subordination that originates not from "individual whites acting against individual blacks," but from "the operation of established and respected forces in the society." Ture and Hamilton explained:

> When a black family moves into a home in a white neighborhood and is stoned, burned or routed out, they are victims of an overt act of individual racism which many people will condemn—at least in words. But it is institutional racism that keeps black people locked in dilapidated tenements, subject to the daily prey of exploitative slumlords, merchants, loan sharks and discriminatory real estate agents. The society either pretends it does not know of this latter situation, or is in fact incapable of doing anything meaningful about it . . . Institutional racism has another name: colonialism.

The introduction of the phrase "institutional racism" was an attempt to shift the antiracist focus from individual attitudes to social structures, in a context of declining individual racism and intensifying structural racism. And it implied a rejection of the notion that racism could be substantially diminished by pursuing the integration of some Black people into the white middle class: "Helping *individual* black people to solve their problems on an *individual* basis does little to alleviate the mass of black people."[27]

Where did this leave the white New Left who had gathered for the NCNP convention? Al-Amin argued that leadership "should always remain in the hands of the dispossessed." There are "other dispossessed people in America besides Blacks who we need as allies: the Indian, the Mexican American." (The following year, over 10,000 Chicano students in Los Angeles high schools went on a week-long strike to protest racist policies.)[28] But it was no use forming coalitions with white left organizations that were unrepresentative of the dispossessed in the US and, as such, were committed to reform rather than radical change. Instead, the role of white left organizations should be to support the Black and Third World revolution by "civilizing" their own white communities.[29] The Black Caucus at Chicago took up this argument by calling upon the white delegates to pass thirteen resolutions reflecting SNCC's message and to allocate 50 percent of the voting power at the NCNP convention to the Black Caucus. After a series of lengthy debates, the majority of white delegates voted to do this.[30] A small group walked out in protest at being asked to condemn Israel's "imperialist Zionist war"—SNCC leaders had begun working with representatives of the Palestinian cause that summer, the first major Black organization to do so.[31]

The NCNP convention was a pivotal moment in the history of the New Left. There was a recognition for the first time that the Black movement was the vanguard of whatever radical political possibilities existed in the US. The white delegates agreed to the demand that they organize in their own communities. For James Forman, a comrade of Al-Amin's in the leadership of SNCC who arrived in Chicago after meeting with African leaders in Tanzania and Zambia, the stand taken by the Black Caucus helped to push US white progressives toward a period of "intense work" on tackling racist attitudes in white communities.[32] But, for many others, the NCNP convention came to signify the moment when the civil rights movement tragically fragmented and was overtaken by Black Power, white guilt, and a new mood of separatism. On this view, the civil rights movement's universal values of equal citizenship, symbolized by King, disastrously gave way to more narrowly conceived ethnic identities and political claims, symbolized by Black Power leaders like Al-Amin.[33] Or, in another version, the NCNP signified the moment the Left abandoned the solid economic ground of class politics and descended to the cultural marshes of race, gender, and sexuality, prompting a backlash against the Left from working-class whites, who turned to Nixon, Reagan, and eventually Trump. Some, such as the historian Matthew Frye Jacobson, describe the NCNP convention as the moment when "identity politics was born."[34]

But this is to distort Al-Amin's idea of identity. He wrote that it was necessary for Black people to "begin to define your Black heritage" in order to overcome the self-hatred inculcated by white superiority. But the definition of identity was the first stage in a process that had to go beyond cultural heritage to radical politics. "We must move from Black awareness to revolutionary motion." The recognition or celebration of Black cultural identity was not necessarily antiracist. "To be Black is not to be revolutionary. When you begin to stress culture without politics, people can become so hooked up in the beauty of themselves that they have no desire to fight. It becomes ego-gratifying just to be Black." These were not the words of someone calling for people to abandon a universal struggle and instead embrace their own ethnic identity. The arguments of Black leaders like Al-Amin only looked separatist within a field of vision parochially narrowed to the US alone. Their argument was not that Black people in the US should go it alone, but that they should build solidarity with the majority of humanity—the people of the Third World, with whom they shared a common struggle against colonialism. This was not a divisive separatism but an internationalist, and therefore universalist, politics.

Moreover, it was an argument that was not so much a fundamental break with the ideas of the Marxist Left but a new iteration of the formulations that had circulated since the 1920 Theses on national oppression. In identifying colonialism and racism as aspects of capitalism, Al-Amin was also an advocate of a form of socialism. Racism "can't be destroyed under the capitalist system," he wrote. The "system is the thing which demands exploitation of people. You have to destroy the system."[35] There are "a thousand families" who make up the "ruling class of America," he said. "Our objective is to destroy that ruling class."[36] For the "total wealth of any country and the world . . . belongs equally to all people." The "political principles of socialism certainly have validity," he wrote but, following Fanon, he argued that "we must extend the Marxist analysis when we view colonialism." Al-Amin's anticapitalism led him to oppose the incorporation of Black leaders into the system if doing so left underlying economic structures intact. "The only constructive thing a Black mayor can do is to organize Blacks to destroy the system that oppresses Black people."[37]

The struggle of workers against capitalists has often been assumed to be unrelated to the cause of Black liberation, if not actively opposed to it. But both King and Al-Amin were anticapitalist antiracists. Both saw in the anticolonial struggles fought in Africa a model of analysis and action that could be applied to the Black freedom movement in the US, and this struggle against "internal colonialism" was for them a struggle against the capitalist class that ruled the US. Only by wrongly assuming that class struggle and antiracism are unconnected political causes can the civil rights movement be reduced to a simple demand for equal opportunities in capitalist markets, or Black Power misrepresented as a movement to diversify the ruling class through the creation of a Black wing of the establishment.

The last public statement signed by Martin Luther King before his assassination in 1968 was a call for an end to the government's persecution of Al-Amin and his release from New Orleans Parish Prison.[38] In the following years, Al-Amin continued to organize for revolutionary transformation, even as a federal judge imposed an order on him not to travel outside of Manhattan and the South Bronx. In 1971, imprisoned at the Queens House of Detention in New York City, he converted to Islam and changed his name from H. Rap Brown to Jamil Abdullah Al-Amin. Upon his release in 1976, he settled in Atlanta and, over the subsequent years, became one of the major leaders of the US Muslim community. In the 1990s, by which time the national security agencies had designated Islam the new enemy, he was targeted again, with the FBI sending informants into the mosque where he was the imam. In 2002, he was convicted on charges of murdering a law enforcement officer, despite fundamental weaknesses in the prosecution's case. Another officer, who survived the shoot-out, said he was completely sure that the perpetrator had gray eyes and was wounded. Neither of those were true of Al-Amin, but an earlier arrest warrant wrongly described Al-Amin as having gray eyes—suggesting the officer had matched his description to what he had been told Al-Amin looked like rather than to what he could actually recall seeing. Aside from the weak identification evidence, prosecutors relied on forensics. But the forensics officer on the case was later fired for inaccurate work. And the trial did not hear from Otis Jackson, who had confessed to being the shooter in a signed affidavit and whose account of what had happened was a good fit with what witnesses had said they saw on the night of the shooting. Like thousands of other Muslims in the US who were prosecuted in the years after 9/11 as part of the domestic War on Terror, there was little chance of Al-Amin receiving a fair trial, with Muslim defense witnesses treated suspiciously during the trial and the judge not allowing defense attorneys to refer to the long history of the FBI's targeting of Al-Amin. After spending years in solitary confinement at the supermax prison in Florence, Colorado, he is today imprisoned at a federal penitentiary in Tucson, Arizona. One of the great figures of radical antiracism in the US has been almost entirely forgotten.[39]

8

What Is Racial Capitalism?

The radical antiracism of groups like SNCC introduced to a mass public in the US the idea of a racist and imperialist social structure held up by the power of the capitalist classes. Yet, by the mid-1970s, the possibility of revolutionary change, along the lines that the Kings and Al-Amin had called for, seemed to recede. Nixon was in the White House crafting a new brand of conservative "law and order" politics. The Black Power movement was stymied by sectarian conflicts. Many activists chose to work with the Democratic Party machine they had earlier denounced. To radicals, it felt like defeat, at least for the time being. For them, it was a moment to take stock, reflect on the unexpected resilience of the system they were fighting, and develop new, more effective modes of struggle. This required a more complex analysis of how the structures of racism and capitalism were actually configured. As SNCC veteran Cleveland Sellers wrote in 1971, it had become obvious that "the problems were more defined than just around freedom and equality" and consequently there was "a new degree of seriousness" in the movement and "a more analytical approach among Blacks who were seriously trying to determine scientifically the what, where and why of our situation, to examining concrete economic, political and social problems" with "the emphasis on economic analysis."[1] The question of the relationship between racism and capitalism became a central intellectual puzzle.

For many on the left, the best solution to this puzzle was the notion that racism was a tactic used by capitalists to divide and thereby weaken the working class. Take, for example, Marxist theorist Ellen Meiksins Wood's version of this argument.

Racism, she says, serves capitalist interests because "it obscures relations of class exploitation in capitalism" by "deflecting attention away" from the fundamental conflict between capitalists and waged workers. She defines capitalism, correctly, as a system in which those who work and those who profit depend on the market for the most basic conditions of their lives. In a capitalist society, the dominant parts of the economy are dependent on the investment of capital, not just for trade but for production as well. In particular, such a society is characterized by a fundamental class relationship between workers and owners, mediated by the market—the capitalist buys labor power for a wage while the worker has no means to survive except through selling their labor power. Race, on the other hand, Wood says, is a "civic status." Civic status had a deep social significance in pre-capitalist societies, including slave societies, because they involved exploitation through direct coercion: the feudal lord or slave-owner took a share of the society's products through military, political, and judicial power, and civic status determined what share he was entitled to take from different groups of people. But, Wood argues, under capitalism "civic status is not constitutive of capitalist class relations." Capitalist exploitation does not work through a hierarchy of civic status but through the market, in which workers are, in principle, interchangeable units of "abstract labor." The basic tendency of capitalism is to sweep away "ancient and venerable prejudices," as Marx and Engels put it in the *Communist Manifesto*.[2] In Wood's analysis, racism is an ideological "legacy" of pre-capitalist societies in which plantation slavery prevailed. Today, at most, it is relevant in certain contexts as a way of ideologically dividing the working class and thereby impeding the emergence of the consciousness and unity necessary to bring down capitalism. Capitalism's core relationship between capitalist and worker, on the other hand, is a deep structure that shapes the whole of society. Racism is contingent and varies from one particular context to another;

capitalism is universal and its underlying logic is the same everywhere. Racism and capitalism are, in this view, separate and unequal in their social power.[3]

By contrast, James, Césaire, Fanon, Jones, the Kings, and Al-Amin all used the word "racism" to refer to a set of social practices that were closely bound up with capitalism, not just a kind of ideological trick or propaganda tool to foster divisions among workers and deceive them about their true interests. Racism was not primarily a matter of beliefs, attitudes, and doctrines at all. It was a material force present in the economic structures of the societies they were trying to transform. None of them believed that the racial aspects of those economic structures could, ultimately, be understood just in terms of race itself; structural racism was, for all of them, bound up with other economic and political motives. They did not think that racism could be explained as a kind of impetus to domination that was just innate to white people. For James, racism was the ideological reflection of material differences in the relationship of different kinds of workers to capitalist production. For Fanon, race was a constituent feature of the economic structures of colonial capitalism. Nkrumah posed the question of the racial segmentation of rights to welfare through neocolonial methods. For Jones, racism, like gender oppression, was a means for capitalism to achieve higher rates of exploitation. For Al-Amin, racist violence was intensifying as Black workers' labor became unnecessary to capitalists. These various ideas flowed into the new attempts in the 1970s to understand how racism was imbricated with capitalism. In trying to answer this question, two places were especially important as case studies and as locations for creative thinking: South Africa and Britain.

Marxists grapple with apartheid

South Africa made apartheid its official policy in 1948 while the rest of the world was at least claiming to eradicate racism after the defeat of Nazism. By the 1970s, the apartheid regime seemed impregnable. The Sharpeville massacre in 1960, in which 250 unarmed African protestors were killed or wounded by police officers, put an end to mass protests, and then, over the next decade, the regime imprisoned or exiled leaders of the underground liberation movement. There was also rapid industrial growth, at levels resembling that of Europe or the United States.[4] That combination of structural racism and capitalist industrialization seemed to confound Marxist and liberal theories of economic development, both of which tended to see racial prejudice as a legacy of the more tradition-bound societies that existed before the industrial age. Capitalist development was, according to the theories, a rationalizing force in the sense that it organized itself according to abstract rules that were, in principle, generally applicable; in this sense, it ran counter to racism's apparently irrational and arbitrary differentiations. But in South Africa, the force of racism seemed to increase the more advanced its capitalist economy became. The apartheid system was not a legacy from the nineteenth century that had survived into the 1970s; it was the creation of a modern capitalist state in the 1940s. Apartheid could not be explained as simply the expression of age-old prejudices or hatreds: in very specific ways, it was a formation of the twentieth century. Apartheid South Africa thus posed in a particularly stark way the question of how capitalism and racism were related.

There was an additional problem for Marxists seeking to understand apartheid South Africa. The prevailing social antagonism did not appear to be, as orthodox Marxists would expect, owners of industrial capital arrayed against an industrial waged workforce, but a white minority ruling over a Black majority. Nor could one plausibly claim that apartheid racism was only an ideological superstructure concealing a material base of non-racial class antagonisms, along the lines of Wood's argument. Apartheid's racist legislative program—imposing on Black workers special regimes of surveillance and monitoring under the "pass laws," removing millions of Black people from their homes and resettling them in specially designated areas, and racially segregating land and property ownership—was not an ideological maneuver to manipulate white workers, but rather constituted the material infrastructure of the entire South African political and economic system.

In the Marxist tradition, a possible answer to the question of how structural racism and advanced capitalism could coexist lay in the theory of national oppression that emerged from the 1920 Comintern discussions. Taking that approach meant seeing the apartheid system as a form of internal colonialism: white South Africa as an advanced capitalist sector subjecting the Black and "colored" peoples of South Africa to national oppression and blocking the regions where they lived from industrial development. If that had been what South Africa looked like, it could have implied a left political strategy based on Lenin's two-stage program: first, a national liberation struggle to achieve democratic rights and the end of the apartheid policies; second, an anti-capitalist class struggle to create a socialist society. In fact, this was the program that the South African Communist Party adopted in 1962.[5] But the internal colonialism thesis was not a plausible explanation of South African apartheid. It could not explain the fact that, by the 1970s, the majority of the workforce employed in modern industrial production in South Africa, such as auto plants, textiles, and steel production, came from the nonwhite sections of South African society that were supposed to be colonized. Nearly half a million Blacks worked in the gold mines, the most important sector of South Africa's economy, producing more than half of the world's output.[6] The situation of these Black wage earners was quite different from that of the masses of peasants in other colonial societies; an analysis that equated the two seemed to be missing the mark. South Africa refused to fit orthodox Marxist categories. At the same time, there were developed revolutionary organizations in South Africa seeking to topple the apartheid system. The combination of these two facts forced on Marxist theory a productive creativity.

In 1976, the London branch of the anti-apartheid movement published a pamphlet entitled *Foreign Investment and the Reproduction of Racial Capitalism in South Africa*. At this time, the anti-apartheid movement was calling for an international boycott of South African exports, though many opposed the boycott on the grounds that the best way to weaken the influence of racial prejudice in South Africa was to encourage economic growth and industrialization. Harry F. Oppenheimer, for example, chairman of Anglo-American Corporation, the world's largest mining multinational, argued in 1974 that "the rapid economic development of South Africa would in the long run prove incompatible with the government's racial policies." The pamphlet set out to show, on the contrary, that South African racism was strengthened, not weakened, by capitalist growth. Capitalism was not the solution to racism but the soil upon which it grew. Apartheid "was a consequence of capitalist development," the pamphlet argued. Its "design is not a product of irrational racial prejudice" but the outcome of a plan to control African workers and maximize profits within a system the pamphlet called "racial capitalism."[7] The pamphlet's authors, Martin Legassick and David Hemson, were part of a group of South African Marxists working in the 1970s—including Neville Alexander, Bernard Magubane, and Harold Wolpe—who started using the term "racial capitalism" to analyze the political and economic structures of apartheid South Africa. The pamphlet appears to mark the first time the term appeared in print.

In their analysis of apartheid, Alexander, Legassick, Magubane, and Wolpe began with what seemed distinctive about

South Africa in the first half of the twentieth century: the apparent coexistence of an urban, industrial capitalist economy, centered upon white consumption, with Blacks and "coloreds" the majority of the waged workforce, and a Black-centered, rural, non-capitalist economy. They noted that, in the areas where African people were concentrated, land was held communally and worked by social units based on extended family networks. What these farmers cultivated was distributed, not through market exchange, but directly according to kinship rules.[8] Much of this non-capitalist, subsistence economy existed in the so-called "reserves"—areas that had successfully resisted European conquest until the late nineteenth century but were then declared "tribal homelands" and organized by the South African government on the model of Indian reservations in the US.[9]

The normal way that Marxist scholars have understood the existence of an urban, industrial capitalist sector alongside a rural, non-capitalist subsistence economy is in terms of "primitive accumulation." In Volume 1 of his *Capital*, Marx described the process in which, for three or so centuries from the late 1400s, an emerging class of English agricultural capitalists, aided by the state, expelled farmers from communally owned land, which they then turned into their own private property. In the century before 1845, the members of parliament in Westminster, most of them landowners, passed 4,000 individual acts of "enclosure," transforming about one-fifth of the area of England from common to private ownership.[10] The "great masses" of peasants who had rights to use this land for independent cultivation in the feudal economy were, Marx wrote, "suddenly and forcibly torn from their means of subsistence, and hurled onto the labour-market as free, unprotected and rightless proletarians." Dispossessed of any means of subsistence of their own, these peasants were forced to sell their labor power to capitalists as waged workers. These processes were necessary conditions, Marx argued, for the transition to capitalism, which required both a capitalist class of owners of the means of production and a proletarian class of workers who, through "ruthless terrorism," were dispossessed of their rights to make use of land. "So-called primitive accumulation, therefore, is nothing else than the historical process of divorcing the producer from the means of production." The general assumption was that, as capitalism expanded across the world, it would dissolve the subsistence economies it encountered, repeating the processes of primitive accumulation Marx described in England. For a time, a subsistence economy might survive "in a state of decay" as an "antiquated mode of production" that existed "side by side" with capitalism. But the usual pattern was of capitalists violently uprooting any other form of economic life.[11]

But in their analysis of South African racial capitalism, Alexander, Legassick, Magubane, and Wolpe showed that the capitalist sector and the subsistence sector had combined in a single, stable economic and political structure. In South Africa, they argued, a precondition of capitalism was the preservation of non-capitalist economies, not their destruction. By employing temporary migrant workers from the reserves, capitalists were able to pay for labor power far below the cost of its "reproduction"—that is, the cost of ensuring that the worker was sufficiently housed and fed to continue working, and that children were cared for. The African non-capitalist economy could meet these needs, enabling capitalists to profit from an exceptionally high rate of exploitation. In effect, the subsistence economy subsidized the capitalist economy.

What emerged then was a differentiated economy. Of the 4 million whites in South Africa in 1970, 90 percent resided in cities. White male workers in the cities only related to the capitalist mode of production, being the kind of waged workers Marx described in *Capital*. Magubane wrote, for example, of

> the typical white miner in South Africa [in the 1970s]: he is married, his wife may or may not be working, he has young children, he needs a house and other material things, and

wants to be steadily employed from the time he enters the labor market until his retirement. When he retires, he expects government benefits, such as social security and insurance, which are partly made up of his employers' contributions and partly a redistribution via taxation of someone else's wages. From his total income he must sustain himself until he dies, and his children until they themselves enter the labor market.[12]

On the other hand, of the 15 million Blacks in South Africa, two-thirds were based in the rural areas. Of these, many temporarily migrated from the rural reserves for waged work in the urban industrial sectors or in the gold mines where nearly 400,000 were employed, but their subsistence was met largely by a non-capitalist economy.[13] The "typical African miner," wrote Magubane in 1979,

> is a migrant, who is recruited only for a term of work. His wife and children are in the reserves . . . The social costs of reproduction—of caring for children, wife, and old age—are all borne by the household in the reserves. Thus, the typical income of an African miner is made up of what his employer pays him as a single man and what his wife ekes out from the subsistence sector. Unlike the white miner, the African is not able to claim from his employer a viable income to sustain him and his family during his productive years, much less throughout his life cycle.

Moreover, while working at the mines, for periods of six to twenty-four months, he is housed as cheaply as possible, sleeping on concrete bunk beds in twenty-four-man dormitories, and unable to form a trade union.[14]

In this way, South African racial capitalism was a system for providing cheap labor: the average per capita income for the white minority in 1971 was over £1,000 a year; for Blacks it was around £53, which meant most were continuously at risk of starvation.[15] The labor of a heavily impoverished Black peasantry, Legassick and Hemson noted, "could be tapped without imposing the 'social welfare costs' on the state that were the necessary consequences of urbanisation."[16] For this arrangement to be sustainable, the non-capitalist economy needed to be productive enough to enable the reproduction of a labor force for capital. Otherwise, there would be permanent African migration to the urban areas and demands for the same subsistence wages as whites. But at the same time, it could not be so productive that Africans became self-sufficient and escaped the orbit of capitalism altogether. Apartheid was a political means to maintain this divided but combined social system. As Wolpe put it, it was

> the attempt to retain, in a modified form, the structure of the "traditional" societies . . . for the purposes of reproducing and exercising control over a cheap African industrial labour force in or near the "homelands," not by means of preserving the precapitalist mode of production but by the political, social, economic and ideological enforcement of low levels of subsistence.[17]

The apartheid regime controlled the movement of labor through the pass laws to ensure the preservation of the racial division of labor, while granting the reserves a quasi-autonomy as "Bantustans," with so-called tribal chiefs constituting a comprador, or intermediary, class to manage and sustain the non-capitalist sector on the terms set by racial capitalism.

This argument implied a capitalism that differed markedly from its conventional portrayal, not wiping out preexisting, non-capitalist modes of production but folding them into a subordinated position within its own structures. This also began to suggest an account of the structural reasons why capitalist development was imbricated with racism in South Africa. It was not that pre-capitalist civic status distinctions survived anachronistically into the capitalist era to obscure what would otherwise be capitalism's homogeneous working class of interchangeable units of "abstract labor." Rather, with its two different modes of production—capitalist and subsistence—there were two materially different social relationships between workers and capitalists in the South African social system. Racism was how apartheid managed these different relationships.

Therefore, racist ideology was not, as Marxist scholars such as Wood argued, simply a mechanism to divide Black and white waged workers, whose relationships to capitalism were fundamentally identical. Instead, racism defined the ideological and *material* boundary between two different kinds of relationship to capitalism. And racist ideology was the story South African capitalism told about its own failure to make itself universal: it narrated the boundary between the capitalist sector and the subsistence sector as the boundary between European modernity and African backwardness. Moreover, because waged labor was not made universal in South Africa, neither was liberal democracy, which, in Western Europe at least, had been forged in the conflicts between waged labor and capital. State racism, violence, and mass coercion of subordinate workers were the correlates of this failure to universalize waged labor. Thus, whatever the older histories of racial prejudice, racism under South African capitalism was not to be conceived as an archaism or legacy from the past persisting into the capitalist present. Rather, racism could be explained as a material force within the current South African social system, dividing Black and white labor materially as well as ideologically. Their respective relations to the means of production were of a quite different character from each other. There was therefore little prospect that Black and white could become conscious of their true, shared interests and, as in the old slogan, "unite and fight." Rather, there would have to be an autonomous Black struggle against racial capitalism.

In recent years, the term "racial capitalism" has proliferated among scholars and activists. Articles in the *New Yorker* and *Vox* have introduced the term to wide readerships.[18] It is beginning to carry institutional weight in universities, with a plethora of research initiatives emerging and funding from the Mellon Foundation. But the meaning of "racial capitalism" in these projects is often unclear. The website of the Research Initiative on Racial Capitalism at University of California, Davis, has a page titled "What is racial capitalism?," but it is entirely blank.[19] The scholars who use the term agree that it refers to the mutual dependence of capitalism and racism. The historian Walter Johnson writes that racial capitalism is "a sort of capitalism that relies upon the elaboration, reproduction, and exploitation of notions of racial difference."[20] Another historian, Peter Hudson, writes: "Racial capitalism suggests both the simultaneous historical emergence of racism and capitalism in the modern world and their mutual dependence."[21] All agree that the framework of racial capitalism is a challenge to the narrative that capitalism matured out of the racism and violent coercion of the slave plantations to a system based upon labor that is "free," waged, and homogeneous. As historian Robin Kelley has written, "capitalism was not the great modernizer giving birth to the European proletariat as a universal subject" that digs capitalism's grave.[22]

"Deep in the bowels of Western culture"

As a student at the University of California, Berkeley, in the late 1950s and early 1960s, Cedric Robinson was swept up in the wave of domestic and international movements, from San Francisco to South Africa. He became active in confronting racial discrimination in the Bay Area and resisting the House Un-American Activities Committee's witch hunts at the university. Through his quiet but engaged involvement in groups on and off campus, he met Malcolm X, whom the university sought

WHAT IS RACIAL CAPITALISM?

to ban from speaking; the Kenyan leader Jomo Kenyatta; and William L. Patterson, the coordinator of the Civil Rights Congress's 1951 petition to the United Nations. While others in his circle took direct action on the streets in 1967 and 1968, he sensed his own contribution would be in the development of ideas, and he began to work on a critique of Western political systems. Yet even while he was employed at the State University of New York at Binghamton's Afro-American and African Studies department and then later as director of the Center of Black Studies at the University of California, Santa Barbara, it was hard to find a journal willing to publish his work. One that did was the London-based *Race and Class*, edited by the Sri Lankan–born antiracist activist and writer A. Sivanandan. In 1980, Robinson joined the journal's editorial working group and *Race and Class* published a good deal of his work over the following decades. The pages of *Race and Class* in the early 1980s reflected a milieu in Britain in which there was a convergence of the energies of Third World liberation movements, the ideas of the US Black Power movement, and the struggles of Asian, Caribbean, and African immigrant workers, with their shared experiences of British imperialism. In this scene, the word "Black" denoted, as Sivanandan put it, not only the color of one's skin but also "the colour of one's politics, irrespective of whether one was Afro-Caribbean, Asian or African—an experience unique to Britain."[23] Robinson was living in England in 1981 when its cities erupted in uprisings against a system that denied young African Caribbeans access to waged work and policed them with an authoritarian violence that had been perfected in the colonies and then brought back home.[24] This context shaped Robinson's 1983 book *Black Marxism*, most of which was written in England. The current prevalence of the term "racial capitalism" largely derives from recent interest in this long-neglected work.[25]

While the South African Marxists were working on the basis that South Africa presented an exception to traditional Marxist

Cedric Robinson

assumptions, Robinson turned the argument on its head. The exception was, in fact, the rule. What the South Africans had called "racial capitalism" was to be found not only in South Africa but wherever capitalism prevailed: all capitalism was racial capitalism. The orthodox Marxist account had to be rethought, not just in colonized settings, but even in Western European countries like England, where, Robinson claimed, racial divisions of labor had existed throughout the history of its capitalist development.

For Robinson, racial capitalism was first a question of labor. The exploitation of waged labor that Marx analyzed in Volume 1 of *Capital* was an incomplete account of capitalist societies, he said, because capitalism had never been able to make this relationship universal—a fact Marx recognized empirically, even if he drew from it different theoretical conclusions.[26] At no point in the history of capitalism has most work been organized through the institutional framework of wage labor as *Capital* described it. As Robinson wrote:

Certainly slave labor was one of the bases for what Marx termed "primitive accumulation." But it would be an error to arrest the relationship there, assigning slave labor to some "pre-capitalist" stage of history. For more than 300 years slave labor persisted beyond the beginnings of modern capitalism, complementing wage labor, peonage, serfdom, and other methods of labor coercion . . . From its very foundations capitalism had never been—any more than Europe—a "closed system."

The picture is of multiple forms of labor, involving varying degrees of coercion, from "free" wage labor to slave labor. (We might add to the list migrant labor that operates under violent threat of deportation.) Moreover, those differentiations were organized through race. "The tendency of European civilization through capitalism was thus not to homogenize but to differentiate— to exaggerate regional, subcultural, and dialectical differences into 'racial' ones." All of this was what Robinson meant by "the non-objective character of capitalist development," or "racial capitalism."[27]

Like the South African Marxists, Robinson introduced the idea of the coexistence of modes of production within a single social system. Like them, he saw capitalism not as a universal modernizing force but instead as one preserving aspects of pre-capitalist society. And he shared with them the idea that racism was a means by which capitalist societies organized their incorporation of other modes of production, and the associated forms of labor. Capitalism, on this view, constantly recreates itself through differentiations of labor: waged industrial workers, enslaved plantation workers, workers who migrate back and forth between temporary waged work in a capitalist economy and work in other modes of production, and various kinds of "surplus populations," such as the never-employed Black youths who had risen up in England in 1981.[28] These different labor relationships to the capitalist mode of production are correlated to differential regimes of rights and privileges, with boundaries between citizens and non-citizens, the free and the unfree, the protected and the disposable.[29] Race, in turn, provides a conceptual framework to represent and legitimate these varied relationships of workers to capitalism.[30]

The power of this argument is that it enables a unitary explanation of the existence of racism and capitalism rather than proposing that they are two autonomous systems with their own separate mechanisms and effects, which then requires having to confront the difficult task of explaining how these two systems interact with each other. And it is a unitary explanation that can account for the constant regeneration of new forms of racism in capitalist societies, rather than just seeing racism as an ideological legacy of earlier modes of production without any material basis in the present. It is worth noting that there is a sort of parallel to this racial capitalism argument in the way that socialist feminists have theorized the processes of social reproduction. They point out that accounts of capitalism that focus only on the waged worker's relationship to the capitalist are necessarily incomplete because behind the sphere of production, where this encounter takes place, there has to be a sphere of reproduction where another kind of labor takes place: the work needed to ensure the waged worker is nurtured and replenished—the work of cooking, cleaning, raising children, caring for the sick, and so on. That work may not itself be waged but it is necessary for waged work—and therefore capitalism—to be possible. Under capitalism, a spatial division tends to stand between the spaces where the work of production takes place and the spaces where the work of reproduction takes place, such as hospitals, day cares, and homes. And this boundary is assigned gender meanings: men are workers; women are nurses, nursery school teachers, and housewives. On this view, gender oppression and capitalism are not two autonomous structures that might intersect, but instead belong in a single, unitary account.[31]

Robinson's initial premise about racial capitalism led him to consider two further problems in understanding the relationship of racism to capitalism: what can be called the "problem of origins" and the "problem of reproduction." With the problem of origins, Robinson was concerned with identifying racism's founding moment, its initial constitution. With the problem of reproduction, he was concerned with how racism constantly reworks itself in new circumstances, how it overcomes the inevitability of resistance, how it stays the same while changing.

On the problem of origins, Robinson argued that European racism—or, using his terms, "racialism" or "racial sensibilities"—historically preceded capitalism, colonialism, and the transatlantic slave trade, and it lies at a deeper level in the structures of Western culture. A "racial calculus," he wrote, was "reiterated and embellished" by "one European ruling order after another, one cohort of clerical or secular propagandists following another" from at least the twelfth century. Once the transatlantic trade started, the "Negro" was invented as a legitimating figure, but that invention was built on preexisting racial forms within Europe, such as images of Slavs, Irish, Jews, Muslims, and so on. Racism, Robinson claimed, runs "deep in the bowels of Western culture" and inevitably reverberated through the relations of production and forms of consciousness that emerged from that culture.[32] The suggestion was that capitalism expresses economically the racism at the core of European culture. Capitalism did not melt away those preexisting structures of racism but instead mediated them. In this aspect of Robinson's work, he understood racism as hard-wired into Western culture from its inception.

The other concern in Robinson's work was the problem of reproduction. Here the focus was upon the constant work of reconfiguring race in new contexts. He introduced the term "racial regimes" to address this, defining them in the introduction to his book *Forgeries of Memory and Meaning* as constructed social systems in which race is proposed as a justification for the relations of power. While necessarily articulated with accruals of power, the covering conceit of a racial regime is a makeshift patchwork masquerading as memory and the immutable. Nevertheless, racial regimes do possess history, that is, discernible origins and mechanisms of assembly.[33]

They sometimes "'collapse' under the weight of their own artifices, practices, and apparatuses; they may fragment, desiccated by new realities."[34] The end of the slave system in the US, for example, led at the end of the nineteenth century to the consolidation of a new racial regime, Jim Crow segregation, which preserved racial domination in new forms. Moreover, racial regimes, for Robinson, can be quite straightforwardly grounded in economic relations:

> The creation of the Negro was obviously at the cost of immense expenditures of psychic and intellectual energies in the West. The exercise was obligatory. It was an effort commensurate with the importance Black labor power possessed for the world economy sculpted and dominated by the ruling and mercantile classes of Western Europe.[35]

Another example was his claim that the "needs of finance capital" in the late nineteenth and early twentieth centuries determined the emergence of the new racial regime of Jim Crow.[36]

Yet elsewhere, Robinson was averse to allowing economic relations to be sufficient explanation for racism. What he called the "nastiness" of racial capitalism, its violence and terror, must involve more than modes of production, he wrote. And recognizing this means accepting that racism, in the end, cannot be explained in terms of property and labor relations. There is a tension, then, between Robinson's picture of racism as constantly regenerated through changing economic relations and the picture of racism as ultimately residing in the transmission of Western cultural norms. Both of these are components of Robinson's thought and shape what he means by "racial capitalism."[37]

However this tension might have been resolved, there were clear implications for movements. Radical opposition to capitalism is not generated only from the confrontation between capital and waged labor that orthodox Marxism theorizes, but also from the antagonism between capital and the various other categories of non-waged, coerced, and surplus labor within racial capitalism—from the enslaved to the lumpenproletariat of city-dwellers hustling a living without access to a regular wage, whom the Black Panther Party saw as the vanguard of the revolution in the United States. Moreover, Robinson argued—and it is a logical consequence of his position—the cultural resources that those struggles draw upon will not come only from within capitalism itself but also from traditions that pre-date capitalism. This is where Robinson's attention to what he calls the Black radical tradition came in, as an "evolving resistance of African peoples to oppression" that has a "specifically African character." African resistance to slavery, colonialism, and racism is not meant to be understood as the retrieval of a cultural heritage that survives unchanged beneath the surface of modernity. It involves instead a coherent, ongoing, collective intellectual tradition of attempting to make sense of Black life under Western systems of oppression. But crucially, this resistance is fused in the "raw material" of reconstituted African "values, ideas, conceptions, and constructions of reality" whose meanings are "distinct from the foundations of Western ideas." For example, Robinson suggests, it draws on an African "metaphysical system that had never allowed for property" in any sense of the term.[38] Capitalism, for Robinson, does not dig its own grave; its death warrant is written in an altogether alien language.

"Race is the modality in which class is lived"

Disenchanted with the colonial society of middle-class Jamaica where he was born, Stuart Hall arrived in England in 1951 looking for "a sort of final reckoning, a showdown" with "those who had for so long mastered us," he later wrote. As a student at Oxford University, he was active in left-wing circles and, in 1957, helped found the *Universities and Left Review* journal, later the *New Left Review*, which he edited for two years. Animating this work was a strong sense that the basic ideas of the English Left needed to be rethought for a new period in which mass consumption was undermining the possibilities of working-class radicalism. Building the journal, attempting to mobilize its ideas into social movements, and agitating for the Campaign for Nuclear Disarmament—these were Hall's formative political activities. This combination of influences naturally meant that at the center of his thinking was the question of how racism and colonialism related to class exploitation. The investigation of culture seemed to be a way to connect all these different terrains of political struggle and, in 1964, Hall cofounded the Center for Contemporary Cultural Studies at Birmingham University, becoming its director in 1968.[39] In the 1970s, his pursuit of the question of how cultural life related to economic and political structures was a way of easing the stiffness of English Marxism. That created the space to improvise, enabling engagement with, for example, the work of the South African Marxists on racial capitalism and the US discussions of racism's relation to capitalism. Through the 1970s, Hall drew on these references to interpret the growing militancy of Black people in Britain—their increasing strike actions at their places of work and challenges to police harassment on the streets.[40]

Like Robinson, Hall generalized from the South African argument. He argued that there is no inevitable tendency for the capitalist–waged labor relationship to become universal, even in the long run. Instead, the capitalist mode of production can stably operate in combination with a "variety of forms of 'unfree labour.'" This was, in fact, what we find in colonial capitalism, which was marked by a "combination of different modes of production," each corresponding to a different form of "free" or unfree labor. Where capitalism developed in this way, there were different political and legal structures that corresponded to these different forms of labor. In any capitalist society, at least some workers are waged and operate under a legal structure in which the worker "freely" contracts to sell her labor power to any capitalist who chooses to buy it. Marx demonstrated that the vaunted individual freedom of waged workers is a fiction that conceals the exploitation of one class by another. Nevertheless, there is a

Stuart Hall
Open University

legal structure that recognizes the universal right not to be coerced into labor. But in societies where there are other forms of labor, Hall argued, there are "legal structures which elaborate more than one form of citizen status" or enable "restricted franchises," such as the immigrant worker who lacks civil rights or the Black worker under apartheid, or, in other contexts, enslavement, as in the plantation system. There is therefore a complex structure in which different modes of production and corresponding different legal systems coexist, with capitalism dominant but its wage relationship not universal.[41]

This is where racism entered the stage. In a self-contained social system where there are only "free" waged workers, any segmentation by ethnicity can be expected to become less significant over time owing to capitalism's homogenizing force. But no such imperative applies to the mix of free and unfree labor in more complex structures with combined modes of production. In colonial settings, it becomes possible, indeed quite likely, for different ethnic groups to be inserted into the different categories of "free" and unfree labor. Through the ideological process of exaggerating these ethnic differences into racial divisions, the different economic relationships to the means of production and the associated legal regimes begin to acquire racial meanings. For example, US slave plantation owners "participated in a general movement of the world capitalist system: but on the basis of an internal mode of production—slavery in its modern, plantation form—not itself 'capitalist' in character."[42] For systems of colonialism and slavery within capitalism, the concept of race offers a way to make it seem natural that certain groups of people are not free, and to disconnect their lack of freedom from any sense of the historical process that led to their unfreedom, so that it appears this is just the way things always are. In this way, racism resolves—at least provisionally—the contradiction between different legal structures in a single social system. It provides capitalism with a rationale to explain why its ostensibly universal principles of individual rights do not apply to particular categories of people at the plantation, at the prison, at the border, and so on. "Capitalism requires inequality and racism enshrines it," as antiracist geographer Ruth Wilson Gilmore puts it.[43]

This line of thinking ties racism to the history of imperialism.[44] As capitalism developed internationally, there was not a progressive homogenizing of economic conditions but, on the contrary, both a deepening of economic inequalities between the dominant, imperialist centers and the dominated peripheries, and an incorporation of non-capitalist social relations as long-term elements within the imperialist system.[45] In India, for example, colonial capitalism preserved, or even intensified, pre-colonial caste relations, finding in them a stabilizing force. As a consequence of all this, there were material differences in how the various classes within the imperialist system related to capitalism. Between 1910 and 1980, the waged working classes in the core imperialist countries were able to win real wage increases in line with increasing labor productivity, roughly halving the difference between their average incomes and those of their capitalist exploiters. Over the same period, the waged working classes in the peripheral, dominated countries, who were subject to super-exploitation and whose wage levels were disconnected from actual productivity, did not enjoy similar improvements in their average standard of living; imperialist violence in all its forms crushed most of the movements aiming to address this inequality. Even worse off were the peasantries of the periphery, subject to super-exploitation and additionally oppressed within pre-capitalist forms of production.[46]

The relationships between these different classes are all arenas in which racial, ethnic, or caste meanings are mobilized. Nkrumah, for instance, identified as a key fault line the boundary between the proletariat at the center, granted welfare rights and rising wages, and the proletariats and peasantries of the peripheries who were excluded from these privileges. With the end of direct colonialism, new racial meanings were attached to this boundary as the vast terrain of Third World poverty and despair came to be presented as a product not of capitalist economics but of an irredeemably backward Third World culture—an idea that Trump invoked with his phrase "shithole countries." But it is hard to generalize about these processes: we would need to investigate each specific historical setting to lay out how different relationships were structured and how social forces attached particular racial meanings to them. "Racism is not present, in the same form or degree, in all capitalist formations," wrote Hall, and it does not necessarily "take one, single form or follow one necessary path or logic, through a series of necessary stages."[47] This is because capitalists and their political representatives are not calculating machines who read off signals from the economy and then instigate corresponding racist ideologies. Rather, the record from the settler colonial era to the War on Terror is of capitalist elites continuously succumbing to delusions: real threats to capitalist interests have been perceived through the distorting lens of racist paranoia. Thus, in the course of its economic production, capitalism also produces monsters: it deforms the souls of its guardians, turning owners of property into perpetrators of remote racist violence beyond the cold calculation of "economy" in any narrow sense. Despite this, we can still generalize to say, with Hall, that the structure in structural racism is capitalism's relationship to other incorporated modes of production, and racism is the main way that capitalism manages its inevitable failure to make itself universal—this is what we can use the term "racial capitalism" to refer to. To the extent that a general theory of structural racism is possible, it seems to me that Hall offers the most compelling basis for it.

It followed, in Hall's account, that racism is not the timeless cultural force that it could sometimes appear to be in Robinson's work. For Hall, it is a mistake to think that racism was hardwired in Western culture from its formation and that it acted uniformly and mechanically thereafter. He did not think there was such a thing as "whiteness" or "anti-Blackness" if those terms are meant to signify some sort of innate foundation in

Western culture—its original sin. For racism to survive, each new generation must remake it in its own image. This is unlikely to be an entirely intentional or conscious process. It is the work of broad social forces. But however it happens, the past cannot serve as an alibi for the present. There are many candidates for the historic "founding moment" of racism: Bacon's rebellion in seventeenth-century Virginia, when ruling elites mobilized racial divisions to defend themselves from insurrections; the arrival of the first enslaved Africans in Virginia in 1619; Columbus's arrival in the Caribbean in 1492; the crusades; the Battle of Tours in 732, when the concept of "Europe" first appeared; or Aristotle's defense of slavery. But whatever conclusion one reaches about this, it does not settle the question of how and why racism reproduces itself now. Hall wrote: "Unless one attributes to race a single, unitary transhistorical character—such that wherever and whenever it appears it always assumes the same autonomous features . . . then one must deal with the historical specificity of race in the modern world . . . Here one is then obliged to agree that race relations are directly linked with economic processes."[48]

Hall's argument here has a surprising implication: the current fraught debates about the role of race in the foundations of the United States are not as relevant to understanding how racism functions now as they might at first seem. These debates generally involve a contest between those with an optimistic view of the classical liberalism invoked by the US's founding fathers and those who see racism as intrinsic to the nation, running "in the very DNA of this country," as *New York Times* journalist Nikole Hannah-Jones put it, rendering white supremacy as pervasive and unchanging.[49] It is true that racism has permeated the key institutions of US life throughout the country's history. But, Hall noted, to remain at that level of abstraction is to ignore the effects of movements against racism. Or, in the words of Sivanandan: "Racism does not stay still; it changes shape, size, contours, purpose, function—with changes in the economy, the social structure, the system and, above all, the challenges, the resistances to that system."⁵⁰ Racism has only survived by constantly adapting and reconfiguring itself in the face of resistance. Since the traces of that resistance are always registered in its structures, racism cannot be properly understood without acknowledging its disruptions as much as its continuities. To have any chance of success, antiracism cannot deal in abstractions or re-fight the battles of the past; it must address itself to the specific character of the context it operates in.

When Hall turned to analyze the context of the UK in the 1970s, he noted that there was a "racial division of labor" within Britain that correlated to and derived from imperialism's worldwide racial division of labor.⁵¹ In the 1950s and 1960s, African Caribbeans and South Asians were "driven into emigration by endemic colonial poverty, in desperate need for the economic and social rewards" their own countries could not provide. These were "the colonial unemployed" of the cities, "rural workers from the plantations," and "subsistence farmers drawn from the rural masses of the hinterland." They arrived in "a labour-hungry British economy" and settled in "sub-standard and decaying" accommodation in the inner cities. They took on "heavy work in the factories; long hours and hard stints in London Transport; hot, laborious work for women in the kitchens and other service industries." By the mid-1970s, with the growing economic recession, these workers were the "most exposed to the winds of unemployment." Young Black school-leavers were especially affected. The role of school, Hall argued, was to assign its working-class students to different positions in the hierarchy of the job market. For young Blacks, the education system "served effectively to depress the general opportunities for employment and education advancement," placing them at the unskilled and semi-skilled lower end. They were four times more likely to be unemployed, with 60 percent out of work in many urban areas.⁵²

This whole set of processes could not be understood as the result of "discriminatory practices based on racist stereotypes and attitudes." Even Ture's concept of "institutional racism"—which highlighted the way that racism is woven into the fabric of institutional domains such as housing and education—did not fully capture it. What the analysis still needed was a sense of how these different institutions "work together so as to reproduce . . . [the] working class in a racially stratified and internally antagonistic form." This enabled African Caribbean and South Asian workers to be "super-exploited" but also, with the recession of the 1970s, created a Black "surplus" fraction unable to access waged work at all. This wageless population—the same surplus population that Al-Amin had pointed to—in turn became a racial signifier of urban crisis and consequently a target of "police activity." In such a situation, race relations could come to stand in for class relations, not as a way of concealing an underlying class reality, but as a "structural feature of the general division of labor." Thus racism in Britain was not, "in any simple sense, the product of an ideological trick" designed to hide capitalism's putative, non-racial economic core. When ruling-class ideologists succeeded in using racism to disaggregate working-class struggles, they did so "because they are practicing on real contradictions within and inside the class, working on real effects of the structure (however these may be 'misrecognized' through racism)—not because they are clever at conjuring demons." Like Fanon and James, Hall pointed to the deep differences in how Black, white, and other workers related to capitalism and argued that this is the "material and social base on which 'racism' as an ideology flourishes" and comes to seem plausible. Racist attitudes and beliefs derive from capitalism's racial division of labor; they do not produce it. Above all, this approach enables one to identify the material forces that uphold the continuously shifting structures of racial oppression, even as society's leading institutions publicly condemn racism. This also means that one can see how race is the domain in which members of the Black working class "'live,' experience, make sense of and thus *come to a consciousness* of their structured subordination" and "begin to resist the exploitation which is an objective feature of their class situation." Or more pithily: "Race is the modality in which class is lived."[53]

To pursue this analysis requires focusing on how, in the second half of the twentieth century, ruling classes were forced to defend their positions from radical anticolonial and antiracist challenges. Through these improvised defensive maneuvers, guided by intellectuals who described themselves as "neoliberals," capitalism regenerated racism in new forms.

9

The Neoliberal Idea

The white Left today is organized around a standard story of neoliberalism. But it is a story that needs to be "stretched," as Fanon put it, for it to serve the needs of antiracism and anticolonialism. The story goes something like this. In 1947, a group of economists, historians, and philosophers, convened by Austrian polymath Friedrich Hayek, gathered at the Mont Pèlerin spa overlooking Lake Geneva in Switzerland. Among the attendees were Hayek's mentor Ludwig von Mises and the US economist Milton Friedman. What united the participants was a desire to revive what they called "liberalism." By this, they meant the free-market policies of the mid-nineteenth century, which they felt had been diminished by the rise of labor movements in Europe and North America, and the creation of the welfare state as a stabilizing compromise between workers and capitalists. To these "neoliberals," welfare states threatened freedom because, in using taxation to redistribute wealth from rich to poor, they weakened the right to private property and tampered with the proper functioning of markets. Markets needed to be released from the fetters of government, they argued. These neoliberals formed the Mont Pelerin Society and met annually thereafter, bringing together like-minded thinkers. At first, their ideas were largely ignored. European and US governments in the 1950s and 1960s pursued New Deal–style policies, aiming to stimulate demand in the economy through government expenditure and expanding public services. The assumption was that governments had to tame the excesses of capitalist markets in order to provide for social stability. Franklin D. Roosevelt and social democratic governments in Europe had first introduced these policies in response to the Great Depression and then maintained them in the decades after World War II. Politically marginalized, neoliberals honed their arguments at think tanks and in academia, especially at the University of Chicago, where Friedman and Gary Becker, another neoliberal economist, were prominent.

By the 1970s, the New Deal policy program was in crisis. This crisis consisted of an economic element and a political element, according to the definitive version of the standard story, *A Brief History of Neoliberalism*, by David Harvey, the City University of New York–based geographer and one of the world's most influential living Marxist thinkers. Economically, the high rates of growth that Europe and the US had attained in the decades after 1945 came to an end. Inflation and unemployment were surging, and governments struggled to meet their expenditure commitments. Capitalists had agreed to a New Deal–style compromise with workers that at least provided them with a stable share of an increasing pie. But that framework "was clearly exhausted and was no longer working," as capitalists faced declining profits and "everywhere felt threatened." At the same time, writes Harvey, there was a political crisis arising from "the emergence of a socialist alternative to the social compromise between capital and labour." In Europe, he suggests, communist and socialist parties were gaining ground. In the United States, "popular forces were agitating for widespread reforms and state interventions." For all these reasons, the "upper classes had to move decisively if they were to protect themselves from political and economic annihilation." In the event, the "capitalist world stumbled towards neoliberalization as the answer through a series of gyrations and chaotic experiments." The first such experiment came in Chile in 1973 after a US-backed military coup overthrew the democratically elected socialist Salvador Allende and brought Augusto Pinochet to power. The Pinochet dictatorship summoned the Chicago economists as advisers and conducted a neoliberal restructuring of the Chilean economy.

THE NEOLIBERAL IDEA

Gradually, the neoliberals gained influence among journalists and intellectuals in Europe and the US.[1]

Then, in the 1980s, Margaret Thatcher in the UK and Ronald Reagan in the US applied neoliberal doctrines to create a new kind of political and economic system. Their regimes privatized publicly owned assets, deregulated financial markets, cut welfare payments, reduced taxes, and crushed organized labor, with Reagan firing striking air traffic controllers in 1981 and Thatcher violently suppressing a miners' strike in 1984. By the 1990s, the new free-market system was in place across the world. Politicians, government officials, and intellectuals broadly accepted neoliberal ideas. The more egalitarian societies of the mid-twentieth century gave way to a competitive culture in which the poor were held responsible for their own fate. Principles of social solidarity were shredded and every aspect of life subjected to the logic of markets, from dating to democracy. Neoliberalism thus freed capitalists from the restraints of a mid-twentieth-century "class compromise between capital and labour" in Europe and the US, and allowed for "the restoration or reconstruction of the power of economic elites," while workers lost out.[2]

Academic writers have made various criticisms of this standard story. One is that it does not grasp how, in neoliberal societies, the market idea not only shapes government policies but also informs a system of norms governing every aspect of our lives.[3] Another criticism is that the standard story underestimates the range of different and inconsistent neoliberal ideas and assumes too neat an alignment between what neoliberals intended and what they achieved.[4]

However, I want to explore a different problem with the white Left's standard story that remains largely neglected in the vast academic literature: it ignores the centrality of new and distinctive forms of racist and neocolonial domination in the neoliberal project. Harvey paints only half the picture. The impetus for the neoliberal turn came as much from decolonization in the Third World and Black struggle in the US as from the white Left in the

West. And, as neoliberal think tanks, politicians, and intellectuals gained political influence, they worked with Western governments to configure new global and domestic racial boundaries to replace the older ones that had been weakened by decolonization and the Black freedom movement. Central to the neoliberal restructuring of capitalism was a massive expansion in the infrastructures of policing, incarceration, bordering, and militarization—processes that were bound up with new forms of racism and imperialism, even as a language of diversity and inclusion proliferated. As Fanon had predicted, racism became less explicit, not because it was weaker but because it had developed an infrastructure that could operate without the need for routine assertions of superiority. To understand what structural racism is today requires that we develop an account of this new racial and colonial infrastructure, built as part of the neoliberal turn from the 1970s.

In its 200 pages, Harvey's *A Brief History* refers to race only two times. It is worth quoting at length one of those moments:

> Employers have historically used differentiations within the labour pool to divide and rule. Segmented labour markets then arise and distinctions of race, ethnicity, gender, and religion are frequently used, blatantly or covertly, in ways that redound to the employers' advantage. Conversely, workers may use the social networks in which they are embedded to gain privileged access to certain lines of employment. They typically seek to monopolize skills and, through collective action and the creation of appropriate institutions, seek to regulate the labour market to protect their interests. In this they are merely constructing that "protective covering of cultural institutions" of which Polanyi speaks. Neoliberalization seeks to strip away the protective coverings.[5]

This extract can be read in multiple ways, and it would be wrong to assign too much weight to it. Yet what Harvey seems to mean is that neoliberalism renders racial differentiations between workers anachronistic. To the limited extent that Harvey mentions race in this text, it appears as a "cultural" factor that is allowed to distort the logic of markets in earlier periods of capitalism but is stripped away under neoliberalism as social relations are organized according to universal market laws.

In more recent writing, Harvey has argued that, while the "intersections and interactions between racialisation and capital accumulation are both highly visible and powerfully present," studying them "tells me nothing particular about how the economic engine of capital works."[6] Racism varies across time and space whereas capital accumulation can be examined in the abstract as having certain universal features across different societies.[7] Harvey's point is that, because race is not part of the inner logic of capitalism, the system can dispense with it, and this is indeed what he seems to think capitalism does in the neoliberal era. Racism appears as a legacy of the past that is weakened by neoliberalism's emphasis on market-based individualism. Consequently, it becomes impossible to explain the persistence of structural racism and neocolonialism alongside neoliberalism. Harvey's theory would predict a decline in racism in the neoliberal era. Yet it has actually been a period in which, despite many challenges to individual racist prejudices, racism has been restructured through, for example, programs of border fortification and mass incarceration. At the same time, racist political movements have flourished.

Usually, the white Left considers these racist political movements the consequence of the social devastation caused by increasing economic inequalities under neoliberalism. This idea is as old as the word "racism" itself. In his book *Racism*, when he systematically introduced the word in the early 1930s, Magnus Hirschfeld suggested that racism was a way of responding to class inequality. Unexpected economic hardship disoriented people and led them to ask who was to blame. Racist politicians exploited this confusion by providing scapegoats for what were essentially economic problems. In Hirschfeld's analysis, "race war instead of class war" was the central formula in the racism that brought the Nazis to power in Germany.[8] As we saw, that theory was pursued in the 1940s by theorists such as Ruth Benedict and became the standard liberal explanation for the success of racist politics. In 2016, the theory was revived again to explain the Brexit vote in the UK and the election of Donald Trump in the US. But, plainly, racism has thrived in good economic times and bad. And these explanations struggle to explain why white experiences of hardship are so easily diverted toward racist politics rather than, say, increased class struggle, especially when, unlike Europe in the 1930s, racist attitudes are widely rebuked today.

The theorist Wendy Brown has attempted to address this problem with a more sophisticated account of how she thinks neoliberalism gives rise to racist political movements. She views racial inequality as a "tradition" or a set of "legacies," an element of the past that endures into the neoliberal present. These racial legacies are diminished by the spread of neoliberalism to every area of life, she writes. Under neoliberalism, being white no longer provides "protection against the displacements and losses" of the "working and middle classes." Racial "dominance is ebbing," weakened by neoliberal "cosmopolitanism," "mortally wounded" but not fully destroyed. Under neoliberalism, "the world has invaded the nation, weakening its borders." The general sense here is that neoliberalism has a leveling effect on racial disparities.[9] But this leveling process, in turn, generates a "wounded" and "dethroned" white identity that lashes out in a nihilist and resentful form, leading to "neo-Nazis in the German parliament, neofascists in the Italian one, Brexit ushered in by tabloid-fueled xenophobia, the rise of white nationalism in Scandinavia . . . and of course, Trumpism." The tradition of racism, now disembedded from "organically reproducing civilization, securing social bonds, and governing conduct," becomes a weapon of the resentful. These constituencies are "anxious about their ebbing place and privilege" and unrestrained by

THE NEOLIBERAL IDEA

conscience. A refashioning of white supremacy as a "raw entitlement claim," detached from any broader ideological grounding, "converges powerfully with neoliberalism's assault on equality and democracy, the social and the political." This process runs against neoliberalism's own aims, producing raucous populist upsurges quite different from the disciplined behavior she believes neoliberals originally envisaged.[10]

Even though her analysis has quite different philosophical foundations from Harvey's, Brown also presents neoliberalism as weakening past structural racisms and not generating any new racisms of its own, except a populist ideological backlash to the declining power of white supremacy. Brown's account arrives at the same proposition as Harvey's: racism exists because neoliberalism has only partially defeated it. An implication of this framing is that the more neoliberalism saturates social relationships, the less space there is for racist reaction; neoliberalism might cause the conditions for a resurgent racist backlash but, on their accounts, must also be a solution to it. This puts the white Left in a bind: if more neoliberalism ultimately means less racism, then the fight against racism and the fight against neoliberalism pull in opposite directions. The white Left then tends to see antiracism as being not intrinsically linked to the core issue of class; it becomes either a divisive "cultural" matter or a concern to be addressed through soft liberal methods of "diversity and inclusion," which sit uneasily alongside the Left's radicalism on matters of class. This means that, even on the left, antiracism too often devolves into a moralizing discourse focused upon individual attitudes and feelings without addressing structures of wealth and power.

This is where the notion of racial capitalism offers a way forward. If capitalism generates the structure in structural racism, then to understand what structural racism is today requires first understanding how racism was reconfigured as part of the broader transformation of capitalism that the term "neoliberalism" refers to. White leftists have tended not to go through these analytical steps, because their understanding of capitalism does not tie it in any fundamental way to racism. As a result, they are often nostalgic for the achievements of the period before the neoliberal turn—the New Deal period in the US or the 1945 Labour government in the UK—which ignores how those were dependent upon racial and colonial underpinnings.

The crises of welfare capitalism

To develop a more satisfactory account of how racism and neoliberalism interact, we need to go back once again to the 1970s, the decade that is pivotal to the standard story. But this time we need to include in our analysis the political and economic crises that antiracism and anticolonialism produced within the capitalist system—to which neoliberal thinkers and organizations were responding. By the beginning of the 1970s, neoliberal intellectuals believed the very existence of free markets was threatened in two major domains. First, in the West, trade unions had mobilized the power of collective action not only to drive up wages but also to gain political influence, which they used to call for expanding public services and social security programs. An upsurge of labor unrest in the West starting from the late 1960s pushed up wages further and gave rise to a widespread sense that capitalists, governments, and even trade union leaders had lost control over industrial workers.[11] The neoliberals believed this to be unsustainable. They feared that workers' demands for state aid, funded by taxes on the wealthy, would keep escalating until market-based discipline could be imposed. Milton Friedman described this dynamic as the "collectivist belief in the ability of direct action by the state to remedy all evils."[12] It threatened not just the private property of the wealthy but the right to private property itself.

The second area of neoliberal concern was decolonization and antiracism. Between 1945 and 1975, anticolonial nationalists redrew the map of the world, bringing formal independence to the colonized peoples of Africa, Asia, and the Caribbean—and the expectation that with political freedom would come economic uplift. Industrial production did not take place in these regions to a significant degree, but they were essential to the capitalist system for their agricultural crops and reserves of extractable raw materials, especially minerals and oil. These regions were also where most of the world's population lived.

Rather than US modernization policies bringing about a peaceful incorporation of Third World peasants and workers into the Western capitalist system, there had been an upsurge of revolt. In Algeria, the national liberation movement had defeated one of the most advanced military powers in the world, France. In Vietnam, another national liberation movement was on the verge of a similar victory against the US. In Cuba, the revolution of 1958 had proven resilient in the face of US actions against it. In southern Africa, there were armed struggles against Portuguese colonialism and the racist political systems of South Africa and Rhodesia. Insurgencies across Latin America were pushing governments to break with neocolonial dependency. Fifty armed movements for national liberation in the Third World were recorded by the Pentagon in 1969.[13] Mobilized by the anti-colonial independence movements, the people of the Third World had come to expect broad transformations in their lives. Their radicalization was set to deepen so long as a chasm separated the promise of liberation from the reality of their sorrows. This was, as Pakistani political analyst Eqbal Ahmad pointed out, "a triple revolution—political, social, and economic . . . with an unprecedented, actual and potential, involvement by the majority of the people" of the world.[14]

Most worrying to the neoliberals was that, in spite of the neocolonial pressures applied to them, leaders of the newly independent nations were bringing under public ownership private assets owned by foreign corporations or demanding reparations from former colonial powers. Already in 1951, the Iranian parliament had voted to nationalize the country's oil production that had previously been under the control of the British-owned Anglo-Iranian Oil Company. Five years later, in Egypt Gamal Abdel Nasser nationalized the British and French company which owned the Suez Canal. Responding to these developments at the 1957 Mont Pelerin Society meeting in Saint Moritz, Switzerland, the economist Arthur Shenfield, who worked with the British neoliberal think tank the Institute of Economic Affairs, argued that self-determination for European colonies would have to be opposed if it meant independent nations pursuing policies unsupportive of free markets.[15]

The annual number of expropriations of foreign investments in the Third World doubled during the 1960s, and then tripled from 1970 to 1975.[16] By 1974, this trend had been endorsed by the United Nations General Assembly with its ratification of the Charter of Economic Rights and Duties of States, by 115 votes to 6. The charter declared that every state has the right to "nationalize, expropriate or transfer ownership of foreign property." It also placed a mandate on states to eliminate colonialism and neocolonialism; states that pursued colonialist policies were expected to pay "restitution and full compensation" for the damages associated with the exploitation of people and natural resources.[17] Leaders such as Michael Manley in Jamaica and Julius Nyerere in Tanzania had taken up Nkrumah's argument that the West's international exploitation of Third World nations was analogous in certain ways to the domestic exploitation of workers. They called for a new economic system in which principles of welfare would apply internationally as well as domestically.[18]

"The wealth of the imperialist countries is also our wealth," Fanon wrote—reparations for colonialism were justified.[19] But he also thought that, in the absence of a broader social transformation of colonial structures, the expropriation of foreign assets would do little to improve the lives of the Third World masses. For the neoliberals, on the other hand, these initiatives presented the terrifying possibility that Western governments would become welfare states not just to their own nations but to the entire world. Calls for the redistribution of wealth from the West to poorer parts of the world were, Hayek wrote, attempts to apply to the whole of humanity obligations that were "appropriate only to the fellow members of a tribal group."[20] Neoliberals saw organized labor in the West and anticolonial nationalism elsewhere as equivalent and related threats. The smooth operation of capitalism was vulnerable to disruption by collectively organized workers; it was also vulnerable to disruption by collectively organized national liberation movements seeking control over the raw materials the system depended upon. As Lionel Robbins, one of the original cohort of neoliberal thinkers, put it: "'The mines for the miners' and 'Papua for the Papuans' are analytically similar slogans."[21]

By the beginning of the 1970s, these tensions were beginning to register economically. The cost of the raw materials extracted from the Third World was rising, driving up inflation. At the same time, it was becoming clear that, despite its military strength, the US could not easily force Third World governments into accepting its economic system—the Vietnamese were proving that, in fact, such attempts could be so costly to the US as to cause a veritable fiscal crisis. Then, in October 1973, six Arab oil-producing states decided to reduce the supply of oil, ostensibly to pressure the US to halt Israel's ongoing colonization of the Palestinians, creating a world "energy crisis." Their decision was not motivated by any kind of radical politics, but it nevertheless dramatically revealed the vulnerability of Western capitalism to the collective action of Third World governments.[22] Decolonization was the thread that tied together the expropriation of corporate property, the fiscal crisis in the US, and the oil crisis.

What neoliberals were confronting was the breakdown of racial and colonial boundaries that had previously set limits to demands for social justice. Even though the European colonial empires conscripted vast armies of workers around the world, only those residing in Europe were able to gradually acquire the benefits of the welfare state, such as publicly funded education and healthcare systems. The symbiosis between industrialization and imperialism in the first half of the twentieth century depended on Europe violently suppressing demands in the colonies to reduce poverty, while offering workers at home incorporation into the imperialist project and encouraging them to perceive their advantages over the colonized as the entitlements of race and nation. This was the racial boundary upon which the imperial economy rested—as Lenin and Nkrumah had understood. Decolonization destabilized this boundary. Third World peoples were now poised to mobilize redistributive claims of their own, not just within their own countries but internationally. At the same time, Europe's capitalist classes had less leeway with which to meet these demands. They had to a large extent lost the protected imperial markets for their products. Moreover, there were no more stories of imperial grandeur to flatter their domestic working classes. Imperialism had been effective in containing working-class insurgencies, but now it could no longer bind together European societies economically or ideologically. The successful national liberation movements in the colonies had created the conditions for a radicalization of working-class movements within Europe. As Roy and James had both argued, the struggle to decolonize was potentially symbiotic with class struggles in the colonizing countries.

Meanwhile, antiracism was attacking racial boundaries in the US. By the 1960s, it was clear that the Black freedom movement was about much more than ending legalized discrimination and violence in the Jim Crow South. The movement was, in effect, demanding the desegregation not just of the South but of New Deal America. And it was proposing a much broader conception of equality than the end of official discrimination. It regarded poverty as an evil in itself, North and South, not just when it resulted from Jim Crow discrimination. From King to Al-Amin, it was demanding a radical redistribution of wealth. President Johnson presented his program of creating a Great Society as a response to these demands, offering to reinvigorate and desegregate the New Deal framework. The majority of neoliberals saw all this as bad news. James M. Buchanan, for example, the founder of the Virginia School of neoliberal thought, characterized the expanding New Deal as support for "unproductive and essentially parasitic members of society." Demands on government to fund more and more public services were undermining individual property rights. "We are all trapped in a collectivist ideology," he wrote in 1973. The only hope was George Wallace's pro-segregationist 1968 presidential campaign, with its attacks on the "briefcase-carrying bureaucrats" of the federal government.[23] What Buchanan called the "disastrous failure" of the reconstruction period after the emancipation of slaves in the US South indicated, he claimed, that Black people were "afraid to be free" of government dependency. The "thirst or desire for freedom, and responsibility, is perhaps not nearly so universal as so many post-Enlightenment philosophers have assumed," he wrote.[24]

The Johnson administration seemed to support the racial desegregation of New Deal policy-making. However, it sought to uphold gender divisions. In June 1965, President Johnson gave a speech, co-drafted by Daniel Patrick Moynihan, in which he claimed the most important factor in the persistence of Black disadvantage "was the breakdown of the Negro family structure."[25] This reflected the conclusions of Moynihan's then unpublished report *The Negro Family: The Case for National Action*, which argued that Black women had assumed an unnaturally overbearing role in raising children in single-parent households, a problem that originally arose from the destruction of family life in the slave plantations but was now a "tangle of pathology" within Black culture, encouraged by the increasing generosity of welfare payments.[26] Moynihan was at the time a New Deal Democrat. His recommendation was for the government to create jobs for Black men, in order to incorporate them into the New Deal's family wage system with their unwaged wives raising children. But as divorce rates increased across the board in the US in the 1970s and former housewives entered the labor market or claimed welfare, the family model of the New Deal era was itself in crisis.

Neoliberals worried that the demographic erosion of the New Deal family unit would lead to women's movements mobilizing to claim greater government assistance for single and working mothers. They noticed how, in the tailwinds of the civil rights movement, working-class women were organizing through the 1960s and into the 1970s to campaign for greater access to welfare support and an end to the paternalist conditions attached to assistance. Welfare caseworkers often precluded women recipients from having intimate partners or pressured them to not have more children; Black women were disproportionately required to undergo even sterilization as a condition of continuing assistance. "Welfare is a women's issue," wrote Johnnie Tillmon, one of the leaders of the welfare rights movement.[27] Tillmon, a single mother who, from the age of seven, had picked cotton and later worked in a laundry and as a domestic, was familiar with the ways that to be on welfare was to have one's domestic life regularly surveilled. After eight months on welfare in the mid-1960s, she began to organize with other recipients in Los Angeles. Over the following years, the welfare rights movement grew, culminating in the formation of the National Welfare Rights Organization (NWRO) in 1967, headed by Tillmon. Within a year, it had 30,000 members across the US, the overwhelming majority of whom were Black women. Its strategy was to mobilize masses of poor women in direct action campaigns to secure government support. Its tactics were staunchly disruptive: in one incident, NWRO activists stormed into a welfare office in the Bronx, overturned furniture, and ripped telephones off the walls.[28]

These methods worked. Before the NWRO was established, the majority of those eligible did not submit claims to the federal Aid to Families with Dependent Children (AFDC) program, the

Johnnie Tillmon addressing a Mother's Day March
on Washington, 1968 or 1969
Wisconsin Historical Society, WHI-8771

main source of welfare support; by 1971, 90 per cent were submitting claims. By 1974, there were over 10 million people receiving AFDC payments, up from 3.1 million in 1961; malnutrition and hunger among children in the US declined correspondingly.[29] The NWRO was now moving to campaign for a "guaranteed adequate income" from the federal government for anyone who needed it.[30] The aim was to radicalize the New Deal by removing its sexist underpinnings. Rather than base policy on a model of women as heterosexual housewives to be supported by their husband's family wage, society as a whole should pay for the work of raising children, whether in the form of government funds for mothers or through the creation of child care centers as a public service. Recognizing that "women's work is *real* work," Tillmon said, in 1971, and paying women "a living wage for doing the work we are already doing—child raising and housekeeping"—would resolve the "welfare crisis" and "go a long way toward liberating every woman."[31] To neoliberals, this was a dangerous indulgence of collectivist values. Single mothers were another group that, with government support, appeared to be living outside the disciplining effects of market competition. The growth in AFDC claims was "eroding the traditional role of the family," wrote the neoliberal economist Gary Becker. "Welfare is the poor woman's alimony," he added.[32] The issue of welfare thus tied together a series of tensions around race, gender, and the limits to market mechanisms.

"The central values of civilization are in danger"

In response to these linked crises of welfare capitalism, neoliberal organizations and intellectual circles provided spaces where leading capitalists and Western government officials could work through anxieties about the future of the system they believed in, cast off no-longer-viable methods of rule, and develop new infrastructures of racial capitalism that remain the dominant forces in our lives today. Neoliberal intellectuals and think tanks were deeply involved in formulating and implementing government policies in the US and the UK in the 1970s and 1980s.[33] Think tanks developed not just new policies but new stories of neoliberal transformation for popular consumption and mobilized activist networks of fellow travelers. In contributing to the restructuring of the capitalist system, neoliberals were also the architects of a reorganizing of colonialism and racism. Racist domination did not simply survive as a legacy of the past under the seemingly race-neutral auspices of neoliberalism but was actively reworked. New forms of racism emerged that were distinctive to the neoliberal era. Racism today is not, as commonly conceived, a hangover of the past, but an infrastructure of oppression generated over the last half century by neoliberalism's reconfiguring of older structures of racism. Of course, organized labor, Black political movements in the US, and countless movements in the Third World, for whom neoliberalism was nothing but neocolonialism, avidly opposed the attempt to impose this transformation. All these movements had their own alternative programs for resolving the impasse of the 1970s. The neoliberal victories of the subsequent decades were not preordained even if the balance of political forces was in their favor.

To understand how neoliberals helped bring about this restructuring of racial capitalism, we need to begin with the intellectual framework they employed. Their first premise was that, from the late nineteenth century, market rules had been progressively weakened by governments responding to mass collective demands for social justice and wealth redistribution—Friedman called it "collectivism" in his 1951 essay on "Neo-liberalism and Its Prospects."[34] The core neoliberal idea was that the more our relationships to each other are mediated through market systems, the harder it will be for social justice movements to achieve redistributions of wealth, both within and between nations. "The wider the range of activities covered by the market, the fewer are the issues on which explicitly political decisions are required and hence on which it is necessary to achieve agreement," wrote Friedman.[35] With decisions about the distribution of resources removed from the sphere of political contest, they were no longer possible targets of mass mobilization. Over time, neoliberals hoped, this would lead to waning expectations that redistributions of wealth were possible. This is what Margaret Thatcher meant when she told the *Sunday Times* in 1981: "Economics are the method; the object is to change the heart and soul."[36] But there was wide disagreement among neoliberals on what social, cultural, and political conditions were necessary to enable markets to perform this role. For most neoliberals, government was not to be minimized to make space for markets but given a new role: to "police the system" and "establish conditions favorable to competition," as Friedman put it.[37] This distinguished neoliberals from eighteenth-century liberals such as Adam Smith, who believed that, once governments withdrew from intervening in the economy, the "invisible hand" of the market would naturally optimize efficiency and create a just distribution. That was harder to believe in the twentieth century with its mass movements agitating for resources. Instead, neoliberal theories proposed that markets required constant government supervision to ensure they were not departing from the rules of competition. Neoliberals paid special attention to the cultural conditions thought necessary to get people to follow the impositions of market discipline without having to be continuously coerced to do so. They understood that "free" markets depended on whether people were willing to pursue their desires through market mechanisms and accept the distribution of resources that markets generated. That willingness or lack of it was a matter of cultural values.

Friedrich Hayek, the most important neoliberal thinker, was born in 1899 to the ruling class of the Austro-Hungarian Empire. Spreading across most of eastern Europe, the Empire was disassembled by World War I. To compound the loss, in the 1920s, Hayek's home city of Vienna elected socialists to office; they implemented a radical program of public housing, healthcare, and education, funded by taxes on the wealthy. The collective power of a well-organized working class had usurped the liberal trade rules of the old Empire. Hayek knew that there could be no restoration of the nineteenth century, but he wanted to build a new market empire better able to withstand the forces of mass collective action that had taken hold in Vienna. He developed a theory of cultural evolution precisely to explain how people might come to embrace a "market order" and governments might refrain from pursuing social justice.[38] Examining his theory in detail enables us to see how questions of culture were central to the ways neoliberals interpreted the crises of welfare capitalism.[39]

First, what did Hayek mean by a market order? The market mechanism of prices varying according to supply and demand, he said, is the only way that each participant in an economy can channel information about their capacities and desires into a single, coordinated system.[40] Individual autonomy has to be preserved in the system precisely so that this dispersed knowledge can be communicated through the market. Deliberate efforts can be made to enhance the general rules of the market order but only in a piecemeal fashion and not according to some external plan.[41] To develop any kind of broader redesign of the rules—for example, in order to promote social justice—is bound to result in totalitarianism: when a government seeks to impose its plans on the "spontaneous order" of the market, it squashes the knowledge the market produces and, as a result, has to use its own expertise to decide what people need.[42] But, without drawing on the knowledge generated by markets, government experts are never informed enough to effectively decide what people need. Governments then inevitably seek greater and greater political power to impose their ill-fitting designs on the population. For Hayek, any policy of equitably distributing wealth therefore leads to despotism and violence. "All endeavours to secure a 'just' distribution must thus be directed towards turning the spontaneous order of the market into . . . a totalitarian order."[43] The NHS leads inexorably to the SS.

Hayek believed that market orders came into existence through a process of cultural evolution, in which better social norms replaced worse ones in a gradual process of competitive trial and error.[44] The market order is inseparable, he wrote, from the "common cultural tradition" that undergirds it.[45] Free markets require a tacit propensity among a people to obey certain general rules of conduct upon which the market depends. This cultural foundation is a matter of "the whole cultural inheritance which is passed on by learning and imitation."[46] For Hayek, this inheritance is the inheritance of Western civilization. The rules enabling a market order to emerge were first glimpsed in ancient Greece, then revived in the Renaissance, before being consciously articulated for the first time by thinkers like Edmund Burke,

Adam Ferguson, and Adam Smith.[47] The resulting "Open Society" lifted Western culture beyond a "tribal" phenomenon of group belonging, to an abstract universalism that everyone could emulate. As the scope of human interaction increased with new technologies, everyone else imitated the West's values, because they were the only possible means of coordinating modernity's complex systems. In this Plato to NATO narrative, the "genius of the West" and its values formed the universal principles of the world system.[48] For Hayek, the laws of liberty were discovered, not invented. And this discovery was only possible in the Western cultural tradition.[49]

It followed that failing to uphold Western cultural values could endanger the market system. Those who advocated for social justice, Hayek wrote, activated the "savage in us" and caused the West's "relapsing rapidly into the conceptions of the tribal society."[50] They were, for Hayek, "the non-domesticated or un-civilized who have never learnt the rules of conduct on which the Open Society is based, but want to impose upon it their instinctive, 'natural' conceptions derived from the tribal society."[51] There was a recurring association in Hayek's writing between the demand for distributive justice and earlier stages of cultural evolution that were presumed un-Western or anti-Western. Fundamentally, the threat Hayek saw was not a decline in economic profitability or efficiency but a matter of culture. "The central values of civilization are in danger," began the statement of aims of the Mont Pelerin Society.[52] Market freedom and "preserving western civilisation" were directly connected in Hayek's mind.[53] The "whole of Western civilization," he claimed, rested on expanding the realm of free markets as far as possible without endangering the stability of government itself.[54]

"Breeding certain types of mind"

Neoliberals like Hayek dreamed of a global capitalism accepted by all. They wanted an economic system in which capital could move freely across the entire world. For the most part, they did not think it was possible to return to the old style of European imperialism, which segmented the world into economic zones controlled by different European powers and limited the flows of capital between them. Most neoliberals also believed that market competition would tend to reduce racial bias because it placed an economic penalty on acts of discrimination by sellers or buyers: if white people only wished to buy from or sell to other white people, then they narrowed the range of what they could purchase and reduced the potential sales of their products. On this basis, Friedman wrote that the "market is color blind" and "the groups in our society that have the most at stake in the preservation and strengthening of competitive capitalism are those minority groups which can most easily become the object of the distrust and enmity of the majority—the Negroes, the Jews, the foreign-born, to mention only the most obvious."[55] But neoliberals also believed that the market system they advocated was somehow a product of Western cultural values and that the West had a special role in leading the process of implanting it elsewhere. Neoliberals were doomed to continuously wrestle with this contradiction at the core of their philosophy: that markets were both culturally Western and culturally universal. They emphasized a particular side of the contradiction depending in part upon political circumstances and the area of policy they were addressing.

When Third World leaders used their newly won independence to demand changes to the Western-designed international economic system, neoliberals interpreted this resistance as evidence of a cultural deficiency: Third World peoples were not culturally suited to Western market systems. In this way, what was essentially a political problem (who gets to set the rules for the international economic system?) was transposed into a cultural problem (do they have the right values to follow the rules of the system?). With the problem reframed, the challenge was how to deal with this cultural deficiency. This, for neoliberals, encapsulated the entire problem of the Third World.

Clearly, the old imperialist method of imposing market systems through direct political control, in the name of a civilizing mission, was no longer possible. Hayek's theoretical position was that the values needed to underpin market systems would spread outside the West by "voluntary and unhampered intercourse."[56] In his vocabulary, "intercourse" meant competition, which he saw taking place not only within economic markets but also between sets of cultural values.[57] Market values would spread, he thought, by out-competing rival cultural systems. As he put it, "competition is as much a method for breeding certain types of mind as anything else." Peoples whose cultural traditions "lack the spirit of enterprise" would soon enough acquire it, first through "foreign intruders," then by local imitation encouraged by competition.[58] Thus would the "tribal" be civilized and irrational populations made to act rationally. But there was a circularity in Hayek's argument: how could competition itself be the process that generated competitive values?

What neoliberals needed was a way to guarantee that market rules would apply at least at the level of international trade and finance. That way, there would be competitive pressures on the Third World emanating from its trade with the West, and these would activate the process Hayek had described, where market values would spread to peoples not predisposed to "enterprise." To enable this, neoliberal thinkers proposed the creation of a new global infrastructure to enforce quasi-legal trade and finance rules that would protect international flows of capital. By creating first bilateral treaties and later international institutions to uphold market principles and bypass national policy-making processes, global capital flows could be protected from interference by any nation-state that chose redistributive policies. The intellectual roots of the World Trade Organization are detectable in this reasoning.[59] Generally unacknowledged in the neoliberals' philosophical texts, of course, were the actual coercive methods used to construct a worldwide neoliberal infrastructure. Not Hayek's "voluntary and unhampered intercourse" but counterinsurgency warfare and devastating so-called structural adjustment programs, imposed by Western lenders and their favored native autocrats, were the means by which neoliberalism was imposed on the peoples of the Third World; this involved a scale of violence little different from the older forms of imperialism.

Fears that Third World peoples were culturally ill equipped to observe market discipline also shaped neoliberal thinking about borders and migration. One might expect neoliberals to argue that workers in high-wage countries should not be protected, via immigration controls, from having to compete with migrant workers arriving from low-wage countries. Neoliberal principles of market competition ought to imply a rejection of all such controls. Occasionally, neoliberals did indeed argue this. As a young student in 1906, Ludwig von Mises wondered whether "English and German workers may have to descend to the lowly standard of life of the Hindus and coolies to compete with them."[60] He supported the freedom to migrate precisely to encourage this competition. That is, until the 1940s, when, with an upsurge of anticolonial agitation, he was persuaded that peoples outside the West were deficient in their capacity to adapt to the market philosophy. "How can we expect that the Hindus, the worshipers of the cow, should grasp the theories of Ricardo and of Bentham?" he asked in 1944.[61] He now supported immigration controls to protect the West's market order from other cultures. In any case, other neoliberals had by then argued that allowing capitalists to move investments freely around the world, so that they could easily relocate production to places where wages were lower, would allow for effective competition between Western and other workers, even if there were no migration. So long as the price of labor was mobile, actual laborers need not be.[62]

Likewise, given the principles of his philosophical system, Mises's protégé Hayek might have been expected to support the free movement of workers from one nation to another. According to Hayek, any attempt by a government to create a system of explicitly defined privileges that cannot be justified by market principles will, of necessity, undermine the market order and be a step on the road to the "serfdom" of totalitarian government.[63] Controls on labor migration, which selectively grant access to particular labor markets on the basis of national citizenship, are just such a set of rules of privilege. So, from his own principles, Hayek ought to have concluded that immigration controls were dangerously totalitarian.[64] But actually, he believed that the immigration of people with different values was a threat to Western culture. After Margaret Thatcher told a television interviewer in 1978 that many Britons feared being "swamped by people of a different culture" and called for an "end to immigration," Hayek wrote in *The Times* of her "courageous and outspoken warning."[65] He set aside his universal market principles when it came to immigration, arguing that "limitations on the free movement of men across frontiers" are necessary because "liberal principles can be consistently applied only to those who themselves obey liberal principles, and cannot always be extended to those who do not."[66] Immigration restrictions had a legitimate function in preventing people entering who do not share with the West a "common system of basic moral beliefs."[67]

To try to justify this, Hayek introduced a distinction between neoliberal principles in the abstract and the practical need to defer to "prevailing moral standards" that opposed immigration.[68] But this did not solve the problem. Why should conventional morality be respected on immigration but rejected as "tribal" on questions of social justice? What would otherwise be a glaring inconsistency only makes sense in terms of Hayek's belief that the universal market order depends upon preserving Western cultural values. Immigration from outside the West would then only be acceptable to the extent that immigrants end up assimilating rather than undermining market values. As he wrote, when new immigrants were "too visibly different to be readily absorbed" and "numerous enough to form their own communities," the process of "acculturation" was in danger; immigration controls were then necessary to prevent this problem.[69] When Western values were threatened, the universal market order could only be preserved by granting this particular culture special rights to defend itself—paradoxically contradicting the principles of the universal order itself. The Open Society needed to know when to close its doors—and to whom.

Neo-racism

For Hayek, the development of humanity was a competitive process in which, over time, primitive cultures, whose social norms are ill adapted to human progress, are displaced by more universal cultures, culminating in the Western civilization of the nineteenth century. Other cultures thereafter only make progress through imitation of the universal West. This conception was a product of European colonialism—even though Hayek distanced himself from the classical forms of high imperialism. More specifically, it derived from Herbert Spencer's nineteenth-century theory that races are social organisms competing according to Darwinian principles of competitive natural selection, but applied to moral progress rather than the development of species. Spencer, in fact, bestowed upon Darwin's theory the phrase by which it became known: "survival of the fittest."[70] In his account, the West alone is ever progressing, while other cultures have reached the limits of their potential. And more energetic races by nature eliminate or assimilate races that have become stagnant.

Competition is the engine of progress, and any attempts to impede it threaten the forward march of human development. His theory was a profound influence on the various branches of neoliberalism, even as they abandoned its biological elements and shifted to a vocabulary of cultural adaptation.[71]

Hayek's theory of cultural evolution rejected the concept of race in any physiological sense. But his theory nevertheless involved a form of what the scholar Étienne Balibar calls "neo-racism," in which "culture can also function like a nature ... locking individuals and groups a priori into a genealogy, into a determination that is immutable and intangible in origin," while, paradoxically, it is possible and desirable to assimilate the other into Western culture. Balibar aptly notes that behind this kind of theory lies "barely reworked variants of the idea that the historical cultures of humanity can be divided into two main groups, the one assumed to be universalistic and progressive, the other supposed irremediably particularistic and primitive."[72] On the one hand, neo-racism claims that all cultures have their particular, fixed nature; on the other hand, it holds up Western culture—presented as open, enterprising, and individualistic—as a universal standard against which others are judged inadequate.[73]

Hayekian neoliberalism feared that the application of its desired universal market order might be constrained by particular cultures unable to grasp the virtues of competitive society; a neo-racist idea of culture was the necessary means for conceptualizing and making sense of this danger. Such an idea of culture reconciled two contradictory impulses. First, it fostered the assumption of Western culture's universality: this is what guaranteed the viability of its implantation outside the West and therefore underpinned a global market order. Second, it enabled the perception that the limits to the spread of "Western" markets were the result of the immutable inadequacies of other cultures, and granted the superior West special rights to uphold and defend the market order. Neo-racism thus enabled neoliberalism to oscillate between thinking the limits it encountered were the necessary consequence of inferior others and thinking they could be overcome by renewed imposition of its market logic.

Other founding neoliberal theorists also thought of the cultural underpinnings of free markets in these terms. Mises wrote in his 1927 book *Liberalism* that "European civilization really is superior to that of the primitive tribes of Africa or to the civilizations of Asia."[74] The "better races" who have "developed the system of the market economy and cling to it are in every respect superior to all other peoples," he claimed. "Western man" is a "being adjusted to life in freedom and formed in freedom," whereas in "the East" abuses such as "slavery, serfdom, untouchability, customs like sutteeism or the crippling of the feet of girls, barbaric punishments, mass misery, ignorance, superstition, and disregard of hygiene" prevail.[75] (There is an echo of Napier in the reference to sati, or suttee, and the mention of women's rights.) After World War II, Mises used the term "race" less frequently and adopted a more cultural vocabulary. But his idea of culture was a rigid one that rendered Third World peoples as being ill suited to the rigors of free-market economics. Because he thought force would be necessary to impose markets on those not culturally suited to them, he advocated for the establishment of a global governance regime with the power to inflict neoliberalism around the world, even where it faced opposition from democratically elected national governments. "Measures which affect debts, the money systems, taxations, and other important matters have to be administered by international tribunals, and without an international police force such a plan could not be carried out," he wrote in 1944. "Force must be used to make debtors pay."[76]

Wilhelm Röpke, a central figure in the neoliberal movement, likewise thought the problem was that market economics depended upon a "moral infrastructure" that thinned in proportion to one's cultural distance from the West.[77] He believed that Third World societies "in part still belong in the Stone Age" and their populations lacked the "sociological, spiritual and political preconditions" for liberal order.[78] He defended apartheid in South Africa as a means to ensure Africans could not jettison the Western culture that was, he held, the only basis for stable market orders in the non-Western world.[79] The "negroes of South Africa," he wrote, "belong to a completely different type and level of civilization."[80] For similar reasons, Milton Friedman supported white minority rule in Rhodesia in the 1970s and described the imposition of sanctions as "the suicide of the West."[81]

A number of neoliberals certainly harbored racist prejudices. But more significantly, the logic of their political and economic project inexorably led to both liberal antiracism and new forms of structural racism, irrespective of the intentions or attitudes of its founding intellectuals. On the one hand, neoliberal market universalism implied a celebration of cultural diversity and the rejection of racial discrimination. On the other hand, whether or not neoliberals admitted it, their commitment to market mechanisms to block redistributions of wealth set them against the interests of Black and Third World movements. The world the neoliberals wished to create could only be brought into existence and maintained through border, military, and economic violence on a colossal scale. And, within the terms of their philosophy, this violence could only be justified by presenting Third World cultures as *by nature* deficient. The more that the market order failed to find universal consent and had to be imposed by force on unwilling populations, the more neoliberals relied upon racist ideas of culture to manage their anxieties, organize their proposals, and legitimize their aggression.

10

Policing the Wastelands

Swept up in the anticommunism of the 1950s, a young Samuel P. Huntington came to believe that "the foundations of society are threatened" from the Left and, in such circumstances, liberals like him had to take on a conservative defense of governing institutions, especially the military. A lifelong Democrat, he had been appointed to the faculty of Harvard's Government Department in 1950 and remained there, almost without interruption, for half a century. From the 1960s, he began shuttling between Cambridge and Washington as a policy adviser to successive administrations. As chair of the Vietnam subcommittee of the government's Southeast Asia Development Advisory Group in 1968, he advocated a policy of forcibly resettling Vietnamese villagers into cities, to counter the Viet Cong.[1] The same year, he became the first voice in the US foreign policy establishment to interpret worldwide rebellions against the US-led economic system as symptoms of a Third World cultural incompatibility with market orders. His book *Political Order in Changing Societies*, published in 1968, was the most influential account of what had gone wrong and how an alternative strategy might be developed.

In the two decades after World War II, Huntington pointed out, successful coups d'état had occurred in a majority of Latin American countries. The Middle East was similarly unstable. Thirteen coups had occurred in Asia and sub-Saharan Africa. "Revolutionary violence, insurrection, and guerrilla warfare," he wrote, "wracked Cuba, Bolivia, Peru, Venezuela, Colombia, Guatemala, and the Dominican Republic in Latin America, Algeria and Yemen in the Middle East, and Indonesia, Thailand, Vietnam, China, the Philippines, Malaya, and Laos in Asia."

This was because modernization policies had led to "the rapid mobilization of new groups into politics" in the Third World, such as peasant classes, middle classes, and groups of radical intellectuals. Political participation was growing rapidly across Africa, Asia, and Latin America. Too many groups were becoming politically organized and making demands on government resources. And because these governments did not have the effective authority to manage "the escalation of aspirations," they were "at the mercy of alienated intellectuals, rambunctious colonels, and rioting students." Modernization theory had claimed that stable government would grow organically from the consolidation of a bourgeois class. But Huntington contended that the creation of a large middle class was "often a highly destabilizing event." Modernization was not producing a bourgeois civil society but "political instability and disorder," creating the ideal circumstances for "political extremism" to arise. Huntington's argument followed the neoliberal template: it claimed that the key political problem was organized mass movements making increasingly excessive resource demands on governments, combined with a decrease in the extent to which governments could deny these demands, leading to the danger of a collapse into far-left or far-right extremism.[2] What was distinctive about Huntington's position was its emphasis on the need to establish government authority to manage these spiraling demands. Before economic underdevelopment could be addressed, political underdevelopment had to be dealt with.

The root of the problem of political underdevelopment, he claimed, was not the actions of Third World governments themselves. Those that were not in the communist camp followed the well-established rules of international relations and were largely responsive to the various policy mechanisms that the US had at its disposal—ranging from aid-with-conditions to military action. However, it was not just a matter of having a pro-capitalist government in place, but whether it could hold up in the face of the increasingly mobilized Third World masses. To understand this mass behavior, Huntington relied on the assumption that some cultures were ill suited to the rational, anonymous, rule-based orders characteristic of modern economic and political systems. Political instability was prevalent in cultures "marked by suspicion, jealousy, and latent or actual hostility toward everyone who is not a member of the family, the village, or, perhaps, the tribe. These characteristics are found in many cultures, their most extensive manifestations perhaps being in the Arab world and in Latin America."[3] Huntington's argument was that small-group loyalties in the cultures of these regions were irrationally excessive, making the populace harder to govern. It was no coincidence that these two regions were especially troublesome for US imperialism at the time. Arab nationalist movements gained in popularity across the region in the 1960s and succeeded in overthrowing Western colonialist regimes in Algeria and Yemen. And across Latin America, leftist guerrillas were fighting for their own versions of the Cuban revolution. These movements were posing the question Nkrumah raised: Who sets the rules of the international economic system once direct colonialism has ended? This was fundamentally a political question of unequal power, but Huntington's argument reframed it as a matter of more or less fixed cultural differences. It presented opposition to Western power as a symptom of a cultural failure to adapt to modernity rather than a contest over resources and legitimacy: the problem was "their" culture, not "our" politics.

It followed from Huntington's argument that the US would better achieve its goals if it abandoned its policies of supporting education and science in the Third World; these were only helping to grow a middle-class intelligentsia prone to radicalism. Instead, US policy should aim to slow down economic modernization and focus more on establishing pro-US governments able to forcefully impose their will in the face of opposition, especially in those regions where the destabilizing effects of local cultural values needed to be reined in. To this end, the US needed to ally with pro-Western military leaders in the Third World, who were "intelligent, energetic, progressive," and advise them to form governments that were at once modernizing and authoritarian while avoiding "premature" increases in political participation, such as through elections. Huntington proposed that "the military may yet be able to play a constructive role, if they are willing to follow the Kemalist model"—replicating Mustafa Kemal Atatürk's earlier authoritarian molding of Turkey into a pro-Western secular, industrializing nation that officially disdained its earlier Middle Eastern orientation. "The achievements of Ayub Khan in Pakistan, of Calles and Cárdenas in Mexico, of Kemal and İnönü in Turkey, of Pak and Kim in Korea, and of others such as Rivera in El Salvador, show that military leaders can be effective builders of political institutions," he wrote. The more a culture in a particular region had a reputation for being antagonistic to Western modernity, the more US policies should encourage governments there to be repressive, to prevent that culture from expressing itself in ways that might hamper the success of the purportedly essential new market policies. In the short term, repression could modify a people's behavior to be more responsive to market signals, even if they were not culturally predisposed to act in these ways; over the longer term, the culture itself might be transformed as citizens internalized these new behaviors. Authoritarian regimes were the lesser evil that would stem the growth of extremism and prevent the need for costly US military actions later: having another Kemalist military government was preferable to having to fight another Viet Cong.[4]

Huntington's argument was representative of a broad transformation in US foreign policy thinking in the late 1960s and through the 1970s. US foreign policy-makers abandoned the earlier goal of fostering a bourgeois civil society in Third World states. Instead, in line with neoliberal thinking, their new aim was to prevent mass struggles outside the West from making redistributive demands at the international level. And they did this by using the existing tools of neocolonial discipline: the leverage that came from debt, the use of conditions attached to aid, the influence of Western economic advisers, and covert and overt intelligence and military actions. But they deployed these tools to impose a policy package quite different from the modernization policies of the 1950s and early 1960s. The key change was that, rather than using tariffs to protect nascent industries from international competition, Third World countries were to compete to attract foreign investment. Enshrining the principle of competition for foreign investment implied that governments had to pressure their own population to bear the costs of turning the nation into an attractive location for exploitation. In this way, mass movements' demands for resources would be contained. Without a long-term process of planned development, there was no longer any need to nurture a scientifically educated middle class to manage it; instead, military men were needed, and a small elite of MBAs. Creditworthiness and market indicators were the new gods.

Huntington played a direct role in developing the architecture of this neoliberal empire: he was an adviser to the State Department on Southeast Asia in the 1960s, chairman of the Democratic Party's Foreign Policy Advisory Committee in the mid-1970s, and coordinator of security planning for the National Security Council in President Carter's administration in the late 1970s. By 1975, he had come to believe that the issue he identified in the Third World applied also to the US itself, where an "excess of democracy" had led to Americans "progressively demanding and receiving more benefits from their government." Crucially, Huntington was one of the first to argue that the "democratic distemper" of the 1960s caused the "inflationary tendencies in the economy" of the 1970s. A too-vigorous democracy meant too much welfare, paid for, he claimed, with too much government borrowing—inflation was the consequence.[5] The argument was questionable: as the Kings had argued, government programs to tackle poverty would have been affordable were it not for the cost of fighting the war in Vietnam; and government debt did not necessarily cause inflation. Nevertheless, Huntington's presentation of inflation as a symptom of political disorder and overly generous welfare payments became a leitmotif of neoliberal commentary in the late 1970s and early 1980s.

The approach Huntington advocated had its initial trial run in Indonesia. There, after the defeat of Dutch colonialism in 1949, left-wing ideas about national development dominated the political scene. The existence of the largest communist party outside of China and the Soviet Union—with approximately 3 million members by 1965—reflected Indonesians' desire for a radical transformation of colonial structures. The Asia-Africa Conference in Bandung in 1955 proclaimed a new kind of Third World solidarity made possible by successful struggles against colonialism. Then, in 1966, the military leader Suharto took power amid the systematic extermination of between a half million and 1 million Indonesians suspected of affiliation to the Communist Party or holding left-wing sympathies. The CIA provided direct assistance to the death squads, including supplying lists of targets.[6] With left opposition annihilated, Suharto embraced a new set of economic policies aimed at enabling US corporations to gain access to Indonesia's natural resources and the potential profits to be made from selling to the sixth largest population in the world. The Ford Foundation and the CIA had already been working with the Indonesian military to lay the ground for this policy shift. A group of Indonesian economists—known in the new government as the "Berkeley mafia," because they had initially studied at the University of California, Berkeley—were trained by the Ford Foundation at the Indonesian Army Staff and Command School in Bandung, which served as a base of operations for the army's usurpation of political power. After the coup, Suharto appointed these economists to work alongside Ford Foundation–sponsored US economists in drafting Indonesia's new economic policy.[7] A select list of US and European capitalists were flown to attend a meeting in Geneva where the new Indonesia was marketed—they were told its selling points were "political stability ... abundance of cheap labor ... vast potential market ... treasurehouse of resources."[8]

In 1967, Suharto's government introduced the Foreign Investment Law, which protected the rights of multinational corporations in Indonesia, opening the door to the exploitation of its natural resources, especially oil, and later its low-wage workforce. The rubber and tea plantations that had earlier been taken under government control were returned to their previous Dutch, British, and US corporate owners.[9] Foreign direct investment increased dramatically from the 1970s onward. Thereafter, to maintain its competitiveness in attracting foreign capital, Indonesia kept wages low, increased its tax incentives to foreign investors, banned strikes, and made Indigenous lands available to corporations for timber and palm oil cultivation. By the 1990s, Indonesian workers were assembling Nike sports shoes for less than a dollar a day. As Huntington had anticipated, Indonesians could only be made to endure these circumstances because an authoritarian government had forced them to do so. Today, Indonesian factory workers receive an average wage that is a fifth of what similar workers earn in the US. When more than 2 million workers organized a general strike in 2012 to raise their wages, the IMF responded by warning that "rising unit labor costs" would affect "competitiveness," and the Indonesian government introduced new bans on industrial action.[10]

What was done in Indonesia from 1966 was repeated in a host of other countries through the late 1960s and 1970s, as Washington used the same combination of covert action, military rule, and free-market policies to discipline organized demands for social and economic progress in the Third World. The 1973 overthrow of Salvador Allende's socialist government in Chile and its replacement by Pinochet's military dictatorship, advised by Hayek and Friedman, was the most well-known example. Across Asia, Africa, and Latin America, new authoritarian regimes emerged and existing ones hardened, with US government agencies supplying armored cars, tear gas, and other weapons of internal political warfare, along with training in the techniques of repression.[11] In each case, the US-friendly regime oriented the economy to exporting raw materials and foodstuffs, offered a cheap labor force as an incentive to foreign investment, and treated any opposition to the interests of foreign capitalists as a national security problem.[12] The repressive apparatuses of colonial government were, as Fanon had predicted, repurposed by new indigenous elites who, lacking any other means of securing their legitimacy, relied upon force. These were the elites with whom US policy-makers allied in order to implement neoliberal policies in the Third World. Neoliberal intellectuals cheered it all on. As well as supporting Pinochet, Hayek publicly defended the Suharto regime in Indonesia and the generals in Argentina.[13]

Petrodollars and Palestine

The decisive moment in the emergence of a neoliberal empire came in 1973 when six Arab oil-producing states announced they would impose an embargo on shipping oil to the United States until Israel evacuated the Palestinian territories it had occupied in 1967. This was the opportunity and basis for a neoliberal restructuring of racial capitalism. To understand how this happened requires reckoning first with what gave the Palestinian struggle a special significance within the imperialist system.

The Zionist colonization of Palestine occurred in the same period that the majority of the Third World achieved formal decolonization, in the years from 1947 to the end of the 1960s. From the Nakba of 1947–49 to the occupation of the West Bank, East Jerusalem, the Gaza Strip, and the Golan Heights in 1967, Zionism appeared as a regression to the exclusivist settler colonialism that characterized the early colonization of North America and Australasia. Palestine represented an exception to the seeming drift of history: a reminder of some of the most devastating episodes of the colonial past, an example of the limits of decolonization in the present, and a harbinger of neocolonial dangers in the future. Until the late 1960s, hopes for the Palestinian cause were vested in the diplomatic and occasionally military efforts of the governments of neighboring Arab countries. But these were in vain. The Arab states were discredited after their defeat by Israel in the June 1967 war. The Palestinians were forced to mobilize their own resources. The existing Palestinian armed groups formed the Palestine Liberation Organization (PLO) coalition, united under the leadership of Yasser Arafat with the demand for a single, secular, and democratic state in Palestine.[14] The struggle now presented itself as being specifically rooted in the aspirations of the Palestinian people, rather than tied to a state-centered Arab nationalism. The PLO was soon the best funded and most widely supported of all the insurgencies engaged across the Third World.

Among US policy-makers, the shift from Arab diplomacy to Palestinian insurgency was associated with the fear of a broader radicalization of Arab politics. In 1972, the Nixon administration issued a set of directives, known as Operation Boulder, that enabled the FBI and CIA to coordinate with the pro-Israel lobby, subjecting nonviolent Arab American political activists to surveillance and harassment.[15] The great anxiety was that a growing culture of Arab radicalism would lead governments in the most important oil-producing region of the world to use their control of oil to advance radical political goals. Capitalism's dependence on Arabs for oil was perceived as analogous to its dependence on miners for coal. Because of the centrality of coal to industry, striking miners could shut down an entire economy, and they leveraged this power to redistribute national wealth from capitalists to workers; radical Arabs could do the same with oil to force international redistributions of wealth from the West to the Third World.[16] From the beginning of the 1970s, Arab oil-producing states had been reducing supply as a way to negotiate better terms of trade with Western corporations. But the 1973 embargo deployed the "oil weapon" not for economic motives but ostensibly on behalf of the Palestinian national struggle, suggesting that the world's oil supply was now vulnerable to Arab political radicalism. In fact, the Gulf Arab elites had no such intentions. Their aim was to integrate themselves as loyal and wealthy subordinates in the US empire. The embargo was a face-saving performance of pan-Arab solidarity; within a few months it was suspended without any gains for the Palestinians. But even a gesture in this direction sent shockwaves through the capitalist system, as the price of oil lurched upward.

On the pages of its house journal, *Foreign Affairs*, the US foreign policy elite had already begun to raise the danger of a revolutionary Arab spirit gaining control of the world's oil, perhaps in a Third World Marxist alliance with China. Nervous discussions of Arabic and Islamic identity were launched, on the assumption that the political management of Arabs rested on an understanding of their culture. Islam appeared as the factor that determined the fate of oil, from the Arab Gulf states and Iran to Indonesia. Matters of Islamic jurisprudence were suddenly considered relevant to the international economy.[17] A flurry of commentaries with titles like "The Depth of Arab Radicalism" appeared, discussing the meaning of Islamic terms like "sharia" and "jihad," "the compatibility of Islam itself with the 'modern' outlook," and "problems [with] their whole culture."[18] The political antagonism between US-led imperialism and Third World radicalism was beginning to be reframed as a cultural antagonism between the West and Islam. The "Muslim problem" began to take the form that became ubiquitous in the twenty-first century with the War on Terror.

What seemed like a moment of danger was also an opportunity. James E. Akins, the US ambassador to Saudi Arabia and the most important diplomat in relation to Arab oil, persuaded policy-makers that the era of cheap oil was anyway at an end, because, as he wrote in *Foreign Affairs*, it had become "plainly evident" to the producing states that it was in their interests to raise prices. The resulting dramatic increase in the oil price meant that a historically unprecedented amount of wealth—expected to be over $200 billion from 1973 to 1980—would be redistributed from consumers around the world to oil corporations and Arab elites, particularly in the Gulf. "What will be done with this money will be a matter of crucial importance to the world," Akins wrote.[19] And so it proved: Wall Street absorbed these "petrodollars" and sent them free-wheeling around the world in pursuit of resources to extract, labor to exploit, and governments to indebt. The neoliberal principle of global market competition was brought to life with this injection of funds from the oil crisis in a context where the older modernization policies had been discredited. A more globalized and financialized capitalism for the first time became possible.

In the US, rather than acting to subsidize the price of gas, which shot up from thirty-eight to fifty-five cents a gallon, the government told the public that the market had to adjust to new circumstances—an education in the market principles neoliberals were trying to inculcate. The oil crisis was the hook upon which were mounted neoliberal arguments about allowing commodities, including labor, to find their "true market price."[20] US news media reworked older stereotypes of Arabs to produce a new image of the wealthy "sheikh," able to manipulate the world economy—an analogue of the anti-Semitic conspiracy theory of Jews secretly running the world.[21] Public anger about the crisis was thus redirected outward to new racial enemies. Moreover, the hunger for investment opportunities in financial markets implied easy credit and a new era of indebtedness. In the US, the growth in household debt, such as student and healthcare loans, went hand in hand with the neoliberal decline in publicly funded education and collectively bargained healthcare plans, which fostered in workers the more individualized relationship to economic processes that neoliberals desired. In addition, the oil funds were pumped into loans to financially weakened Third World governments; Western lenders then took advantage of the leverage they had over them to impose neoliberal market principles. Moreover, the oil funds circulated in a system of market discipline that would now be upheld by regional surrogates, armed to the teeth and empowered by the US to carry out the brutal suppression of local insurgencies. Following the US's defeat in Vietnam, the Middle East became the testing ground of this new imperial strategy, with Israel offering the paradigm of a regional power allying with the US in the name of mutual security.[22] Israel's new strategic role was to counter the danger of Arab radicalism. To this end, the US government dramatically increased its military support: between 1949 and 1968, the US supplied half a billion dollars in arms to Israel; from 1969 to 1976, it supplied $22 billion.[23] Thus neoliberalism took shape in the crucible of oil, Palestine, and imperial crisis.

"Superfluous humanity"

As Third World authoritarian regimes, such as Suharto's, started to offer Western multinationals highly policed cheap labor forces, the potential arose for an epochal relocation of the world's industrial manufacturing. Multinational corporations were now able to move production to wherever in the Third World they could find low wages. With its Border Industrialization Program, launched in 1965, Mexico was a pioneer in seeking to attract such investment. It led to the development of maquiladoras, the foreign-owned assembly plants situated in "free trade zones" along Mexico's northern border, where US corporations could take advantage of wages that were a fraction of those north of the border.[24] Corporations centralized their administrative, financial, research, design, and marketing functions in their home country while subcontracting labor-intensive manufacturing and assembly via global supply chains to low-wage, export-led production zones in Southeast Asia, Turkey, and Mexico. Western capitalists profited from a new form of super-exploitation of

Third World workers, made possible by, first, the difference in the wages prevailing where products were made and where they were sold being greater than the difference in productivity and, second, capital and goods being free to circulate while labor's movement was restricted by progressively fortifying racist border regimes.[25] By 2010, there were 541 million industrial workers in the global South compared to 145 million in the North.[26] In Juárez, Mexico, for example, the cost of employing a manufacturing worker in 2015 was two dollars an hour; in El Paso, Texas, the cost was five times higher.[27] The border cutting through the middle of the Juárez–El Paso conurbation allows capital and goods to move freely but not labor, making the wage difference possible and giving it a racial meaning.

By offering well-policed, low-wage labor, it has been possible for some Third World countries to achieve a sustained growth in their industrial production. But corporations can relocate easily if labor costs rise too high. In the garment industry, for example, the cost of manufacturing labor is such a small proportion of the final retail price that, if workers were to be paid three times as much, the retail price would only have to increase by around 4 percent to pay for it. Yet wages are nevertheless kept crushingly low. The entry-level wage in the Bangladeshi garment industry—which employs about 3.5 million workers and makes clothes for companies like Walmart, H&M, Tesco, Levi Strauss, Tommy Hilfiger, and Marks & Spencer—was about $43 a month in 2010.[28] As such, industrialization in most Third World countries has not provided the basis for rising standards of living, as had happened in Europe and the US in the nineteenth century.[29] Instead, a new imperialism has operated through a global racial division of labor and unequal exchanges in global supply chains. The earlier wealth drain from the colonial periphery to the core has continued in this new form into the twenty-first century, amounting to a total drain of $62 trillion from 1960 to 2018, according to one estimate.[30] And over this period, the new imperialism greatly increased the inequality between the richer and poorer nations (China excepted), with the per-capita GDP gaps between the US and Latin America, sub-Saharan Africa, and South Asia each roughly tripling.[31]

While some regions of the Third World were incorporated into global capitalism as zones of low-wage industrial production, the larger part was still defined by communal land relations and subsistence farming in rural areas. This served as a bulwark against capitalist market discipline—it preserved a sense of non-capitalist rights and entitlements, even among those who left the rural areas for the cities. And food and energy prices tended to be set by government policy at levels lower than those of international markets. All of this added up to the "collectivist" culture that neoliberals wished to dissolve. The Oxford University economist S. Herbert Frankel summed up such neoliberal concerns when he complained at the 1958 Mont Pelerin Society meeting that people wait outside West African banks for their relatives to draw money, "ready to pounce on them like vultures, because they believe they have the 'right' to be supported or assisted by a relative who has some wealth." What was needed was a cultural shift to break up the communal cultures that, according to neoliberals, cushioned individuals from the imperatives of market competition.[32] The role of Western governments was to design the institutions that could deliver this process of cultural reform.

By the end of the 1970s, US development policy was wholly focused on using market mechanisms to break the social expectations of Third World peasants and workers. To achieve this goal, there needed to be what World Bank head Robert McNamara in 1979 called the "structural adjustment" of Third World countries: privatization of government-owned businesses, privatization of land tenure, abolition of government subsidies on food and energy, cuts to public healthcare and education, abolition of labor and environmental protections, abolition of tariffs and capital controls, and fiscal austerity.[33] The way to bring about this structural adjustment was for Western banks and agencies like the IMF and the World Bank to shift from lending for specific projects to using debt as a lever to impose broader policy changes. US Treasury secretary William Simon wrote privately in 1976 that the IMF had "to change the policies of countries that have wandered from the reservation in terms of conduct of their affairs."[34] It was an apt idiom, unconsciously linking neocolonial economic policies to settler-colonial rule. Not only did international financial institutions adopt neoliberal policies, the neocolonialism Nkrumah had described also made it possible for these institutions to impose neoliberalism on the Third World. Increasingly, the acceptance of the IMF's directives was necessary even to obtain private bank loans. Third World debt, as Nkrumah had cautioned, was not simply one side of an economic transaction but a means by which powerful agencies could directly control and secure the indebted; it authorized surveillance, judgment, and domination.[35] In most cases, Third World governing elites were made up of profiteers and kleptocrats whose wealth derived from trade relationships with multinational corporations; they were therefore enthusiastic to implement the unpopular austerity and trade liberalization policies that the IMF insisted upon. In other cases, where Third World leaders sought international redistributions of wealth, they faced sharp rebuke from US policy-makers. "It is time we asserted that inequalities in the world may be not so much a matter of condition as of performance," wrote Daniel Patrick Moynihan in 1975, then the US ambassador to India.[36] He was subsequently appointed ambassador to the United Nations, where he led a counter-offensive against Third World efforts at creating a more equal international economic order.[37]

The consequences of this neoliberal transformation of the Third World were devastating, especially in Africa. Ghana, for example, completed sixteen structural adjustment programs with the World Bank and the IMF during the 1980s. By the end of it, it still had an external debt of $3.5 billion and was, as it had been at independence, entirely reliant on cocoa exports.[38] Ghana's tropical forest was reduced to just a quarter of its original size, in the process wiping out both the wild game that provided food for the majority of the population, and the supply of fuel and medicines that was previously harvested from the trees.[39] Meanwhile, the privatization of education forced two-thirds of children in rural areas to stop attending school.[40] Inequality and absolute poverty both rose in what was nevertheless described by the IMF as one of its few success stories in Africa.[41] Across the continent, the abolition of subsidies for agriculture and the privatization of land tenure displaced great swathes of people from subsistence farming. Uprooted from the terrain on which their existing rights and entitlements were entrenched, these rural evictees put their hopes for survival in the cities.[42]

The epic displacement of the Third World's rural masses, a consequence of the neoliberal privatization of communally owned resources, was another iteration of what Marx called "primitive accumulation." Indeed, neoliberalism produced the most intensified and wide-ranging processes of primitive accumulation in world history, as capitalists seized both state-owned and communally owned resources.[43] This process of dispossession and eviction was, as Marx had described, necessarily violent. But there was an important difference between the primitive accumulation at the dawn of English capitalism, which Marx analyzed, and that of the neoliberal era. In Marx's analysis, those dispossessed from subsistence economies on the land were generally absorbed as waged workers in capitalist agricultural and industrial production. Those who were not emigrated to the settler colonies of North America or Australasia or fell into the reserve army of labor as disposable workers, brought in to waged work temporarily as needed and then expelled. But neoliberal primitive accumulation has functioned differently. The Third World dispossessed arrived in cities that could not provide waged work even for their existing workforces, as cutbacks in the public sector took hold. There was, then, only the informal economy of street vendors and day laborers, and a life of surviving hand to mouth in the slums that had become a permanent feature of Third World cities.[44] The United Nations Human Settlements Programme found in 2003 that one-third of the world's urban population lived in slums, and four out of ten inhabitants of the global South were informal settlers.[45] Some of these dispossessed Third World city-dwellers—such as those settling in Juárez, Mexico, to work in the maquiladoras—were connected through subcontracting chains to major capitalist corporations. But the majority were deemed to be surplus to capitalism's needs. Capital did not engage them as waged labor, even as a reserve army. The Cameroonian theorist Achille Mbembe writes they "are unable to be exploited at all. They are abandoned subjects, relegated to the role of a 'superfluous humanity.' Capital hardly needs them anymore to function."[46] For the Indian economist Kalyan Sanyal:

> The dispossessed are left only with labor power, but their exclusion from the space of capitalist production does not allow them to turn their labor power into a commodity. They are condemned to the world of the excluded, the redundant, the dispensable, having nothing to lose, not even the chains of wage-slavery.

Neoliberalism thus produced "a vast wasteland" inhabited by those who have lost the entitlements of subsistence economies but "for whom the doors of the world of capital remain forever closed"; this wasteland is a space outside of capitalism's labor relations and a challenge to its claims to universality.[47] There, women especially have had to take on the task of improvising survival strategies in the face of multiple crises of food and health—in short, of social reproduction.[48]

Anti-Muslim racism

By the end of the century, neoliberal intellectuals, activists, and politicians could survey the world they had built with some satisfaction. Soviet communism had collapsed. Labor movements in the West had been disaggregated. The industrial working class in Europe and the US could no longer call upon "its pristine form, shape, size, homogeneity of experience, unity of will, clout," as Sivanandan, the London-based antiracist activist and writer, wrote in 1990.[49] Meanwhile, the workforces of the newly industrializing global South were held firmly in check by the force of authoritarian regimes sponsored by Western governments. In any case, Sivanandan noted, neoliberalism had succeeded to some extent in inculcating new cultural values in the global South. The "food you eat, the clothes you wear, the music you hear, the television you watch, the newspapers you read," he wrote, trained the mind to celebrate "individual greed in place of collective good."[50] Across the global South, elites were enthusiastic to be incorporated into the "liberal world order" that a victorious neoliberalism proclaimed. Some were able to join the top 10 percent of income-earners, which by the twenty-first century was less dominated by elites from Europe and the US, with East Asians making up around one in ten.[51] The position of China in the world system was dramatically transformed. Most significantly, the earlier redistributive demands of Black and Third World radicalism—which had so troubled neoliberals—were no longer on the agenda. The collectivism that neoliberals had attacked for decades was politically dead. Even the leaders of the African National Congress, upon the success of its struggle against apartheid in South Africa, decided to implement neoliberal policies of reducing import tariffs, offering tax incentives for foreign corporations, and cutting social spending.[52]

Yet the neoliberals' triumphs did not diminish their sense that the market system was endangered by the dispossessed and excluded masses of the global South. The wealth gap between the poor and the rich countries of the world remained at a similar level to what it had been in the heyday of European imperialism a century earlier. The poorest half of the world's population, largely in South Asia and Africa, possessed barely any wealth at all while the richest tenth owned three-quarters of everything.[53] Neoliberalism was haunted by these impoverished masses, most of whom were deemed surplus to capitalism. They signified a limit to neoliberalism's reach, a failure of its claims to universal validity, and a space within which anti-market cultures might thrive. Neoliberal concern expressed itself in a farrago of publicly circulated fears about population explosions, out-of-control migration, extremism, underclasses, ethnic conflict, and fundamentalism—all issues that neoliberals interpreted in terms of a cultural failure of surplus populations to follow the rationality of the market order.[54]

But it was Palestine that once again became the major focus of disquiet in the 1990s. The Palestinian national struggle stood out as the one remaining antagonism that could not be resolved through incorporation into the neoliberal order. The hope was that the Oslo accords signed in 1993 would achieve in Palestine the pacification that had been effected elsewhere in the global South. But the mass of the Palestinian movement outside of the PLO leadership opposed the accords, on the grounds that they gave the Palestinians only "a series of municipal responsibilities in bantustans dominated from the outside by Israel," as Edward Said wrote.[55] The radical energies of twentieth-century Third World nationalism had not entirely dissipated. Once again, the US foreign policy establishment set aside the political nature of the conflict—a struggle over land and rights—and interpreted Palestinian resistance to Israel's military occupation as nothing but mindless terrorism inspired by Islamic values that were ill adjusted to modernity. Prior to the 1980s, the concept of terrorism had not yet solidified as a major term in US policy-making discourse and, when people did refer to "terrorism," it was not especially associated with Arabs or Muslims.[56] But by the early 1980s, the image of the Muslim extremist began to be crafted from the earlier figure of the Arab radical. A pivotal moment was the 1984 Jonathan Institute conference on terrorism, held in Washington, DC, and organized by Benjamin Netanyahu, then the Israeli permanent representative to the United Nations, where delegates argued that terrorist violence was endemic to Islamic culture.[57] President Reagan's secretary of state, George Shultz, and his ambassador to the United Nations, Jeane Kirkpatrick, attended the conference. The Reagan administration began to present terrorism as the number-one foreign policy issue. *Time* magazine published excerpts of the conference, and the ideological link between Islam and terrorism began to form—as images of mad mullahs, suicide bombers, and angry turbaned crowds circulated in Hollywood movies and news reports.[58] Then, in the early 1990s, with the Cold War over, Samuel P. Huntington developed his earlier thinking about the role of culture in political development to argue that what threatened the West was not only Palestinian intransigence derived from Islamic culture, but also Islam in general; it was, drawing on Bernard Lewis's phrase, a "clash of civilizations."[59] On this account, culture played the same role as race: a force that drove a whole people's behavior and could be used to mechanically explain anything they did. Huntington wrote that, with communism defeated, Islam was the "ideal enemy" for the US as it was "ideologically hostile, racially and culturally different, and militarily strong enough to pose a credible threat to American security."[60]

This narrative about Islam served to shield Israel from domestic criticism in the US, especially after Israel's invasion of Lebanon in 1982, its laying siege to Beirut, and its direct responsibility for the Sabra and Shatila massacres.[61] But anti-Muslim racism also offered what Stuart Hall called a "lay ideology" that could be used as a framework to make sense of random and shocking events, such as acts of terrorism, in ways that disavowed those events' political meanings—their origins in conflicts over land, rights, and resources—and instead explained them as products of an unchanging alien culture.[62] Since the neoliberal ordering of the world inevitably generated political violence and chaotic movements of peoples, it was not hard to find the crisis events around which such a framing could be organized, from acts of Palestinian resistance to the 9/11 attacks to Syrians seeking asylum. Within the US media system, national security agencies and associated "terrorism experts" were granted a particular authority to interpret the meaning of those events. From the 1990s, they consistently placed events involving Muslims within the framework of an assumed Islamic propensity to extremism.

With the launch of the War on Terror in September 2001, anti-Muslim racism was solidified in the global machinery of counter-terrorism. National security think tanks and pro-Israel lobby groups organized and coordinated the representation of Islam in this way. But there were deeper reasons for anti-Muslim racism's grip on US public culture. These reveal themselves when the War on Terror's ideologists detail their justifications. The journalist Robert Kaplan, for example, one of the most effective defenders of the 2003 Iraq war and an adviser to the Pentagon, described the War on Terror as "really about taming the frontier."[63] Yale University military historian John Lewis Gaddis argued that the Iraq war had its origins in the wars that cleansed the US frontier of "native Americans, pirates, marauders, and other free agents." Defense secretary Donald Rumsfeld told US troops in 2003 that, in "fighting terrorists in the mountains of Afghanistan," they had "lived up to the legend of Kit Carson"— the nineteenth-century US army officer responsible for the deaths of thousands of Navajo people.[64] And when Deputy Assistant Attorney General John Yoo wrote his 2003 memo seeking to justify torture, he turned to an 1873 case involving Modoc Indian prisoners for a legal precedent.[65] Propagandists for the War on

Terror repeatedly conceived of Muslim extremism as an analogue of the Indigenous insurgencies against US settler colonialism in the nineteenth century. Not for nothing was the operation to kill Osama bin Laden named "Geronimo," after the nineteenth-century Apache leader who organized armed resistance to US colonialism.

The ideological traffic between the War on Terror and histories of US settler colonialism flowed through another site of settler colonialism: Palestine.[66] Israeli colonization had occasionally assimilated Palestinians as citizens or exploited them as a subordinate migrant workforce, but its primary drive was to remove them entirely from occupied land. By their very existence in Israel and the occupied territories, the Palestinians signified a barrier and a limit to the Zionist project. They were a kind of surplus population.[67] Thus, through a series of displacements, the Muslim extremist stood in for the Palestinian who stood in for surplus populations in general—and all were conceived in the US, at a more or less unconscious level, as the savages at the frontiers of civilization, once again standing in the way of modernity's expansion. Israel's colonization of Palestine became a microcosm of the broader US-led imperial structure. Fundamentally, anti-Muslim racism took hold in the US because, via these linkages, it offered a systematic framework for working through and responding to the problem of surplus populations at the core of the neoliberal world. The Muslim extremist became a metaphor for Third World radicalism, and the global policing of Muslims meshed with the broader problem of policing neoliberalism's surplus populations, within and without the West. The violence upon which US capitalism depended to manage surplus populations—its support for authoritarian regimes, its wars of pacification, its fortification of borders—found a new rationale in the inflated danger of Muslim extremism. Ostensibly liberal governments could now understand their mass violence as a proportionate response to the inherently aggressive and threatening nature of the fanatical Muslim enemy. The necessary violence of an imperialist system was projected onto the personality of the Muslim and seen as emanating from outside its own processes. A Western self-image of innocence and beneficence could be maintained by way of the fantasy of securing the civilized from the menace of savage violence.[68]

For Israel, this set of relationships enabled it to develop techniques of policing the dispossessed surplus populations of the global South, specializing in programs of surveillance, police violence, border fortification, aerial bombardment, and propaganda. Israel's treatment of the Palestinians, once hoped to be the last gasp of a dying European colonialism, became the model for the neocolonial present. As Roei Elkabetz, a brigadier general for the Israel Defense Forces, told a security conference in El Paso, Texas, in 2012: "We have learned lots from Gaza ... It's a great laboratory." In the US, security agencies and police departments have adopted methods of repression that Israel pioneered. When the Obama administration needed to find a legal justification for its program of using drones to carry out "targeted" killings, it explicitly cited the arguments developed by the Israel Defense Forces for its analogous program.[69] When the Customs and Border Protection agency needed to step up its policing of the US-Mexico border in 2014, it hired the Israeli security company Elbit Systems to build the same network of fixed towers containing cameras, radar, and motion sensors that Israel has built in the West Bank.[70] And when the New York Police Department sought to initiate a program of mass surveillance of every aspect of Muslim life in the city, it emulated the methods used by the Israeli military and internal security service, Shin Bet, in the Occupied Palestinian Territories.[71] In all its years of operation, the NYPD surveillance program generated no leads of potential terrorist activity to investigate; its main effect was to instill in Muslim New Yorkers the fear that they would be targeted if they spoke out against the injustices of the War on Terror.[72]

11

A War on the Urban Dispossessed

As it became possible from the 1970s to relocate a large share of industrial production from the West to East Asia and Central America, Western workers were subjected for the first time to wage competition with workers in the Third World, especially in manufacturing. This had long been a neoliberal goal. Its consequences were profound. First, it led to the erosion of older racial boundaries dividing the world economy. No longer did wages for Western workers rise steadily with increases in productivity while Third World workers remained at subsistence levels. By the end of the 1970s, the divergence in the average wage levels between the West and the Third World was frozen, rather than increasing further. In the US, there was a decline in the real wage rate from the 1980s onward.[1] Second, with capitalists free to relocate production, they were also emancipated from having to grant the modicum of rights and privileges won through workplace militancy in the West. The threat of relocation, as much as relocation itself, helped deprive Western labor movements of their bargaining power.[2] Third, with industrial manufacturing gradually disappearing from the US, there emerged a large population deemed surplus to capitalism. This constituted another "wasteland" space of the permanently excluded from waged work, no longer functioning as a reserve army of labor but forced to survive entirely on welfare provisions and hustling in the informal economies of the cities.

The waning of manufacturing jobs, as Al-Amin anticipated, hit Black people hardest. Campaigning to remedy this discarding of people as surplus to capitalism's needs was a deep concern of Coretta Scott King in the years after her husband's assassination.

She helped to develop and lead the National Committee for Full Employment and, in 1977, organized a national week of demonstrations to end unemployment, in which over a million people participated across the US. Whites, she emphasized, constituted the majority of unemployed people; they had always made up a majority of the poor in the US. But one in three Black families were recorded as below the federal poverty line in the 1970s.[3] The next year, the Humphrey-Hawkins Full Employment Act became law. In its original formulation, which Scott King helped develop, it committed the federal government to minimizing unemployment; it eventually passed in only a defanged version. With its roots in the Black Left of the 1940s, Scott King's political agenda represented an alternative to the neoliberal path out of the crises of the 1970s. "True homeland security," she wrote, was about "providing health care for every citizen . . . feeding the hungry, housing the homeless, and making sure there is quality education for every child and a job at a decent wage for everyone who wants and needs one."[4] To meet these human needs would require downsizing the US's agencies of national security. "This nation has never honestly dealt with the question of a peacetime economy," she noted in 1975.[5]

To the Nixon administration, the solution to Black poverty was Black capitalism. "We have to get private enterprise into the ghetto," declared Nixon during his 1968 presidential campaign. "But at the same time we have to get the people of the ghetto into private enterprise—as workers, as managers, as owners."[6] Under his administration, the federal government and the Ford Foundation issued grants to Black-owned businesses, while the Federal Housing Authority ended its longstanding practice of segregation through redlining and adopted new policies designed to help low-income Black people become homeowners. This inclusion was premised on the notion that access to a free market in real estate was a pathway to equality. The market system was valorized in a new fable of color-blind fairness. As liberal antiracism was succeeding in removing some overt forms of discrimination, and racial abuse in interpersonal relationships was beginning to diminish, neoliberals could dress these up as victories for market rationality. But Nixon also understood that free markets would, in fact, preserve patterns of segregation. In a 1971 statement on federal housing policy, he argued that, so long as there was not active racial discrimination, racial segregation in housing may still legitimately arise. "An open society does not have to be homogeneous, or even fully integrated," the statement claimed, because there was nothing wrong with the wealthy using their wealth to choose to live in racially exclusive neighborhoods.[7]

Yet this new form of structural racism could be couched as a civil rights victory because overt discrimination was no longer a part of it. To do this credibly, the civil rights movement's demand that wealth be redirected to the poor had to be erased from the collective memory—hence the deradicalization of King's life in most popular history during the neoliberal era. The "integration" that the civil rights movement had fought for in the 1960s meant Black inclusion in the New Deal's system of benefits and protections. But the neoliberal response in the 1970s was to dismantle the New Deal itself and to redefine "integration" to mean entry into a competitive market system. The racist segregation the civil rights movement had fought against was likewise reframed as a matter of different individuals making different choices as to where to live, based on their diverse tastes and preferences, within a single market order. "We are richer for our cultural diversity," said Nixon in defense of this market-based segregation. Neoliberalism was simultaneously shaping new forms of structural racism and making use of a liberal antiracist politics of diversity. Over the following decades, a burgeoning Black middle class did benefit to some extent from the new opportunities, but "color-blind" market inclusion preserved racial inequality in housing in new forms: the extent to which home values correlated to the racial composition of neighborhoods actually increased in the neoliberal era between 1980 and 2015.[8]

Developing this nascent politics of diversity, Nixon sought to co-opt the upsurge in affirmations of Black identity. He argued that "much of the black militant talk these days is actually in terms far closer to the doctrines of free enterprise" and reflects a desire for "'pride,' 'ownership,' 'private enterprise,' 'capital,' 'self-assurance,' 'self-respect'—the same qualities, the same characteristics, the same ideals, the same methods, that for two centuries have been at the heart of American success, and that America has been exporting to the world."[9] Responding to this, Al-Amin wrote that the concept of Black Power "has been diluted and prostituted" to the point where even conservatives support it because they mistakenly think that "Black Power is attainable through Black capitalism."[10] Al-Amin had hoped that the turn to Black identity in the 1960s would spark a process of radical change. The term "identity politics" was first defined a decade later by the Black feminists of the Combahee River Collective. They also saw the turn inward to one's own experience as a combusting force, catalyzing new levels of radical consciousness to drive a feminist, antiracist, and socialist politics. They wrote in 1977 that identity politics meant "focusing upon our own oppression," adding: "We believe that the most profound and potentially most radical politics come directly out of our own identity, as opposed to working to end somebody else's oppression."[11]

But this turning inward to identity was ambiguous. Some thought of identity as a sense of self that was shaped and modified by social and political circumstances. On this view, you could, within certain limits, set aside or transform your identity through the conscious choice to join a movement: you could *become* Black, which, as Al-Amin had argued, was essential but insufficient if it did not also open up revolutionary solidarity with others. Your cultural identity lubricated connections to other people's struggles without losing the specificity of your own. Black identity, wrote Stuart Hall, "was a social, political, historical and symbolic event, not just a personal, and certainly not simply a genetic, one."[12] Others conceived of identity as a basic element in one's personal sense of self that was simply there—a kind of automatic internalizing of the fixed norms of a broader cultural bloc, near enough a genetic inheritance. The psychologist Erik Erikson had first introduced the term "identity" to the general public in the 1960s with more or less this second meaning, drawing on Franz Boas and Ruth Benedict's theories of culture.[13] Nixon's attempt to co-opt Black pride implied this second conception of identity: a stabilizing process in which the market order integrated marginalized groups as consumers of their own distinct culture. A positive sense of one's own identity, inculcated by a consumerist multiculturalism and sympathetic representations in popular culture, was supposed to be the key to individual empowerment and uplift. This form of incorporation involved pruning Black and Third World cultures of their radical edges, isolating them from each other, and packaging them up as commodities. As Fanon anticipated, the effect was to "objectivate, encapsule, imprison and encyst" these cultures and thereby deradicalize them.[14]

For liberal antiracists, the new emphasis on diversity was once again about elites leading a process of educating away racist attitudes among ordinary people; it was meant to happen now through the symbolic power of representation in political leadership, corporate leadership, and popular culture. On this basis, liberals saw the growing number of elected representatives from Black, and later Latino and Asian, backgrounds as in itself a measure of antiracist progress, irrespective of whether that increasing representation brought about any deeper changes.

Even though Nixon presented markets as spaces of individual freedom and Black empowerment, they were to neoliberals essentially mechanisms of discipline. The more a society was organized through the market, the more waged workers were forced to compete on wages and stay creditworthy; their standard of living depended less on what could be obtained through collective political or industrial action and more on what could be gained by individual efforts. But market competition did not apply to those who never entered waged work. And this latter group had increased in size as a result of the neoliberals' policy of introducing global competition. In 1969, the unemployed population of the US was 2.8 million, according to official figures; about half a million were Black. Fourteen years later, with the shift to neoliberal policies in full swing, there were 10.7 million out of work, about 2.6 million of whom were Black. Roughly half of Blacks aged sixteen to nineteen years old were unemployed.[15] The neoliberals had thus created a dilemma for themselves. Their expansion of worldwide market competition had generated within the US a growing number of people who lived within the market order but were not disciplined by it. Welfare assistance, it seemed to neoliberals, protected these people from the "civilizing" functions of market competition. Under the New Deal, this did not matter much because unemployment insurance was seen as a cushion for workers whose lack of waged employment was temporary. But once neoliberalism had generated a surplus population chronically excluded from waged work and dependent on welfare, the welfare recipient became a fraught signifier of the anxieties and tensions thrown up by the neoliberal order. Racial capitalism had always generated a distinction between the deserving and undeserving poor. But in the neoliberal era this was transformed into a distinction between those who followed market signals (because they depended on a wage) and those who did not (because they depended on welfare). That economic benefits could be received outside of any market mechanisms was a scandal to neoliberal thought. That there even existed mass movements—led by figures like Coretta Scott King and Johnnie Tillmon—to defend and expand the right to those benefits was an outrage.

The most important neoliberal think tank to focus on what to do about these surplus populations within the US was the Manhattan Institute. Originally named the International Center for Economic Policy Studies, the Institute was founded in New York in 1977 by the attorney William J. Casey, who later ran Ronald Reagan's presidential campaign and was appointed his director of the CIA, and Antony Fisher, a disciple of Hayek and the wealthy founder of the most important neoliberal think tank in Britain, the Institute of Economic Affairs.[16] The Manhattan Institute proposed to address the challenges of the US's surplus populations through two areas of policy: welfare "reform" and "broken windows" policing.

"A very different set of values"

It "would appear that large numbers of young Black males stopped engaging in the fundamental process of seeking and holding jobs—at least, visible jobs in the above-ground economy," wrote Charles Murray in *Losing Ground*, a 1984 book funded and promoted by the Manhattan Institute. Although he is best known for coauthoring *The Bell Curve* a decade later, with its racist argument that Black poverty might be explained by genetic racial differences in intelligence, *Losing Ground* is more significant in the emergence of neoliberal welfare "reform" policies.[17] In fact, the proscriptions he presented in *Losing Ground* were, like Huntington's, seeded in the hothouse of US imperialism in Southeast Asia. Murray arrived in Thailand in 1965, shortly after graduating from Harvard, working first for the Peace Corps, and then for the Agency for International Development, which was essentially deployed to prevent communist insurgency in the countryside. In 1969, he joined the American Institutes for Research, a social science firm contracted by the Pentagon to develop counterinsurgency strategies. Later he claimed that his studies of Thai villages taught him that government welfare assistance did not help; what he neglected to mention was that his work in Thailand was effectively in service to a pro-US military government that was hated in the countryside.[18]

Losing Ground began with the proposition that, from 1966 to the late 1970s, young Black men withdrew from participating in the labor market. This "population of disproportionately poor youngsters behaved conspicuously differently from the way poor people in previous generations had behaved." The change in their market behavior was "perhaps the most curious of the phenomena" of the late 1960s and "certainly one of the most significant." Murray took what was in fact an effect of the neoliberal transformation of the US labor market and reinterpreted it as a cultural shift among the Black long-term unemployed: they were refusing to follow market signals by reducing the price of their labor to a more competitive level. This new set of cultural values could, he suggested, be traced back to the movements of the 1960s and their attempts to go beyond a narrow focus on racial discrimination to seek redistribution of wealth through the welfare state. What had resulted, he claimed, was an "underclass" in which "the principles of personal responsibility, penalties for bad behavior, and rewards for good behavior" were not applicable. This underclass was "living by a very different set of values from those of mainstream society." The "increase in single-female black families from 1968 onwards" was one measure of this underclass culture, he argued, picking up Daniel Patrick Moynihan's earlier argument about Black families. Murray's fear was that "the problems we now associate with the black inner city will metastasize into the much larger white population, with disastrous results for American society." Thus the distinction between those who followed market signals and those who did not was in his reinterpretation a matter of cultural disposition, which itself was understood in racial terms. Murray's conception of race at this point was cultural rather than biological. But because he interpreted Black behavior as dysfunctional for cultural reasons, it was, from a certain angle, all the more dangerous: since cultural values, unlike biologies, could be adopted by others, there was the possibility of Black disorder spreading to poor whites. Murray's recommendation was "to end welfare altogether." By abolishing welfare payments, there would no longer be a way for members of the underclass to avoid market pressures on wage levels. Market discipline could be reimposed. Even if it would take a long time to dismantle the culture of the underclass, its behavior could be altered immediately by a contraction of the welfare system.[19]

Murray's proposal to abolish welfare was too much even for the Reagan administration. Instead, the pivotal moment in this overhaul of welfare policy came in 1996 with the Personal Responsibility and Work Opportunity Act, signed into law by President Clinton. The act, largely drawing on Murray's and Moynihan's framing of the issue, ended the New Deal–era federal cash assistance program, Aid to Families with Dependent Children, and replaced it with a new state-administered system that had tighter eligibility restrictions and time limits. Immigrants, teenage mothers, and convicted felons were excluded from receiving assistance. The act's advocates courted public support by emphasizing the existing system's burden on taxpayers. But cost reduction was not the purpose of the reforms. The aim was rather to use the idea of "personal responsibility" to ensure the poor followed labor market dictates and took any job at any wage. Inappropriate cultural attitudes—a lack of ambition, entrepreneurial spirit, family stability, orderliness, or thriftiness—became the reflex explanations for Black and Latina poverty.[20] Meanwhile, the equalizing effects that free markets were meant to deliver never came. Measuring the disparity in the wealth of white and Black people in the US does not adequately capture the extent of racial inequality. Yet even on this measure, neoliberal markets have worsened racial inequalities. Researchers at the National Bureau of Economic Research found that, during the 1960s and 1970s, racial wealth disparities improved as a result of "Black activism and civil rights legislation, expansions of the social safety net, and improved labor standards." But with neoliberal policies from the 1980s to today, there has been "a widening of the racial gap." The ratio of white to Black wealth is now six to one, roughly the same level that it was in 1950.[21]

"We are today fighting a war within our own boundaries"

At the end of the summer of 1967, James Q. Wilson—a faculty member of Harvard University's Department of Government and chair of President Johnson's Task Force on Crime—announced, in effect, the death of the liberal argument that spending government money to tackle poverty would reduce racial conflict. The focus on the "underlying causes" of unrest had reached its limits, he stated. The problem was that "a modern economy, however affluent, has great difficulty in doing much for anybody who finds life on the street corner more attractive than life in the factory. This is true of a substantial fraction of Negro men who now operate most of the big-city hustles—pimping, petty gambling, pushing dope, defrauding the tourists (and each other)." The government, he wrote, "is going to have to make it much clearer than it has so far that it is capable of maintaining order in the cities." The best way to do this, he suggested, would be for military units to patrol the cities in the summers.[22] Over the previous two years, Black city-dwellers had organized hundreds of uprisings. The property damage amounted to almost a billion dollars in today's money, while 45,000 people were arrested.[23] In Newark and Detroit, white troops, who were sent in tanks to re-occupy Black neighborhoods, launched a reign of terror, killing dozens of Black residents in their own homes.[24] Politically, the uprisings discredited President Johnson's civil rights and anti-poverty initiatives, which were meant to have put an end to racial turmoil.

Wilson represented a growing sense in the Johnson administration that establishing order on Black streets was an under-acknowledged prerequisite for the broader goal of tackling poverty. His description of Black people choosing the informal economy of the streets over the formal economy of the factory resonated with Moynihan's concerns but also implied there was a cultural limit to the project of integrating Black men into the New Deal labor market. Oscar Lewis's 1965 book *La Vida*, about Puerto Ricans in New York City, added to the sense that poverty was really, as he put it, a "subculture . . . a way of life which is passed down from generation to generation along family lines."[25] This implied that the poor would benefit less from shifting the social distribution of wealth and more from policies to transform their cultural behaviors and values. The growing number of New Deal liberals who embraced this cultural explanation for poverty came to be known as neoconservatives, but neoconservatism and neoliberalism have always blurred into each other.

At the FBI, J. Edgar Hoover was describing a rise in violent crime in the US in the late 1960s as "the most serious domestic problem confronting the United States," and argued it had "been intensified by the recent growth of black-extremist organizations . . . whose manifesto is Frantz Fanon's 'The Wretched of the Earth'; and whose preachers of the gospel of hate include Stokely Carmichael [and] H. Rap Brown."[26] Johnson shared with Hoover the belief that Black radicals such as Carmichael (Kwame Ture) and Rap Brown (Jamil Al-Amin) had somehow instigated the urban uprisings. The Kerner Commission, established by President Johnson to investigate the 1967 revolts, disagreed and proposed stepping up efforts to tackle poor housing, jobs, and education. But its recommendations were ignored. President Johnson instead began to talk about a "war on crime." "We are today fighting a war within our own boundaries," he said. "This nation can mount a major military effort on the other side of the globe. Yet it tolerates criminal activity, right here at home, that costs taxpayers far more than the Vietnam conflict."[27] The result of these concerns was the Safe Streets Act of 1968, which Wilson helped draft. It created a new agency called the Law Enforcement Assistance Administration that distributed billions of dollars to increase the personnel of police departments, professionalize them, and upgrade their weaponry.

All of these trends were replicating domestically what Huntington was arguing with regard to the Third World—that economic development did not necessarily produce political order and authority. Rather than seeing poverty as the cause of crime and disorder, New Deal liberals increasingly reversed the equation and saw crime and disorder as the cause of poverty, because it discouraged investment. A neoliberal account of crime and poverty was beginning to take shape, in which impoverished neighborhoods had to compete for investment within the US as much as Third World countries had to compete for investment abroad. In both cases, the need to be competitive implied a mandate for an authoritarian transformation of cultures to mold them to the needs of the market. As Walt Whitman Rostow wrote to President Johnson in 1967, while serving as his national security adviser, there are "parallels between your formulation of domestic policy and those you have applied to foreign policy . . . At home your appeal is for law and order as the framework for economic and social progress. Abroad we fight in Vietnam to make aggression unprofitable while helping the people of Vietnam[—]and all of Free Asia—build a future of economic and social progress."[28]

The seeds of anxiety about Black crime, radicalism, and culture that had grown amid the New Deal liberalism of the Johnson administration came to fruition under Nixon. Moynihan was appointed by President Nixon to head his newly created Urban Council, which was supposed to do for domestic policy what the National Security Council did for foreign policy.[29] By now, Moynihan was suggesting that government initiatives to help integrate Black men into the capitalist economy had failed. "During the past year intense efforts have been made by the administration to develop programs that will be of help to the blacks. I dare say, as much or more time and attention goes into this effort in this administration than any in history. But little has come of it," Moynihan wrote in a January 1970 memo for the White House. The problem was that, rather than take up the new opportunities, Blacks had adopted a culture of militancy. "It would be difficult to overestimate the degree to which young well-educated blacks detest white America," he wrote. So far as social assistance was concerned, an attitude of "benign neglect" of racial issues was warranted, claimed Moynihan; only law enforcement could remedy the problems of the Black poor.[30] On Moynihan's recommendation, his Harvard colleague Wilson was appointed in 1969 to Nixon's Model Cities Task Force with responsibility for formulating urban policy. The following year, the Nixon administration embraced Wilson's proposals for police foot patrols as a more effective way of maintaining order, rather than after-the-act investigations of criminal violations—the beginning of what would become broken windows policing.[31] Then the creation of the Drug Enforcement Administration in 1973 heralded the beginning of what Nixon called "an all-out global war on the drug menace."[32] Until this moment, rates of incarceration in the United States had been declining. But now they began to increase. Nixon commenced a plan to expand federal prison capacity, which reverberated with states initiating their own expansions. The new punitive mood in US urban policing and the growth in rates of incarceration were stewarded by law enforcement leaders who often had backgrounds working for the US programs that supported authoritarian regimes abroad, running police training or advising on repression techniques.[33] This was Césaire's "boomerang" once again, bringing to the streets of US cities a fascism first deployed in neocolonial settings. Prison expansion went hand in hand with a transformation in the racial composition of the prison population, as the proportion of Blacks and Latinos shot up from the early 1970s.[34]

A WAR ON THE URBAN DISPOSSESSED

In 1982, the *Atlantic* magazine published the definitive statement of broken windows policing, written by James Q. Wilson and George L. Kelling, a fellow at the Manhattan Institute. They began by making a distinction between two separate problems: the issue of crime, and the fear of those who were not necessarily criminals but "disreputable or obstreperous or unpredictable people: panhandlers, drunks, addicts, rowdy teenagers, prostitutes, loiterers, the mentally disturbed."[35] What united these various categories of persons was that they lived outside of waged work; their unpredictability consisted in their not being disciplined by wage competition. Broken windows policing or, more accurately, what Wilson called "broken windows government" was directed at those people whom neoliberalism had rendered surplus.[36] It was not primarily aimed at investigating and prosecuting crimes they might commit, but at responding to the more nebulous fears and anxieties surplus populations generated. It proposed that the criminal justice system ensure that a price of some kind be paid for even the smallest gains acquired in the informal economies of the cities. To break a window "costs nothing" yet is "fun," wrote Kelling and Wilson. It was getting something for free. Where windows could be broken without any cost, they argued, a culture sprang up that encouraged more valuable things to be taken. To prevent this escalation, there needed to be a system to make the disorderly follow "informal but widely understood rules," so that "private possessions are cared for" and "mischievous behavior is costly."

In this way, Kelling and Wilson, in effect, interpreted street disorder and crime through the neoliberal lens of a slippery slope of escalating resource demands that needed to be disciplined through a market-like mechanism. Police officers had to patrol the streets where the surplus populations gathered and be given the discretion necessary to impose costs on their disorderly behavior.[37] To prosecute minor infractions meant expanding city budgets to cope with more and more prosecutions but, since this was a market-order-upholding tax burden rather than one aimed at redistributing wealth, that was not a problem for neoliberals. Thus broken windows government was a solution to the distinctly neoliberal problem of what to do about groups of people who were outside the formal order of market signals. It was a means of interpreting the behaviors of these groups in neoliberal terms, managing the anxieties they threw up, and shifting police work to impose a form of market discipline on them, not in monetary terms but in a newly constituted quasi-economy of urban pleasure and pain. Policing the cities of the US, like policing the Third World, meant using authoritarian force to ensure that cultures antagonistic to market discipline did not hamper competition for outside investment. In the neoliberal city, the answer to poverty was not to be found in government action to create jobs but in policing the poor so that they did not endanger capital investment.[38]

When it was founded in 1977, the Manhattan Institute's welfare and policing ideas were on the fringes of urban policymaking. By the end of the 1990s, they represented the orthodox view of how to run a neoliberal city.[39] Rudy Giuliani's term as mayor of New York City in the 1990s was presented as a model—he had become close to the Manhattan Institute prior to his election, and on taking office implemented its policy program. The institute publicized broken windows policing throughout the 1980s and 1990s as the solution to the impoverishment of cities (which neoliberalism had in fact fostered).[40] The punitive infrastructure that had first taken shape under Presidents Johnson and Nixon was, in the last two decades of the twentieth century, mobilized in newly intensified ways. The number of people incarcerated in state and federal prisons jumped from 196,000 persons in 1970 to more than 1.4 million persons in 2010, not even counting those in jails.[41] By the end of the twentieth century, the Manhattan Institute was sending figures like Charles Murray around the world to promote welfare reform and broken windows policing.[42] A new kind of neoliberal government emerged: its purpose was to assemble the kinds of unorganized, indebted, and deportable workers necessary for global capital, and to violently contain the growing numbers of people who were surplus to neoliberal labor markets.

It would be wrong to suggest that the intellectuals of the Manhattan Institute directly and exclusively shaped policy decisions in the US or elsewhere, independently of any other factors. What the Institute provided above all was a space where governing elites, corporate interests, and neoliberal intellectuals could come together to grapple with the crisis of an older set of structures, develop a shared narrative of the neoliberal transformation they sought, plot the paths through which their new order might be established in particular local settings, win over constituencies to their cause, and work through the anxieties and tensions thrown up by the limitations of their new vision. Broken windows policing was certainly not a response to rising crime rates—it was, after all, not primarily aimed at crime but at anxieties of disorder. Nor was it simply a way of filling a policy void once the anti-poverty programs of the 1960s were discredited as ways to deal with the poor. Rather, in its definition of the problem and its conception of the solution, broken windows policing expressed a thoroughly neoliberal logic.

In the US, broken windows policing helped generate spiraling rates of racially disproportionate mass incarceration. Al-Amin's dire warnings about the fate of the Black surplus populations turned out to be essentially accurate: from the 1970s, the US removed millions of Black people from their communities and incarcerated them. The geographer Ruth Wilson Gilmore noted in her book *Golden Gulag* that the neoliberal transformation of US capitalism generated disproportionately Black "surplus populations" of "workers at the extreme edges, or completely outside, of restructured labor markets," who were no longer needed as a subordinate industrial workforce and represented a crisis to be contained, not with the social safety net of earlier decades but with a criminal dragnet.[43] From 1926 to 1976, the Black-to-white prison admission ratio was remarkably consistent at three to one;

thereafter it shifted upward until, by 1997, it was six to one.[44] As the historian Barbara Ransby has pointed out, the police's targeting of poor and working-class Black people reflected their being "deemed expendable and disposable" in a "society that had no place for them in a downsized, neoliberal labor market." Broken windows policing implied a brutal targeting of those working in the informal economy. Thus Eric Garner was killed by police officers in Staten Island, New York, in 2014 after intervening to break up a fight, but he was known to them as a cigarette street vendor. And Alton Sterling was killed by the police in Baton Rouge, Louisiana, in 2016 while he was selling CDs.[45]

The racist effects of broken windows policing did not derive from Wilson and Kelling adopting racist formulations in their theory, not even through coded language. Nor could it be explained in terms of conservatives introducing law-and-order policies as a way of playing to racial attitudes among Southern or working-class white voters—in fact, liberal politicians as much as conservatives implemented broken windows policing and mass incarceration. Rather, the racist outcomes were inevitable in any program in the US aimed at disciplining neoliberalism's surplus populations, because Blacks and Latinos were over-represented among them and because Black men and women had come to ideologically signify the problem of surplus populations in the neoliberal era. Once a racial idea of culture had become the explanation for the failure of groups to adopt neoliberal norms, violent attempts to repress, contain, and reform that culture naturally followed—and a new vocabulary of racist labels emerged to refer to the imagined outcomes of that culture: "welfare queens," "super-predators," and so on.

12

Why Neoliberals Build Borders

The opening salvo of the neoliberal campaign in Britain was fired in 1958. Three years earlier, the first neoliberal think tank in the world, the Institute of Economic Affairs (IEA), had been founded in London by Antony Fisher. Fisher had acquired his wealth introducing the factory farming of chickens to Britain. He was also a devotee of Hayek, having been introduced to *The Road to Serfdom* via *Reader's Digest* in 1945. Two years later, the two met and Fisher mentioned his plan to go into politics to advocate for Hayek's ideas. Hayek advised him instead to establish a policy research organization that would publicize neoliberal ideas among intellectuals and through the media, laying the groundwork for politicians to follow.[1] In 1958, Fisher and his colleagues began a campaign to persuade Harold Macmillan's Conservative government to end increases in social spending. But senior ministers were too pragmatic to be swayed in that direction. The incident did, though, prompt some resignations from ministers sympathetic to the IEA's position, including Enoch Powell, the financial secretary.

Powell grew close to the neoliberal activists at the IEA and made a series of speeches criticizing public ownership, economic planning, and social security, and espousing floating exchange rates and legal restrictions on trade unions—what he called the "doctrine of the market."[2] At the time, these were outlandish positions to take, even in the Conservative Party. Trade unions were generally respected as pillars of social stability in the postwar British political system; Powell, on the contrary, described them as pursuing "fascism" and "mob rule."[3] He attended meetings of the Mont Pelerin Society and worked closely with Diana

Spearman, a key neoliberal organizer in London who introduced him to the Hayekian concept of the "spontaneous order." They reveled in the discovery that there was an intellectual alternative to the belief, held widely across the political class, in a steadily expanding welfare state.[4] Sounding distinctly Hayekian, Powell spoke of the market system as "the largest and most wonderful working computer the world has ever known." Its inputs are "millions of facts" from around the world, he said. "The answers tumble out of it in an unending stream," telling "every buyer and seller, manufacturer and consumer" what activities can be "competitively" carried out. To seek to override "this machine and the implications [it] signalled," as the Labour Party proposed, was "at heart totalitarian."[5] With speeches such as this, Powell distinguished himself as the most articulate and vocal exponent of the neoliberal agenda in British politics. The 1959 Mont Pelerin Society meeting in Oxford noted that his speeches were one of the signs that neoliberal ideas were gaining support in the UK.[6] By 1965, the *Spectator* was describing Powell as the IEA's "political prophet."[7] Five years later, Milton Friedman wrote that Powell had "a clearer conception of the relation between economic and personal freedom, than any other major political figure I have ever met."[8] He was, a decade before the election of Margaret Thatcher, Britain's first neoliberal politician.

Powell had been a passionate imperialist and, for two and a half years from 1943 to 1946, a military officer in colonial India, including a stint as assistant director of military intelligence. It was a terrible blow to hear the news of the subcontinent's independence. "I walked the streets all that night," he later told an interviewer. "The world as I had known it was coming apart. Occasionally, I sat down in a doorway, my head in my hands."[9] But a decade later, he understood that Britain could no longer trade, literally and metaphorically, on its empire.[10] Gamal Abdel Nasser's nationalization of the Suez Canal in 1956, in particular, and the failed British, French, and Israeli bid to recapture it by military force had brought home the weakness of Britain's international position. Powell knew that, from the late nineteenth century, the empire had been the economic and ideological basis for whatever social peace had been achieved between workers and capitalists in England. The question that preoccupied him through the 1950s and early 1960s was what kind of cultural and political entity Britain might now be, without its imperial advantages. The answer he landed on would have profound implications for the reconfiguration of structural racism and the emergence of neoliberalism in Britain.

Powell suggested that empire had been a dream from which England was now awakening.[11] The imperial definition of Britain of the late nineteenth and early twentieth centuries was a seductive but harmful illusion. Empire was an indulgence that protected the British people from having to live within their means. Instead of "the imperial delusion that we can consume what we have not produced," Britain now had to stand on its own "ingenuity, effort, and initiative," unaided by the subsidies and privileges that empire made possible.[12] The predominant elite view at the time was that the Commonwealth, the voluntary international association of Britain's former colonies, would preserve the unequal trade relationships of the imperial economy, enabling profits to continue to flow to the UK. Powell thought otherwise. In a series of speeches and articles in the mid-1960s, he argued that the multilateralism of the Commonwealth would lead to the expectation that Britain distribute "international charity" to the formerly colonized of Africa, Asia, and the Caribbean.[13] The "monstrous progeny of a closed Imperial trading area" had to be ended, not rebranded "under the name of Commonwealth preference."[14] Powell was laying out a neoliberal case for the virtues of free trade and for Britain succeeding through its own enterprise.

Waking from the imperial dream, said Powell, meant the real England, on the strength of its values of individual enterprise and self-discipline, could now rise.[15] Making "a clean break with the imperial past" was necessary to reactivate this deeper set of cultural dispositions. The market was for Powell not an abstract, universally valid set of rules but an organic expression of English values. This version of Englishness would be the replacement for empire and the basis for "a new patriotism" that would "be a salve to the wound of Suez."[16] It was also an answer to the question of how neoliberal politicians could embed an acceptance of market discipline in a British culture still dominated by "collectivism." To deflate the overblown welfare state and curb the indulgences of the trade unions required, in an age of mass democratic politics, finding a way to persuade a substantial section of the English working classes to go against the grain of their history and their collective interests. Powell's solution was to present values of "ingenuity, effort, and initiative"—words that really meant consent to market forces—as the central elements of an imagined unchanging Englishness. That way, trade unionism and the welfare state were cast as un-English, and those who disagreed with neoliberalism were not simply holders of different opinions on matters of policy but enemies of the nation. Powell's instinct was that, by such means, neoliberals could raise enough working-class support to make their project politically viable. As Powell's friend and admirer, the journalist Peregrine Worsthorne wrote, if a Conservative government was going to "re-activate the class war" by attempting to implement neoliberal policies, it would need to mobilize "the patriotic theme" to secure a "hold over working class votes."[17]

The next step in Powell's reasoning took him onto the terrain of racism. His strategy for the neoliberal transformation of Britain ran up against a cultural barrier: the increasing number of Asian, African, and Caribbean immigrant workers in England who, he thought, could never be won over to his "new patriotism" because they and their descendants would never have an affiliation to ideas of Englishness. Powell was echoing the neoliberal theorizing of the border that thinkers like Mises and Hayek developed: the border was a tool to protect the West's market order from other more "communal" cultures. In Powell's inflection of this argument, a small number of Third World immigrants could be assimilated, but that possibility ended when the visible appearance of whole neighborhoods began to change. "Color is the uniform," he said, that signals "a separate and strange population."[18] Without assimilation, the immigrants constituted an "alien wedge," their "communal values" fracturing the cultural homogeneity of England's political order and endangering Powell's neoliberal project.[19] Appeals to Englishness could potentially bring white workers into a coalition of support for neoliberalism but not Third World workers; that was the real source of the threat the immigrants represented. And even though Third World immigrants made up a small proportion of the working class, there was nevertheless a danger that their "communal values" could spread, influencing a broader political radicalization among whites. "All revolutions are made by minorities, and usually by small minorities," warned Powell.[20] What made matters worse was that their very presence in England was an outcome of the empire that Powell now thought it essential to forget. By the end of the 1960s, he was drawing parallels between the movement of Asian, African, and Caribbean peoples to Britain and the movement of African Americans from the Deep South to the Northern cities. The urban violence in the US, which he saw as the inevitable consequence of the great migration, was set to appear in England in twenty or thirty years, he predicted.[21]

This was a new crisis of the border. Britain introduced its first immigration legislation in 1905, aimed at blocking the migration of Jews from eastern Europe, and then the Aliens Restriction (Amendment) Act of 1919 was a response to fears of Chinese migration. But these were limited affairs. The main feature of immigration policy in the century prior to the 1960s was the absence of controls on British Empire and Commonwealth subjects. The empire had meant a constant and large-scale movement of people from England to its colonies; Powell himself had made that journey. In the eight decades from the middle of the nineteenth century through to the first quarter of the twentieth, just under 17 million emigrated from the British Isles, about 41 percent of the 1900 population. The largest part of this movement was emigration to the settler colonies of North America and Australia.[22] This emigration acted as a safety valve for British capitalism, releasing surplus populations who could not be absorbed as waged workers; in the territories where they settled, it went hand in hand with the expulsion or elimination of Indigenous peoples. The free movement policy also enabled an industrial reserve army of workers to enter and leave Britain, absorbed into the margins of the labor market during economic upturns and ejected from work in subsequent downturns. Irish workers in England were key to this process in the nineteenth century, representing between one-fifth and one-third of the working populations of London and Manchester in the 1840s.[23] A century later, workers from the Caribbean and South Asia were recruited to this role in large numbers. In legal terms, these were not foreign nationals migrating from one sovereign nation to another but imperial subjects moving from one part of the British Empire to another. The empire had been a multi-racial project that placed African, Asian, and Caribbean peoples under a single sovereignty with the English, even as they were ordered into a racist hierarchy and ruled from London. For Powell, that flow of people between England and empire now threatened to destroy Englishness itself. The Third World presence in England, which had once signaled traffic within an imperial hierarchy, could, at the end of the empire, only symbolize the loss of prestige and power. Yet, Powell noted, these questions of race and immigration were not discussed in mainstream politics. Instead, a silent consensus held that, apparently for the sake of Commonwealth goodwill, there should continue to be relatively free movement between the former colonies and Britain.

Diversity and deportation

Gradually, cracks in that consensus started to appear through the 1960s, as Parliament introduced a series of laws to limit who could enter from the former colonies. The first of these, the Commonwealth Immigrants Act of 1962, did not explicitly distinguish between the white settler countries of the Commonwealth—such as Canada and Australia—and its Third World members—such as India and Ghana. But for the first time it prevented Commonwealth immigrants from entering the UK unless they had a government employment voucher, and these were granted primarily to whites. In a private memo for cabinet colleagues, the home secretary Rab Butler wrote that the "great merit" of the act was that, while it did "not legislate openly on grounds of colour . . . its restrictive effect is intended to, and would in fact, operate on coloured people almost exclusively."[24] Claudia Jones, then exiled to Britain, wrote that the act "discriminates heavily against coloured Commonwealth citizens" and, in doing so, "has established a second-class citizenship status for West Indians and other Afro Asian peoples in Britain."[25]

This was Powell's political opportunity to activate his "new patriotism." Moreover, he understood that he could present opposition to Third World immigration without making an explicit claim to racial superiority, which by the 1960s was easily discredited by association with Nazism. Instead, he could argue that different cultures cannot stably coexist in a single political order and therefore that English culture needed to be protected from unduly mixing with others. By placing multiple cultures under a single sovereignty, the empire had depended on claiming the opposite. But the end of that kind of direct imperialism made possible a new form of racist ideology. Whereas imperial racism was linked to the expansion of England's sovereignty to other parts of the world, the new racism was turned inward and defensive, directed toward the cultural threat of Third World peoples in England, who were presented as engaging in colonialism in reverse. To make this argument work required a highly static idea of culture as a force that determined one's whole being and did not alter its characteristics through contact with others—a "neo-racism" in which culture was a kind of nature.[26]

On April 20, 1968, Powell addressed a small meeting of Conservative Party activists in a Birmingham hotel and called for the "re-emigration" of the million or so Asian, African, and Caribbean people then living in the United Kingdom. "In this country in fifteen or twenty years' time, the Black man will have the whip hand over the white man," he quoted a "quite ordinary working man employed in one of our nationalised industries" as saying. "As I look ahead, I am filled with foreboding," he added. "Like the Roman, I seem to see 'the River Tiber foaming with much blood.'"[27] His words, infamously dubbed the "rivers of blood" speech, shattered the postwar consensus on race relations. He was the first mainstream politician in Europe to claim that an out-of-touch, weak-willed liberal establishment had wrought upon the (white) working class the calamities of immigration and multiculturalism, and that only decisive, urgent action could save the nation from this crisis before it was too late. His instinct that this "new patriotism" could connect with a section of white, working-class opinion proved correct. Thousands of London dockworkers and meat porters marched on Parliament to demand the implementation of his racist expulsion policy. Racist attacks on the streets surged in number and remained a regular feature of British life, at least until the 1990s.

The political and cultural establishment reacted with revulsion at Powell's open appeal to racist prejudice. He was sacked from his post as shadow defence secretary and never again held ministerial office in the Conservative Party. But the way that England's liberal intellectuals and politicians responded to Powell was not straightforward rejection, since there were a series of subterranean linkages between their positions and Powell's. First, the static idea of culture that was central to Powell's argument overlapped with the liberal antiracist concept of culture that Franz Boas and his colleagues had promoted in the 1940s. To counter Nazism, they had argued that social relationships were determined by culture, not race as a physical fact. For them, cultures could not be ranked according to any external hierarchy but had to be seen as organic wholes, meaningful only on their own terms. Powell could agree with both of these claims and simply add that, by the same token, there could be no justification for weakening the coherence of a culture by introducing alien elements.

Second, because liberals thought of racism as a doctrine of superiority, they were unable to counter the innovative core of Powell's argument: that borders were necessary to protect the shared cultural values he held to be necessary for a market order. Generally, liberals accepted this premise but then disagreed with some of the policy implications Powell drew from it. They argued that, with suitable policies, Third World immigrant cultures could be successfully integrated. The most prominent liberal politician of the era, Labour's Roy Jenkins, argued that "cultural diversity, in an atmosphere of mutual tolerance" was the best way to achieve this.[28] But he added: "There is a clear limit to the amount of immigration this country can absorb and it is in the interests of minorities themselves to maintain a strict control."[29] Acceptance of diversity, in other words, was conditional on forcefully limiting Third World immigration. With this thinking, the meaning of "integration" as an objective of British race relations shifted subtly but fatefully from a program of equal civil, political, and economic rights to a project of managing cultural diversity and fostering shared values. Liberals, in effect, transformed the fight against racism into a fight for the official recognition of "minority" cultures. The politics of "diversity" in the UK was born in this moment—umbilically tied to an acceptance of Powell's core contention that the basic danger was people of other cultures overwhelming the tolerance of liberal England.

As Fanon had warned, the celebration of Third World cultures could be perfectly compatible with structural racism.

In addition, there were the neoliberals who emphasized what they called the "economic contribution" of immigrant workers. Their argument was that immigrants did not threaten market values but, on the contrary, were more likely to accept the imperatives of "market signals" by taking on low-wage, precarious work that British workers rejected. These neoliberals also held that borders had to be increasingly strengthened to ensure that migrant workforces were so vulnerable that they did indeed act "competitively"—that is, by accepting low wages and limited social protections. All these liberal and neoliberal responses to Powell accepted his underlying concerns about the relationships between borders, cultures, and markets.

Third, because liberals located the sin of racism in individual attitudes, they had no qualms about carrying out a dramatic expansion of the infrastructure of racist immigration control, as Powell advocated, so long as it was done by decent, technocratic politicians who did not whip up racist sentiments. Thus, the surface disavowal of Powell went hand in hand with an acceptance of much of his immigration control agenda. Before Powell's speech, the Labour government had already introduced the 1968 Commonwealth Immigrants Act. It prevented the entry of around 200,000 British subjects of Asian origin who had been expelled from Kenya after independence; their British passports no longer entitled them to pass through British ports. White settlers leaving Kenya were allowed in. Edward Heath, the leader of the Conservative Party, then in opposition, had initially disowned Powell but a year later warned of the "fear of the people of this country that those ultimately responsible for their welfare—the elected government of Westminster—has insufficient control of the situation." He added: "For the sake of the nation I call on the government to act without further delay" and "restrict and control the entry of Commonwealth immigrants."[30] The surprise victory of the Conservative Party in the 1970 election was generally credited to Powell's popularity. The Heath government went on to pass the 1971 Immigration Act, which divided the British Commonwealth population into two categories: "patrials"—those born in the UK, or whose parents or grandparents had been—and "nonpatrials"—those without this connection. Since patrials were usually descendants of British colonizers, they were overwhelmingly white; nonpatrials, descended from the colonized, were not. The act removed the right of nonpatrials to settle in the UK; those already legally in the country—such as my father, who had come a few years earlier—were allowed to stay but offered cash if they agreed to "voluntary repatriation." Everyone understood that the concept of "patrials" was simply a legal device to avoid explicit reference to the act's actual purpose: racial segregation of the Commonwealth bloc of Britain and its former colonies. And turning the border into a racial battleground meant the inevitable spread of those battles to the rest of British society.

Thus, in spite of significant differences in the analysis of immigration across liberal and neoliberal politics, since Powell's intervention the consistent, cross-party aim of immigration policy has been the use of borders to constitute populations of workers in Britain who are predisposed to market discipline. To this end, a constant flurry of immigration legislation has continuously increased and expanded the powers and resources available to police Britain's borders through searching, surveilling, arresting, imprisoning, and deporting; and the UK has become a key player in building the global infrastructure of militarized migration control. The 1971 act has never been repealed. Since its passing, every leader of the major English parties has sought to reassure the public of their support for strong controls on (implicitly nonwhite) immigration.

Britain's new immigration restrictions were not initially mirrored elsewhere in Europe. West Germany began to reduce its "guest worker" migration a decade later; it did so for straightforward industrial-reserve-army reasons: with the recession of the 1970s,

West German industry needed fewer workers. That was the standard pattern of industrial capitalism: upsurges of anti-immigrant sentiment and vigilantism in moments of economic downturn. A different dynamic prompted the shift in Britain in the 1960s. Working at the border, neoliberalism constructed new racial boundaries from the wreckage of the British Empire's hierarchies. Third World peoples were no longer seen as docile, interchangeable units, able to straightforwardly serve as an industrial reserve army. The terminology changed: they were not "immigrant workers," a category that referred to their location as a reserve component of the working class; they were "Indians," "Afro-Caribbeans," and "Muslims," categories that referred to a conception of cultural values in terms of ancestry. The emerging neoliberal project saw the Third World's "communal values" as a problem to be carefully managed. Powell gave this anxiety its most prominent political expression. In the 1960s, he could do no more than clear the ground for the neoliberal transformation that fully flowered with the election of Margaret Thatcher in 1979. But his successful attacks on an earlier consensus were essential to that transformation. His lasting achievement was turning the border into a new object of political contestation and an arena of racial meanings. The vote in favor of Brexit in 2016 was one of its long-term consequences.

"Cultures have color"

The new politics of racial and cultural identity at the border that Powell developed in the 1960s was a harbinger of what recurred across the West from the 1970s to the 1990s. In country after country, the same pattern repeated: conservative political activists or parties, typically with strong ties to neoliberal think tanks or intellectual circles, launched attacks on an existing immigration policy consensus that had been crafted to facilitate the use of immigrant workforces as reserve armies. They accused the liberal elite of allowing the nation to be overwhelmed by culturally distinct immigrants. Then, liberals and other neoliberals responded in the same ways they had in Britain, establishing the conditions for a permanent culture war at the border. The end result was the dramatic expansion of border enforcement infrastructures, enabling new forms of racial differentiation and super-exploitation of workers.

The path that each country took varied. In the United States, in the century prior to the 1960s, immigration was organized in a quite different way from the British Empire's free movement policy. The United States had two aims in its policy during this period: to maintain an adequate supply of labor for westward colonial expansion and industrial development, and to control the racial makeup of participants in the US's settler-colonial enterprise. The Naturalization Act of 1790, which remained in force through most of the nineteenth century, allowed for any "free white person" to become a US citizen through settlement.[31] As California governor Leland Stanford put it in his 1862 inauguration speech: "While the settlement of our State is of the first importance, the character of those who shall become settlers is worthy of scarcely less consideration." That year California passed an Anti-Coolie Act to restrict Chinese immigration, the beginning of a series of state and later federal measures to counter migration from Asia.[32] The Johnson-Reed Immigration Act of 1924 was the first comprehensive immigration control policy; it established a national quotas system to favor the settlement of western Europeans in a US that now understood itself as a bounded territory with surveilled borders.[33] Meanwhile the policy at the Mexico border operated in terms of a reserve industrial army calculus. In the 1900s and 1910s, the US allowed Mexicans to freely enter as their labor power was needed in mining, railroad construction, and agriculture. But in the early 1930s, 400,000 persons of Mexican descent were repatriated in response to the Great Depression's contraction of labor demand; according to estimates, half of those repatriated were US citizens.³⁴ From 1942 to 1964, the demand for highly exploitable labor in agriculture was met through the Bracero Program, which facilitated temporary "guest workers" from Mexico while segregating them from the rest of the US working class.³⁵ In what were referred to as "medical exams," government officials stripped aspiring braceros naked in public, checked them for venereal diseases, and "disinfected" them with DDT.³⁶

In the 1960s, as Britain was ending its free movement policy and racially segregating the Commonwealth with immigration controls, the US racially desegregated its immigration policy through the 1965 Hart-Celler Act. The act introduced a quota system to allow more professionals to migrate from the Third World. And it enabled close relatives of US citizens and permanent residents to join their families, leading to a sharp rise in Asian immigration in particular. Prior to the act, there were five times more immigrants arriving from Europe than Asia; by 1971, more Asians were migrating than Europeans. But the act also heavily curtailed migration from Mexico. In the early 1960s, the US had admitted 200,000 Mexicans a year under the Bracero Program and an additional 35,000 a year for permanent residency. The 1965 act set an annual limit on migration from Mexico of 20,000. By 1968, the number of deportations of Mexicans had increased by 40 percent, to 151,000. In 1976, the US expelled 781,000 Mexicans.³⁷ Now, the militarization of the US-Mexico border began in earnest. Under the Carter administration, the budget for the Border Patrol rose by 24 percent, leading to the deployment of new military sensor technologies, the construction of border walls, and joint patrols with the armed forces; and the Supreme Court approved the Border Patrol's racial profiling policies.³⁸ This paved the way for a further escalation of these trends during the Reagan administration in the 1980s and the full blossoming in the US of the border politics that Powell had developed. The 1986 Immigration Reform and Control Act added tighter controls to the Mexico border and Congress doubled Border Patrol funding. By the 1990s, political discussion on immigration in the US was a theater of anxieties over cultural values. It was no longer possible to "frame US racial issues in strictly Black-white terms," wrote former SNCC activist Elizabeth Martínez in 1998. "Racism evolves" and, in this new landscape, she wrote, "cultures have color." Cultural markers, such as not speaking English, came to symbolize differences in values that, in turn, were regarded as deep and fixed—that is, they were racial differences even if the language of race itself was absent.[39] Echoing Powell, Samuel P. Huntington wrote of the "profound differences" that exist "between Mexican and American values and culture," which are the primary source of Mexican Americans' "lagging educational and economic progress and their slow assimilation into American society." A "de facto split between a predominantly Spanish-speaking America and English-speaking America" is "a major potential threat to the cultural and possibly political integrity of the United States."[40] Similarly, John Vinson of the American Immigration Control Foundation complained in 1998 that "multiculturalism" was replacing "successful Euro-American culture" with "dysfunctional Third World cultures."[41] Books like Allan Bloom's 1987 *The Closing of the American Mind* and *Illiberal Education* by Dinesh D'Souza, of the neoliberal American Enterprise Institute, attacked liberal elites for failing to defend a common set of Western values in the face of a growing Third World immigrant presence in the US.[42] By a strange series of displacements, campaigns to uphold a Western literary canon on university campuses became a space within which to work through the anxiety that the US had lost a vaunted cultural homogeneity, supposedly dating from the founders.

Neoliberals were split between those who, following the Powell template, thought a multicultural America could not provide the stabilizing cultural ballast for a liberal (that is, market-based) order and those who made the "free market" (that is, cheap labor) case for increasing immigration from outside the West.[43] For the pro-immigration side, policies of celebrating and recognizing diversity became ways to manage the issue of cultural difference. Both sides in these debates served "to uphold racial regimes through a social organization of difference," notes activist and writer Harsha Walia. To respond to anti-immigrant arguments with the claim that "our economy needs immigrants," she points out, is also to treat immigrants "as commodities to be traded in capitalist markets and discarded if deemed defective."[44] A commitment to expanding the infrastructures of border enforcement was shared by both sides in the neoliberal immigration debate. And it was striking that advocates on both sides received financial support from brothers Charles and David Koch—the billionaire energy tycoons and major funders of neoliberal think tanks.[45] The belief, widely held on the Left, that neoliberals "are completely for open borders" is mistaken.[46]

In this context, President Clinton's Antiterrorism and Effective Death Penalty Act and Illegal Immigration Reform and Immigrant Responsibility Act, both passed in 1996, radically remade immigration enforcement. Since then, the US has forcibly removed over 5 million people from the country—more than double the number of people it deported in the previous 110 years.[47] The border policing budget in the US increased from $1.2 billion in 1990 to $25.2 billion in 2019, with the Customs and Border Protection agency allowed to apply its racial profiling powers anywhere within a hundred miles of borders and coastlines—an area that covers 200 million people in the US.[48] Moreover, through a series of international border control "partnerships," especially across Latin America, the US has worked in tandem with other governments to "manage" migration transnationally. The resulting global border system includes more than seventy-seven border walls, many billions of dollars' worth of surveillance technology, and tens of thousands of armed agents.[49]

The vast border infrastructure that expanded across the West, especially from the 1980s onward, has served as the most important means by which states have produced racial boundaries between different kinds of laboring populations in the neoliberal era. Western governments have blocked the majority of neoliberalism's surplus populations in the global South from gaining access to the protected core of racial capitalism where welfare and labor rights are stronger. Even as those rights have been reduced in the neoliberal era, they have remained significantly valuable to their beneficiaries. With freedom of movement for capital and constraint of movement for people, multinational corporations have been able to find cheap labor in the global South that Western borders keep in place—a form of super-exploitation, enabled by bordering, that is a neoliberal form of imperialism. Thus the racial boundary between those inside and outside the protected core, which decolonization had challenged, has been restored in a new form through the strengthening of border regimes. The racial segregation produced by the neoliberal border has been as absolute and violent as that produced by South African apartheid or the Jim Crow laws of the US South—illustrated most recently by the Biden administration allowing thousands of Ukrainians to live in the US while in the same year arresting more than a million Black and Brown migrants at the border and removing them.[50] The maintenance of neoliberalism's global racial division of labor has depended upon the mass imprisonment of migrants in detention centers, the regular violent bundling of migrants onto deportation flights and buses, and the vast death tolls along the fortified entry points to the West. It has also meant that the safety valve of emigration that existed for European capitalist development in the nineteenth century, through settler colonialism, has been closed off for the global South.

At the same time, the border enables capitalists access to criminalized, cheap labor within the West by creating distinct zones of "crimmigration," sectors in which criminalized migrants work under the constant threat of removal. The purpose is not, as with the older immigration policies, to remove an industrial reserve army of migrants when the economy enters a depression. Rather, the neoliberal border seeks to continuously maintain the conditions ideal for coercively exploiting a section of the working class, by subjecting it to the full panoply of border enforcement powers—surveillance, searches, arbitrary arrest and imprisonment, and the threat of deportation.[51] Through this system, neoliberal governing agencies working on behalf of capitalists assemble migrant workforces that are segregated from the "free" workforce and subjected to direct control. In the US, these are the quarter of all workers in meatpacking who lack documentation, the quarter of all dishwashers, and of construction workers, 17 percent of cleaners, 12 percent of food preparers, about a third of garment workers, and 1.5 million farm workers—all of whom, having survived the violence of the border to come to the US, live in fear of discovery and deportation by Immigration and Customs Enforcement agents.[52] Walia writes that these workers often

> have their identification confiscated, are held captive in their place of employment, and are traded between employers like goods ... Migrant workers are segregated from citizen-workers in a divergent labor pool and are unable to access labor protections or public services. They typically cannot bring their families and, in the case of domestic workers, perform the gendered labor of caring for others' families while forcibly separated from their own. This combination makes it possible for capitalism to exploit the divisions.[53]

The boundaries between super-exploited workers in the global South, unfree migrant workers, and "free" citizen-workers are essential to the neoliberal form of capitalism. To create and maintain these boundaries, neoliberalism requires a reconfigured racism to program and administer its differentiations.[54] The vilification of migrants as terrorists, criminals, drug dealers, "illegals," and "bogus asylum seekers" is the ideological counterpart to the global racial division of labor that neoliberalism maintains. To cross the border without authorization is to transgress against the racial ordering of the neoliberal system.

13

A Darker Red

Acts of individual racist discrimination and abuse remain common enough. But they are not the primary means through which racial domination is effected. Neoliberalism has given racial capitalism ways to organize itself without the need for the explicit vocabulary or attitudes of white supremacy. Neoliberal racism operates through the hidden hand of property ownership and the iron fist of security agencies. The mute compulsions of market pressures are upheld through the intensified brutality of racially coded bordering, incarceration, policing, and war. The "rigour of the system makes it superfluous to make a daily assertion of superiority," as Fanon put it.[1] We fail to grasp this reconfiguration of a whole structure if we understand racism today as solely a pattern of unconscious biases and micro-aggressions.

Racism has been essential to organizing the complex, dispersed boundaries between different laboring and surplus populations in the neoliberal world system. New racial regimes have emerged to police, shore up, and make sense of the boundaries between the "free" citizen-worker and the unfree migrant worker, between waged workers in the global North and those in the South, and between the exploitable working classes and a superfluous humanity. Only in its own fantasies has neoliberalism produced a homogeneous market order.

The need to manage the masses of surplus populations who are of almost no value to neoliberal markets has meant a dramatic increase in governments' capacity to carry out policing, carceral, border, and military violence, domestically and globally. Organized in the name of "law and order," "securing borders," and "national security," the neoliberal order has developed a transnational security infrastructure, led by the United States but dispersed globally through the nation-state system. Within these arenas of security, complex fears and tensions generated by neoliberalism and its discontents have been projected onto racial "threats." Individuals such as Samuel P. Huntington, Daniel Patrick Moynihan, Charles Murray, Enoch Powell, and James Q. Wilson have not been the originators of new governing ideologies so much as effective articulators of these real anxieties in the structures of power, and definers of the possible means of trying to address them. As part of this process, neoliberalism has come to represent the dispossessed surplus populations through a series of racist figures—"welfare queens," "Muslim extremists," "illegals," "narcos," "super-predators," and so on. These figures of economic dependency, property violations, and threats to Western culture have been produced through a reworking of older repertoires of racial demonization to generate images distinctive to the neoliberal era. What these figures have in common is they are violators of neoliberal market rules, and in each case, the violation appears as a problem of fixed cultural dispositions among racial groups. They have emerged not as a result of clever people in the corridors of power conjuring them up as propaganda tools, but through a more complex and partially unconscious process of cultural displacement—from actual political insurgencies or social antagonisms to the racist fantasies with which they are misrepresented. Thus, behind the images of the Black woman on welfare, the radical Muslim, and the violent immigrant lie fears of actual Black feminist radicalism, of the actual Palestinian national movement, and of the actual politicization of working classes induced by migrant organizing. In this sense, these images have been displaced signifiers of neoliberalism's failure to find universal acceptance. The global policing of Blacks, Muslims, and migrants has thus synchronized with and come to stand in ideologically for the broader problem of policing neoliberalism's surplus populations, within and without the West.

Despite their antiracist rhetoric, neoliberal ruling elites have been committed to violently maintaining a racial ordering of laboring and surplus populations. Bordering regimes, with their huge death tolls in the seas and deserts to the south of Europe and the United States, and their warehousing of millions of refugees in camps conveniently far from the West; projects of broken windows policing and mass incarceration, another form of warehousing of surplus populations; and global wars of counterinsurgency, such as the wars on terror and drugs, causing the deaths of millions—all these are the macro-aggressions that have been inextricable from neoliberalism's market order.[2] It is no coincidence that the think tank networks involved in advocating for neoliberal economic frameworks have typically also been the key mobilizers of projects of racist policing, incarceration, and counterterrorism. Moreover, racism has enabled state violence *in general*: by associating poverty, deviancy, and radicalism with Blackness, for example, the neoliberal order has more easily managed the poverty, deviancy, and radicalism of all surplus populations, including whites.

Neoliberal ideology has been wracked by a tension between its aspiration to establish a universal market system and its well-founded fear that such a system would not be widely accepted. When movements of the global South or peoples of color in the North have opposed market systems, neoliberals have called upon a racial idea of culture to interpret that opposition as no more than the acting out of cultures inherently lacking in traits of individualism and entrepreneurialism—as Hayek's theory of cultural evolution exemplifies. Race has enabled neoliberal ideology to strip opposition movements of their political meanings, remove them from the histories that gave them shape, and see them as no more than the outbursts of lesser peoples. The political problem of opposition to neoliberalism has been reframed as a problem of cultural values, and racism has increasingly taken the form of cultural arguments about aptitudes to thrive in market-based societies. Neoliberal racism has worked ideologically by displacing the political conflicts it generates onto the more comfortable terrain of clashes of culture.[3] The more neoliberalism fails to resolve its own contradictions, the more it is caught in its own web of financial, ecological, and health crises, the more it will deploy racist state violence and call upon racist ideology.

There has been a continuous oscillation in neoliberalism between an optimistic mode of racial incorporation, in which Black and global South cultural values have been deemed assimilable to a market rationality, and a pessimistic mode of racial exclusion, in which securing the market system requires violently suppressing the behaviors that those values produce. The former mode leads to celebrations of diversity; the latter leads to militarized policing, mass incarceration, and border fortification. These two modes have been mutually reinforcing rather than antagonistic. In contexts of intensified insurgency against the neoliberal project, practices of violent exclusion have become dominant; when insurgencies have been defeated, their remnants have been incorporated through diversity politics. In this sense, diversity is conditional on deradicalization. What characterizes the politics of race under neoliberalism, above all, has been this flexible and adaptive racial regime that alternates in different settings between diversity and despotism. This oscillation has been organized through a framework in which a racial concept of culture represents both a fixed and determining source of disorder as well as an object of assimilating intervention by corporations and governing agencies.

In its racial incorporation mode, neoliberalism has drawn on the liberal theory of antiracism as its organizing framework. It has outlawed racist discrimination and abuse, which it interprets as offenses against market rationality; in any case, racial capitalism no longer needs explicit discrimination to reproduce itself. It has also proposed the principle of recognizing Black and global South cultural identities—so long as they are first desiccated and depoliticized. As Fanon wrote, there has been a "respect for the traditions, the cultural peculiarities, the personality, of the enslaved peoples" if these cultures are represented in a "mummified" way.[4] Radical antiracism had produced a fluid identity politics in which the turn to Black and Third World cultures was a way to strip away a personal sense of inferiority and open one out to revolutionary movements in other parts of the world. Figures like Roy, James, Césaire, Fanon, Nkrumah, Jones, the Kings, and Al-Amin were, wrote Sivanandan, "all stars of a common constellation, and the struggles of one continent flowed and ebbed into the struggles of the other."[5] Neoliberalism has given the term "identity" a quite different meaning as a fixed inner personhood that statically defines who we are. Sivanandan noted that this reframing meant also redefining racism as no longer "a matter of racial oppression and exploitation, of race and class, but of cultural differences and their acceptability."[6] The possibility of forging solidarity on the basis of shared experiences, shared interests, or simply imagining the pain of others was replaced by a notion that people could only truly act together if they shared an identity. The term "racism" lost its earlier power to find resonances between different oppressions; instead, liberal antiracism became a space where different identities competed for attention and recognition by emphasizing whatever in their experiences of victimhood appeared distinctive. This narrowing of antiracist politics in turn enabled processes of incorporating small elites of Black leaders, not as representatives of oppressed peoples to be evaluated in terms of how much they relieved that oppression, but as representatives of identities in the abstract. This diversity politics was only possible because the representation of Black identities had been violently emptied of the radicalism of earlier mass struggles. Its hallmark was vapid claims to authenticity rather than concrete commitments to justice and accountability. The historian Keeanga-Yamahtta Taylor has pointed out that, by the 1990s, Black elected representatives in the US "lined up to sign off on legislation that was literally intended to kill Black people": President Clinton's 1994 Violent Crime Control and

Law Enforcement Act expanded the use of the death penalty, mandated life sentences for nonviolent criminal offenses, and added a hundred thousand police officers to American streets.[7] Meanwhile liberals have clung to the fantasy that the solutions to racism lie in better representations in Hollywood movies and more diversity among corporate executives.

Nevertheless, diversity has been an anxious politics, continuously vulnerable to being undermined by the structural racisms it coexists with. On the one hand, there has been the risk of a re-radicalization of Black and global South identities, making it harder to smoothly manage their assimilation. On the other hand, there has been the constant danger that white people might reject what Oliver Cromwell Cox called liberals' "idealistic preachments" of diversity and instead receive a different message from the system: they might look at the vast infrastructures aimed at capturing, incarcerating, deporting, and bombing Black and Brown peoples and conclude that there is indeed something to fear from the dark proletariat.[8] Racist attitudes have continued to exist, not because ruling-class propagandists have implanted them in white-working-class minds, but because, as Stuart Hall wrote, they have been plausible ways to "spontaneously" interpret a social world marked by racist divisions in the "material and social base" of capitalism.[9] The recent electoral successes of racist politicians and parties are not the result of a backlash against antiracist progress; they are winning by making explicit in their political rhetoric what is already implicit in the violently racist practices of nominally liberal states.

"All the great and simple things that make us human"

By the metrics of liberal antiracism, there has been tremendous progress since Myrdal and Benedict laid out their programs. Many more white people are able to have personal relationships with others without attitudes of superiority or prejudice. But as

Sivanandan put it, that amounts to saying that white people have done their "potty training" and learned to function as ordinary human beings.[10] From a structural vantage point, liberal antiracism has proven a failure. It has been fully co-opted by neoliberal forces that have used it to help regenerate racial capitalism and establish immense systems of racist macro-aggression. That in turn has meant that progress in challenging individual racist prejudices has been fragile and vulnerable to reversal. The liberal antiracism that has prevailed since the 1940s has turned out to be, in the end, not a pathway to substantial change but a diversion from it. Our only way forward today is to re-energize the alternative traditions of radical antiracism and anti-imperialism that run through figures like Roy, James, Césaire, Fanon, Nkrumah, Jones, and Al-Amin. Theirs was a struggle for socialism but one centered upon the experiences of racism, colonialism, and imperialism; their flag was socialist red, but it was a darker red.

A socialism of Black and global South struggles cannot involve itself in a nostalgia for the mid-twentieth-century social democracies of the West, which not only depended on the profits of imperialism but were deeply structured through racial and colonial boundaries. The story at the heart of white progressive politics holds up the New Deal in the US or the 1945 Labour government in the UK as representative of a more economically equal period before neoliberalism. But this story does not include any recognition that racism and imperialism have been continuous, structural features of capitalism. The political movements that mobilize this story fail to make addressing structural racism or present-day imperialism a part of their politics—even as they passionately oppose individual racist prejudices. The white progressives who long for the state to be once again a venue of social democratic reform and welfare forget that the reputation of the state as social democratic protector of the working class derives from a period in which these benefits were available only to a white core of workers, the better to exploit the world working class as a whole.

Meanwhile, white liberals do not see racism as linked to capitalism and are parochially indifferent to imperialism; as such, they also limit themselves to opposing manifestations of racism in personal relationships, demanding diversity in media representations, and calling for greater policing of far-right extremism. They fail to see that liberal democracies die not when they are threatened by extremists, but when they see themselves as finished products, needing only to be protected from external dangers. The danger to US democracy comes not from extremist polarization but, as Césaire explained, from a "liberal" imperialism that boomerangs back to the US. Racism, imperialism, and capitalism depend upon each other; they have to be fought together. That does not mean holding off on fighting racism until capitalism is first defeated; rather, the struggle against capitalism has to be intertwined with a struggle against racism. In the words of historian Barbara Ransby:

> There is a symbiosis between US and European capitalism, empire, white supremacy, and hetero-patriarchy. This understanding is a basis for unity; not fragmentation. If only the various white-led Left and labor organizations could truly internalize these historical truths, the political possibilities would be enormous.[11]

Understanding this symbiosis also means understanding the centrality of the state in mediating it. As Sivanandan wrote in a 1985 essay, the power of structural racism

> is derived from racist laws, constitutional conventions, judicial precedents, institutional practices—all of which have the imprimatur of the state. In a capitalist state, that power is associated with the power of the capitalist class—and racial oppression cannot be dissociated from class exploitation. And it is that symbiosis between race and class that marks the difference between the racial oppressions of the capitalist and

A. Sivanandan
Institute of Race Relations

pre-capitalist periods. The fight against racism is, therefore, a fight against the state which sanctions and authorises it—even if by default—in the institutions and structures of society and in the behavior of its public officials.[12]

The racial attitudes of individuals—whether they be deportation officers, police officers, or capitalists—matter very little compared to the structures of law and policy, and broader economic and institutional practices. The border violence of detention and deportation, for example, is driven by the need to maintain a worldwide racial division of labor; it does not diminish in the slightest if the deportation officer who carries out the violence and the capitalist who profits from it have done terrific jobs of examining their unconscious biases. To be antiracist implies working collectively with organizations to dismantle racist border, policing, carceral, and military infrastructures. It also requires a commitment to the international redistribution of wealth—the poor of the global South are equally entitled to the world's resources as the wealthy residents of the North. Decolonization means undoing the inequalities that colonialism created.

Even if the politics of twentieth-century social democracy is moribund, we still need the values that working-class movements forced it to partially honor. The core of socialism is not a doctrine of economic policy, wrote Sivanandan, but a "moral creed" that began with "a simple faith in human beings and a deep knowledge that, by himself or herself, the individual is nothing, that we need to confirm and be confirmed by each other, that only in the collective good our selves can put forth and grow." It values "loyalty, comradeship, generosity, a sense of community and a feel for internationalism, an understanding that unity has to be forged and reforged again and again and, above all, a capacity for making other people's fights one's own—all the great and simple things that make us human." Every movement for liberation has embodied these commitments in one form or another. Buried under decades of neoliberal attacks on "collectivism," they have over the last decade reemerged in the US in the Black Lives Matter movements, in Indigenous struggles, in the upsurge in labor organizing, and in the struggles of migrant workers.[13]

This is a socialism that does not believe multiple struggles can only be united if they conform to a narrow definition of the working class. Nor does it suspect that any attempt to build collective action beyond specific identities must involve an oppressive erasure of their particularities. Rather, it seeks to build from different race, gender, and class struggles to something greater than the sum of its parts. "There are two ways to lose oneself, walled segregation in the particular or dilution in the 'universal,'" wrote Césaire. "My conception of the universal is that of a universal enriched by all that is particular, a universal enriched by every particular: the deepening and coexistence of all particulars."[14]

As a concrete image of what this might look like, Sivanandan offered the example of the Pentonville Five case of 1972, in which five white workers were arrested and imprisoned for organizing unofficial picketing in support of a dockers' strike in London. The trade unions invited Black organizations to join a march to Pentonville prison where the men were held. Black organizers recognized that the unions' struggle was also their struggle—they, too, were workers. But the entrenched racism of the trade unions meant they would not join the official march—four years earlier, the dockers had marched in support of the racist politician Enoch Powell. Moreover, to the Black organizations, imprisonment was an aspect of state racism that impinged on their communities in a distinct way. Instead, Black organizations led a different march down a different road to the same spot on behalf of the Pentonville Five.[15] Same destination, different journey. Not the intersection of identities or oppressions but of movements; not a hierarchy of oppression but an opening out to other struggles while maintaining the specificity of one's own. Unity has to be made in the struggle, not assumed in the abstract.

Understood in this way, antiracism does not fragment class struggle but radicalizes it. Culture is neither a distraction from economic struggles nor a fixed identity that determines a group's political desires. Instead, the socialist tradition is one of making and renewing cultures through our struggles for working people. And because our struggles are unbounded, so is our sense of who we might be.

Acknowledgments

The writing of this book was supported with a grant from the Independent Social Research Foundation. Prior to this award, it was made possible by New York State's unemployment benefits. I am grateful to New York University for firing me so that I could access this funding.

A large number of people have supported my research with their time and energy. I would like to especially thank Aisha al-Adawiya, Jamil and Karima Al-Amin, Lars Cornelissen, Des Freedman, Cortelyou Churchill Kenney, Greg Leslie, Naomi Lorrain, Amara Majeed, and Heather Murray. I am grateful to Mieke Kundnani for her translations from Dutch and to Bart Jonkergouw for his research at the Institute for War, Holocaust and Genocide Studies in Amsterdam. Thanks to Jessica Ratcliff and Nico Silins for giving me a space in their home where I could finish writing the book. Amna Akbar, Patrick Barrett, Jenny Bourne, Jordan Camp, Lars Cornelissen, Avery Gordon, Daniel Renwick, Robbie Shilliam, and Amandla Thomas-Johnson all read sections of the book and added immensely to whatever value it has. Chapters 6 and 7 owe a huge debt to Jeanne Theoharis's radical intellect and her generosity in supporting my work. So much of the book has been shaped by the many years of Deepa Kumar's friendship, support, and political insights. Andy Hsiao first set me thinking about writing this book; his superb editorial work has been invaluable to completing it. Finally, my deep thanks to Stew and Gloria for the innumerable ways they make my work possible.

Notes

Introduction

1. "National: Protestors' Anger Justified Even If Actions May Not Be," Monmouth University, NJ, June 2, 2020, monmouth.edu.
2. Larry Buchanan, Quoctrung Bui, and Jugal K. Patel, "Black Lives Matter May Be the Largest Movement in U.S. History," *New York Times*, July 3, 2020.
3. Amna A. Akbar, "Our Reckoning with Race," *New York Review of Books*, October 31, 2020.
4. "Walmart Center for Racial Equality," walmart.org.
5. Jordan Pouille, "Blackrock: The Financial Leviathan That Bears Down on Europe's Decisions," *Investigate Europe*, April 17, 2019; Carleton English, "Larry Fink Blitzed by War Protesters at Conference," *New York Post*, September 20, 2018; Larry Fink, "Recent Events of Racial Injustice," May 30, 2020, linkedin.com; Morris Pearl, "Dear Larry Fink: It's Time to Stop Lavishing Your Wealth on the Police," *Guardian*, August 1, 2020.
6. "Fact Sheet: US Efforts to Combat Systemic Racism," White House Briefing Room, March 21, 2021.
7. Robin DiAngelo, *White Fragility: Why It's So Hard for White People to Talk about Racism* (Beacon Press, 2018), 20.
8. A. Sivanandan, *Communities of Resistance: Writings on Black Struggles for Socialism* (Verso, 1990), 118.
9. Gary Younge, "What Covid Taught Us about Racism—and What We Need to Do Now," *Guardian*, December 16, 2021.

1. How to Hide a Genocide

1. *Final Destination or Transit Station* (Camp Vught National Memorial, 2002), 11.
2. Pim Griffioen and Ron Zeller, "Anti-Jewish Policy and Organization of the Deportations in France and the Netherlands, 1940–1944:

A Comparative Study," *Holocaust and Genocide Studies* 20, no. 3 (Winter 2006): 457.
3. *Final Destination*, 11.
4. Marnix Croes, "The Holocaust in the Netherlands and the Rate of Jewish Survival," *Holocaust and Genocide Studies* 20, no. 3 (Winter 2006): 474.
5. Peter Meel, "Anton de Kom and the Formative Phase of Surinamese Decolonization," *New West Indian Guide* 83, nos. 3–4 (2009): 256.
6. Anton de Kom, *Wij Slaven Van Suriname* (Contact, 1934), 39, 58, 134–5. Translations by Mieke Kundnani.
7. Meel, "Anton de Kom and the Formative Phase of Surinamese Decolonization," 263–5.
8. Clarence Lusane, *Hitler's Black Victims: The Historical Experiences of Afro-Germans, European Blacks, Africans, and African Americans in the Nazi Era* (Routledge, 2003), 155.
9. Sanne Kortooms, "Not Everything Is What It Seems," nmkampvught.nl.
10. *Inhuman and Unnecessary: Human Rights Violations in Dutch High-Security Prisons in the Context of Counterterrorism* (Amnesty International and Open Society Justice Initiative, 2017), 17.
11. Tinka M. Veldhuis et al., *Terrorists in Prison: Evaluation of the Dutch Terrorism Wing* (University of Groningen, 2010), 3.
12. *Inhuman and Unnecessary*, 8.
13. Craig Haney, "Mental Health Issues in Long-Term Solitary and 'Supermax' Confinement," *Crime and Delinquency* 49, no. 1 (2003): 130–2.
14. "Solitary Confinement Should Be Banned in Most Cases, UN Expert Says," *UN News*, October 18, 2011.
15. *Inhuman and Unnecessary*, 7–9, 14.
16. "Samir A. Klaagt over Regime in Vught," Nu.nl, October 25, 2006.
17. David A. Ward and Thomas G. Werlich, "Evaluating Super-Maximum Custody," *Punishment and Society* 5, no. 1 (2003): 55–6.
18. Brittany Friedman and Zachary Sommers, "Solitary Confinement and the Nation of Islam," *The Immanent Frame*, May 30, 2018.
19. Alan Eladio Gómez, "Resisting Living Death at Marion Federal Penitentiary, 1972," *Radical History Review* 96 (Fall 2006): 62–4.
20. George Jackson, "Towards the United Front," in *Imprisoned Intellectuals: America's Political Prisoners Write on Life, Liberation, and Rebellion*, ed. Joy James (Rowman & Littlefield, 2003), 89.
21. Ward and Werlich, "Evaluating Super-Maximum Custody," 58.
22. Gómez, "Resisting Living Death at Marion Federal Penitentiary, 1972," 58, 75.
23. Ward and Werlich, "Evaluating Super-Maximum Custody," 57; Jean Casella, James Ridgeway, and Sarah Shourd, eds., *Hell Is a Very Small Place: Voices from Solitary Confinement* (New Press, 2016), 5.
24. Casella, Ridgeway, and Shourd, *Hell Is a Very Small Place*, 5, 6, 8.

25. Hannah Pullen-Blasnik, Jessica T. Simes, and Bruce Western, "The Population Prevalence of Solitary Confinement," *Science Advances* 7, no. 48 (November 2021).
26. Casella, Ridgeway, and Shourd, *Hell Is a Very Small Place*, 149.
27. Jill Stauffer, "We Have Invented a New Form of Death, Interview with Colin Dayan," *Believer*, February 1, 2013; Fred Ho and Quincy Saul, eds., *Maroon the Implacable: The Collected Writings of Russell Maroon Shoatz* (PM Press, 2013), 59–61.
28. Angela Y. Davis, *Are Prisons Obsolete?* (Seven Stories Press, 2003), 16.
29. Avery F. Gordon, "The United States Military Prison: The Normalcy of Exceptional Brutality," in *The Violence of Incarceration*, ed. Phil Scraton and Jude McCulloch (Routledge, 2008).
30. Luk Vervaet, "The Violence of Incarceration: A Response from Mainland Europe," *Race and Class* 51, no. 4 (2010): 34.
31. Dan Bilefsky, "A Space Issue in Dutch Prisons: Too Many Empty Cells," *New York Times*, February 12, 2017, A8.
32. Timothy Garton Ash, "Wake Up, the Invisible Front Line Runs Right through Your Back Yard," *Guardian*, September 13, 2007, 37.
33. Daniel Boffey, "Dutch 'Burqa Ban' Rendered Largely Unworkable on First Day," *Guardian*, August 1, 2019; Arun Kundnani, *The Muslims Are Coming! Islamophobia, Extremism, and the Domestic War on Terror* (Verso, 2014).
34. Neta C. Crawford and Catherine Lutz, *Human Cost of the Post-9/11 Wars* (Costs of War Project, Watson Institute of International and Public Affairs, Brown University, November 2019).
35. David Vine et al., *Creating Refugees: Displacement Caused by the United States' Post–9/11 Wars* (Costs of War Project, September 21, 2020).
36. Tony Blair, speech to the Los Angeles World Affairs Council, August 1, 2006; see "In Full: Tony Blair Speech," news.bbc.co.uk, August 1, 2006.
37. *Recruitment for the Jihad in the Netherlands: From Incident to Trend* (Algemene Inlichtingen- en Veiligheidsdienst, December 2002); *From Dawa to Jihad: The Various Threats from Radical Islam to the Democratic Legal Order* (Algemene Inlichtingen- en Veiligheidsdienst, December 2004).
38. Gloria Wekker, *White Innocence: Paradoxes of Colonialism and Race* (Duke University Press, 2016), 55.

2. The Liberal Theory of Antiracism

1. Heike Bauer, *The Hirschfeld Archives: Violence, Death, and Modern Queer Culture* (Temple University Press, 2017), 7.
2. Ralf Dose, *Magnus Hirschfeld: The Origins of the Gay Liberation Movement* (Monthly Review Press, 2014).

3. Magnus Hirschfeld, *Racism* (Kennikat Press, 1973), 26.
4. Tom Reiss, "The First Conservative: How Peter Viereck Inspired—and Lost—a Movement," *New Yorker*, October 24, 2005, 42.
5. Dose, *Magnus Hirschfeld*, 90–1.
6. "Reichstag Fire Trial: Defence Speeches in Paris, Lively Street Scenes," *The Times*, September 12, 1933, 12.
7. Hirschfeld, *Racism*, 35.
8. Ibid., 36.
9. Bauer, *The Hirschfeld Archives*, 28; Mahmood Mamdani, "A Brief History of Genocide," *Transition* 87 (2001).
10. Dose, *Magnus Hirschfeld*, 93; Bauer, *The Hirschfeld Archives*, 23.
11. W. E. B. Du Bois, *The Philadelphia Negro: A Social Study* (Oxford University Press, 2007), 229, 2, 270.
12. Aldon D. Morris, *The Scholar Denied: W. E. B. Du Bois and the Birth of Modern Sociology* (University of California Press, 2015), 185.
13. David Levering Lewis, *W. E. B. Du Bois: Biography of a Race 1868–1919* (Henry Holt & Co, 1993), 379, 410–11, 99.
14. Morris, *The Scholar Denied*, 59.
15. "Wallace Assails Race Prejudice," *New York Times*, October 15, 1939, 48.
16. George W. Stocking, *Race, Culture, and Evolution: Essays in the History of Anthropology* (Free Press, 1968), 201.
17. Robert Knox, *The Races of Men*, 2nd ed. (Henry Renshaw, 1862), v.
18. Herbert Spencer, *Social Statics* (John Chapman, 1851), 416–19.
19. Stocking, *Race, Culture, and Evolution*, 203.
20. Franz Boas, "Some Traits of Primitive Culture," *Journal of American Folklore* 17, no. 67 (October–December 1904): 254.
21. Stocking, *Race, Culture, and Evolution*, 229.
22. Tracy Teslow, *Constructing Race: The Science of Bodies and Cultures in American Anthropology* (Cambridge University Press, 2014), 12–13; Anthony Q. Hazard Jr., *Boasians at War: Anthropology, Race, and World War II* (Palgrave Macmillan, 2020).
23. Teslow, *Constructing Race*, 238.
24. Ruth Benedict, *Race: Science and Politics* (Modern Age Books, 1940), 153, 170–1, 174.
25. Étienne Balibar, "Racism, Anti-Semitism, Islamophobia," verso books.com, September 24, 2021.
26. Benedict, *Race: Science and Politics*, 153.
27. Teslow, *Constructing Race*, 246–53.
28. Ibid., 229.
29. Mary L. Dudziak, *Cold War Civil Rights: Race and the Image of American Democracy* (Princeton University Press, 2000), 9.
30. Morris, *The Scholar Denied*, 216.

31. Gunnar Myrdal, *An American Dilemma: The Negro Problem and Modern Democracy* (Harper & Brothers, 1944), ix, 998, 1003, 1006.
32. Ibid., 69, 1003, 104.
33. Ibid., xlv, 111, 80.
34. Jodi Melamed, "The Spirit of Neoliberalism: From Racial Liberalism to Neoliberal Multiculturalism," *Social Text* 24, no. 4 (Winter 2006): 7.
35. Myrdal, *An American Dilemma*, 1019, 1021–2.

3. Imperialism and the Uses of Diversity

1. William F. P. Napier, *History of General Sir Charles Napier's Administration of Scinde and the Campaign in the Cutchee Hills* (Chapman and Hall, 1851), 42–3, 86.
2. *House of Lords Hansard*, vol. 69 (HC Deb, June 12, 1843), 1323–5.
3. Napier, *Administration of Scinde*, 401.
4. Wendy Doniger, "Presidential Address: 'I Have Scinde': Flogging a Dead (White Male Orientalist) Horse," *Journal of Asian Studies* 58, no. 4 (November 1999): 943.
5. Ibid., 941–3.
6. William F. P. Napier, *The Conquest of Scinde, with Some Introductory Passages in the Life of Major-General Sir Charles James Napier* (T. & W. Boone, 1845), 25.
7. Napier, *Administration of Scinde*, 12, 35.
8. Deepa Kumar, *Islamophobia and the Politics of Empire: Twenty Years after 9/11* (Verso, 2021).
9. Agha Saleem, *Shah Abdul Latif Bhittai—Melody of Clouds* (Rotary Club, 2002), 5–7.
10. Andre Gunter Frank, *ReOrient: Global Economy in the Asian Age* (University of California Press, 1998), 127, 166.
11. H. T. Sorley, *Shah Abdul Latif of Bhit: His Poetry, Life, and Times* (Oxford University Press, 1966), 93.
12. Frank, *ReOrient*, 127, 158; Sven Beckert, *Empire of Cotton: A Global History* (Alfred A. Knopf, 2014).
13. Frank, *ReOrient*, 277–8.
14. Utsa Patnaik and Prabhat Patnaik, *A Theory of Imperialism* (Columbia University Press, 2017), 34.
15. Claude Alvares, *Decolonizing History: Technology and Culture in India, China, and the West, 1492 to the Present Day* (The Other India Press, 1991), 138–59.
16. Beckert, *Empire of Cotton*.
17. Karl Marx, "The British Rule in India," in Karl Marx and Frederick Engels, *Collected Works*, vol. 12 (Lawrence & Wishart, 1975), 128.

18. Karl Marx, *Capital*, vol. 1 (Penguin, 1982), 925.
19. Gail Omvedt, *The Political Economy of Starvation: Imperialism and the World Food Crisis* (Leela Bhosale, 1975), 28, 32–3.
20. A. Sivanandan, *A Different Hunger: Writings on Black Resistance* (Pluto Press, 1982), 143–61.
21. Priyamvada Gopal, *Insurgent Empire: Anticolonial Resistance and British Dissent* (Verso, 2019), 48–9.
22. Barbara Harlow and Mia Carter, eds., *Archives of Empire Volume 1: From the East India Company to the Suez Canal* (Duke University Press, 2003), 480.
23. Mahmood Mamdani, *Define and Rule: Native as Political Identity* (Harvard University Press, 2012), 1–2.
24. *Proclamation by the Queen in Council to the Princes, Chiefs and People of India* (Governor-General at Allahabad, November 1, 1858).
25. Mamdani, *Define and Rule*, 26–7, 42.
26. Bernard S. Cohn, *Colonialism and Its Forms of Knowledge: The British in India* (Princeton University Press, 1996), 8.
27. Mamdani, *Define and Rule*, 30.
28. Uma Narayan, "Essence of Culture and a Sense of History: A Feminist Critique of Cultural Essentialism," *Hypatia* 13, no. 2 (Spring 1998): 100.
29. Utsa Patnaik, "Revisiting the 'Drain,' or Transfers from India to Britain in the Context of Global Diffusion of Capitalism," in *Agrarian and Other Histories: Essays for Binay Bhushan Chaudhuri*, ed. Shubhra Chakrabarti and Utsa Patnaik (Tulika Books, 2019), 278, 302.
30. Dadabhai Naoroji, *Poverty and Un-British Rule in India* (Swan Sonnenschein, 1901), viii.
31. Mike Davis, *Late Victorian Holocausts: El Niño Famines and the Making of the Third World* (Verso, 2001), 7, 38–41, 51.
32. *Famine Inquiry Commission: Report on Bengal* (Government of India, 1945): 110.
33. Madhusree Mukerjee, *Churchill's Secret War: The British Empire and the Ravaging of India during World War II* (Basic Books, 2010), ix.
34. Utsa Patnaik and Prabhat Patnaik, *Capitalism and Imperialism: Theory, History, and the Present* (Monthly Review Press, 2021), 212–15.
35. Spencer, *Social Statics*, 416.
36. Samar Attar, *Debunking the Myths of Colonization: the Arabs and Europe* (University Press of America, 2010), 9.
37. Mukerjee, *Churchill's Secret War*, 246, 233.
38. George Orwell, "Not Counting Niggers," *Adelphi* (July 1939).

39. Urvashi Butalia, *The Other Side of Silence: Voices from the Partition of India* (Penguin Random House India, 2000).
40. Patnaik, "Revisiting the 'Drain,'" 311–12.

4. Marxists Confront Colonialism

1. Karl Marx and Frederick Engels, *Manifesto of the Communist Party*, in *Collected Works*, vol. 6 (Lawrence & Wishart, 1975), 496.
2. Kevin B. Anderson, *Marx at the Margins: On Nationalism, Ethnicity, and Non-Western Societies* (University of Chicago Press, 2010), 3–4.
3. Pranav Jani, "Karl Marx, Eurocentrism, and the 1857 Revolt in British India," in *Marxism, Modernity, and Postcolonial Studies*, ed. Crystal Bartolovich and Neil Lazarus (Cambridge University Press, 2002).
4. Karl Marx, "The Future Results of British Rule in India," in Marx and Engels, *Collected Works*, vol. 12 (Lawrence & Wishart, 1975), 221.
5. Rachna Bhola "Yamini," *The Life and Times of Madam Bhikaji Cama* (Prabhat Books, 2016).
6. Hélène Carrère d'Encausse and Stuart R. Schram, *Marxism and Asia: An Introduction with Readings* (Allen Lane, 1969), 129–30, 132–3.
7. V. I. Lenin, "The International Socialist Congress in Stuttgart," in *Lenin Collected Works*, vol. 13, *June 1907–April 1908* (Progress Publishers, 1978), 77.
8. V. I. Lenin, "Imperialism, the Highest Stage of Capitalism: A Popular Outline," in *Lenin Collected Works*, vol. 22, *December 1915–July 1916* (Progress Publishers, 1974), 266–7, 284, 301.
9. W. E. Burghardt Dubois, "The African Roots of War," *Atlantic Monthly*, May 1915, 709.
10. John Riddell, ed., *Workers of the World and Oppressed Peoples, Unite! Proceedings and Documents of the Second Congress, 1920*, vol. 1 (Pathfinder Books, 1991), 284, 288.
11. V. B. Karnik, *M. N. Roy: Political Biography* (Nav Jagriti Samaj, 1978), 6–7, 13.
12. Ibid., 25–35; Tim Harper, *Underground Asia: Global Revolutionaries and the Assault on Empire* (Harvard University Press, 2021), 262–3; M. N. Roy, *Political Memoirs* (Ajanta Publications, 1984), 7–11.
13. Karnik, *M. N. Roy*, 42–3; Harper, *Underground Asia*, 300–303; Roy, *Political Memoirs*, 22–6.
14. Karnik, *M. N. Roy*, 46–7; Harper, *Underground Asia*, 311; Roy, *Political Memoirs*, 37–44.

15. Harper, *Underground Asia*, 312, 336.
16. Karnik, *M. N. Roy*, 61–6, 71; Harper, *Underground Asia*, 379–81; Roy, *Political Memoirs*, 210–13.
17. D'Encausse and Schram, *Marxism and Asia*, 161.
18. John P. Haithcox, "The Roy-Lenin Debate on Colonial Policy: A New Interpretation," *Journal of Asian Studies* 23, no. 1 (November 1963): 95.
19. Riddell, *Workers of the World and Oppressed Peoples, Unite!*, 286.
20. Robin D. G. Kelley, *Freedom Dreams: The Black Radical Imagination* (Beacon Press, 2002), 45–6; Minkah Makalani, "Internationalizing the Third International: The African Blood Brotherhood, Asian Radicals, and Race, 1919–1922," *Journal of African American History* 96, no. 2 (Spring 2011): 151–78; Philip S. Foner, *Organized Labor and the Black Worker, 1619–1981* (Haymarket, 2017), 149.
21. Robin D. G. Kelley, "The Third International and the Struggle for National Liberation in South Africa," *Ufahamu: A Journal of African Studies* 38, no. 1 (2014): 252.
22. D'Encausse and Schram, *Marxism and Asia*, 151.
23. Karnik, *M. N. Roy*, 130.
24. Gail Omvedt, *Understanding Caste: From Buddha to Ambedkar and Beyond* (Orient Blackswan, 2011), 24, 39, 49–51.
25. Kris Manjapra, *M. N. Roy: Marxism and Colonial Cosmopolitanism* (Routledge, 2010), 81.
26. Paul Buhle, *C. L. R. James: The Artist as Revolutionary* (Verso, 1988), 69.
27. C. L. R. James, "An African 'Homeland' for the Jewish Refugees?," *Socialist Appeal*, November 26, 1938, 3.
28. Jamaica Kincaid, *A Small Place* (Farrar, Straus, and Giroux, 1988), 36–7.
29. Karl Marx, "The Eighteenth Brumaire of Louis Bonaparte," in Marx and Engels, *Collected Works*, vol. 11 (Lawrence & Wishart, 1975), 128.
30. C. L. R. James, *The Black Jacobins: Toussaint L'Ouverture and the San Domingo Revolution* (Vintage, 1989), 39, 43–4, 47–8, 80, 89, 98.
31. Ibid., 85–6.
32. Ibid., 60–1, 73, 120.
33. Selma James, "*The Black Jacobins*, Past and Present," in *The Black Jacobins Reader*, ed. Charles Forsdick and Christian Høgsbjerg (Duke University Press, 2017), 76.
34. W. E. Burghardt Du Bois, *Black Reconstruction: An Essay toward a History of the Part Which Black Folk Played in the Attempt to Reconstruct Democracy in America, 1860–1880* (Harcourt, Brace, 1935), 55, 15–16, 700, 30; Bill V. Mullen, *Un-American: W. E. B. Du*

Bois and the Century of World Revolution (Temple University Press, 2015), 83.
35. Buhle, *C. L. R. James*, 72.
36. Anthony Bogues, *Caliban's Freedom: The Early Political Thought of C. L. R. James* (Pluto Press, 1997), 73–5, 97.
37. J. Meyer [C. L. R. James], "The Revolutionary Answer to the Negro Problem in the United States," December 1948, available at marxists.org.
38. Farrukh Dhondy, *C. L. R. James: Cricket, the Caribbean, and World Revolution* (Weidenfeld and Nicholson, 2001), 170.
39. C. L. R. James, *Black Power: Its Past, Today, and the Way Ahead* (Marcus Garvey Institute, 1968), 14.

5. Racism Is a Structure

1. Aimé Césaire, *Discourse on Colonialism* (Monthly Review Press, 2000), 35 7, 41.
2. Adam Tooze, *The Wages of Destruction: The Making and Breaking of the Nazi Economy* (Penguin, 2008); James Q. Whitman, *Hitler's American Model: The United States and the Making of Nazi Race Law* (Princeton University Press, 2017).
3. Anton de Kom, *Wij Slaven Van Suriname* (Amsterdam: Contact, 1934), 58.
4. Peter Hudis, *Frantz Fanon: Philosopher of the Barricades* (Pluto Press, 2015), 19.
5. Césaire, *Discourse on Colonialism*, 78.
6. Aimé Césaire, "Letter to Maurice Thorez," *Social Text* 28, no. 2 (Summer 2010): 147, 150.
7. Hudis, *Frantz Fanon*, 76; Lewis Gordon, *What Fanon Said: A Philosophical Introduction to His Life and Thought* (Hurst, 2015), 85; Penny Von Eschen, *Race against Empire: Black Americans and Anticolonialism, 1937–1957* (Cornell University Press, 1997), 175; David Macey, *Frantz Fanon: A Biography* (Picador, 2000), 266, 279, 293; Alice Cherki, *Frantz Fanon: A Portrait* (Cornell University Press, 2006), 84, 89–90.
8. Frantz Fanon, "Letter to the Resident Minister (1956)," in *Toward the African Revolution: Political Essays* (Grove Press, 1967), 53.
9. Frantz Fanon, "Racism and Culture," *Presence Africaine* 8–10 (June–November 1956): 122–3, 125, 127–8.
10. Ibid., 122–3, 125–6.
11. Ibid., 124, 131.
12. Frantz Fanon, *Les Damnés de la Terre* (Éditions La Découverte & Syros, 2002), 305. All translations by the author.

13. Frantz Fanon, *Black Skin, White Masks* (Pluto Press, 2008), 4–5, 64, 175.
14. Fanon, *Les Damnés de la Terre*, 42–3, 108.
15. Ibid., 146, 148, 168–9.
16. Ibid., 111, 126, 138.
17. Ibid., 40–1, 90.
18. Barnor Hesse, "Im/plausible Deniability: Racism's Conceptual Double Bind," *Social Identities* 10, no. 1 (2004): 14.
19. Oliver Cromwell Cox, *Caste, Class, and Race: A Study in Social Dynamics* (Monthly Review Press, 1959), 482, 521.
20. Ibid., 537.
21. Madeleine Albright, *Fascism: A Warning* (HarperCollins, 2018), 13, 87, 167, 174.
22. Robert Kagan, "This Is How Fascism Comes to America," *Washington Post*, May 18, 2016.
23. Timothy Snyder, *On Tyranny: Twenty Lessons from the Twentieth Century* (Tim Duggan Books, 2017).
24. Kathleen Belew, *Bring the War Home: The White Power Movement and Paramilitary America* (Harvard University Press, 2018).
25. Greg Grandin, *The End of the Myth: From the Frontier to the Border Wall in the Mind of America* (Metropolitan Books, 2019).
26. Haifa Zangana, "Is It Still Worth It?," *Guardian*, April 1, 2006.
27. Robert Kagan and William Kristol, "What to Do about Iraq," *Weekly Standard*, January 21, 2002.
28. Antony Flew, *Thinking about Social Thinking: The Philosophy of the Social Sciences* (Basil Blackwell, 1985), 50–1.

6. Internationalists

1. Kwame Nkrumah, *Neo-Colonialism: The Last Stage of Imperialism* (International Publishers, 1965), 24.
2. Kwame Nkrumah, *Revolutionary Path* (Panaf Books, 2001), 43–4.
3. Nkrumah, *Neo-Colonialism*, ix.
4. Ibid., 255.
5. Nkrumah, *Revolutionary Path*, 449.
6. Arnold R. Hirsh, *Making the Second Ghetto: Race and Housing in Chicago, 1940–1960* (University of Chicago Press, 1998), 254.
7. Kenneth T. Jackson, "Race, Ethnicity, and Real Estate Appraisal: The Home Owners Loan Corporation and the Federal Housing Administration," *Journal of Urban History* 6, no. 4 (August 1980): 430–6.
8. Komozi Woodard, *A Nation within a Nation: Amiri Baraka (LeRoi Jones) and Black Power Politics* (University of North Carolina Press,

1999), 31, 35, 36; Mae M. Ngai, *Impossible Subjects: Illegal Aliens and the Making of Modern America* (Princeton University Press, 2005), 136.
9. Jacquelyn Dowd Hall, "The Long Civil Rights Movement and the Political Uses of the Past," *Journal of American History* 91, no. 4 (March 2005): 1241.
10. Bernard Semmel, *Imperialism and Social Reform: English Social-Imperial Thought 1895–1914* (Anchor Books, 1968), 15.
11. Sidney Webb, "Lord Rosebery's Escape from Houndsditch," *The Nineteenth Century and After* 50 (September 1901): 382; Sidney Webb, *The Decline in the Birth Rate* (Fabian Society, 1907), 17, 19.
12. Nkrumah, *Revolutionary Path*, 449.
13. *House of Lords Hansard*, vol. 484 (HC Deb, February 28, 1951), 2076–8; John Newsinger, "War, Empire and the Attlee Government 1945–1951," *Race and Class* 60, no. 1 (July 2018): 61–76.
14. Nkrumah, *Revolutionary Path*, 449; Nkrumah, *Neo-Colonialism*, 255.
15. *House of Lords Hansard*, vol. 446 (HC Deb, January 20, 1948), 132–56.
16. Nkrumah, *Neo-Colonialism*, x, 257.
17. Nkrumah, *Revolutionary Path*, 450.
18. Nkrumah, *Neo-Colonialism*, 242–3.
19. Leo Panitch and Sam Gindin, *The Making of Global Capitalism: The Political Economy of American Empire* (Verso, 2012), 73.
20. Nkrumah, *Revolutionary Path*, 451.
21. Nkrumah, *Neo-Colonialism*, x, xv, xii, 243.
22. W. W. Rostow, *The Stages of Economic Growth: A Non-communist Manifesto* (Cambridge University Press, 1971), 6, 12.
23. Panitch and Gindin, *The Making of Global Capitalism*, 104–5.
24. Amy C. Offner, *Sorting Out the Mixed Economy: The Rise and Fall of Welfare and Developmental States in the Americas* (Princeton University Press, 2019), 6.
25. Panitch and Gindin, *The Making of Global Capitalism*, 10–11.
26. Eqbal Ahmad, "The Lessons of Vietnam," in *The Selected Writings of Eqbal Ahmad*, ed. Carollee Bengelsdorf, Margaret Cerullo, and Yogesh Chandrani (Columbia University Press, 2006), 65.
27. Branko Milanovic, *Global Inequality: A New Approach for the Age of Globalization* (Harvard University Press, 2016), 130–1.
28. Timothy Mitchell, *Carbon Democracy: Political Power in the Age of Oil* (Verso, 2013), 111, 114; Panitch and Gindin, *The Making of Global Capitalism*, 103.
29. Mitchell, *Carbon Democracy*, 144–5, 148–9.
30. Nkrumah, *Neo-Colonialism*, 245–6.
31. Eqbal Ahmad, "Political Culture and Foreign Policy: Notes on American Interventions in the Third World," in *Selected Writings*, 207.

32. "Book Review: *Neo-Colonialism: The Last Stage of Imperialism* by Kwame Nkrumah," November 8, 1965, cia.gov.
33. John Stockwell, *In Search of Enemies: A CIA Story* (W. W. Norton, 1978), 160, 201.
34. Charles Quist-Adade, "How Did a Fateful CIA Coup—Executed 55 Years Ago This February 24—Doom Much of Sub-Saharan Africa?," *CovertAction Quarterly*, February 24, 2021.
35. Johnson Library, National Security File, Memos to the President, Robert W. Komer, vol. 21, 3/3/66–3/20/66.
36. Erik S. McDuffie, "'For Full Freedom of . . . Colored Women in Africa, Asia, and in These United States . . .': Black Women Radicals and the Practice of a Black Women's International," *Palimpsest* 1, no. 1 (2012): 8; Erik S. McDuffie, "'No Small Amount of Change Could Do': Esther Cooper Jackson and the Making of a Black Left Feminist," in *Want to Start a Revolution? Radical Women in the Black Freedom Struggle*, ed. Dayo F. Gore, Jeanne Theoharis, and Komozi Woodard (New York University Press, 2009), 31–4.
37. Vicki Garvin speech, folder 7, box 11, Komozi Woodard Amiri Baraka Collection, Auburn Avenue Research Library on African-American Culture and History, Atlanta, GA.
38. Dayo F. Gore, "From Communist Politics to Black Power: The Visionary Politics and Transnational Solidarities of Victoria 'Vicki' Ama Garvin," in Gore, Theoharis, and Woodard, *Want to Start a Revolution?*, 76–7.
39. Erik S. McDuffie and Komozi Woodard, "'If You're in a Country That's Progressive, the Woman Is Progressive': Black Women Radicals and the Making of the Politics and Legacy of Malcolm X," *Biography* 36, no. 3 (Summer 2013): 508–14.
40. Carole Boyce Davies, *Left of Karl Marx: The Political Life of Black Communist Claudia Jones* (Duke University Press, 2008), 30, 36.
41. Ibid., 25, 219–20.
42. Carole Boyce Davies, *Claudia Jones: Beyond Containment* (Ayebia Clarke Publishing, 2011), 89–90.
43. Hall, "The Long Civil Rights Movement," 1247.
44. Ashley Farmer, *Remaking Black Power: How Black Women Transformed an Era* (University of North Carolina Press, 2017), 77.
45. Davies, *Claudia Jones*, 74.
46. Ibid., 75, 87.
47. Combahee River Collective, "The Combahee River Collective Statement," in *Available Means: An Anthology of Women's Rhetoric(s)*, ed. Joy Ritchie and Kate Ronald (University of Pittsburgh Press, 2001), 292.
48. Davies, *Claudia Jones*, 76, 78, 81.

49. Ibid., 62.
50. Ibid., 62, 69, 63.
51. Ibid., 115.
52. "Shirley Graham's Keynote Speech, Progressive Party, 1948," W. E. B. Du Bois Papers (MS 312), Special Collections and University Archives, University of Massachusetts Amherst Libraries.
53. Coretta Scott King, *My Life, My Love, My Legacy* (Henry Holt, 2017), 28.
54. Davies, *Claudia Jones*, 104.
55. Newsinger, "War, Empire and the Attlee Government," 73.
56. Davies, *Claudia Jones*, 86, 92, 157.
57. Ibid., 60.
58. Charisse Burden-Stelly, "Claudia Jones, the Longue Durée of McCarthyism, and the Threat of US Fascism," *Journal of Intersectionality* 3, no. 1 (Summer 2019): 48.
59. "The Genocide Convention," United Nations Office on Genocide Prevention and the Responsibility to Protect, un.org.
60. William L. Patterson, ed., *We Charge Genocide: The Historic Petition to the United Nations for Relief from a Crime of the United States Government against the Negro People* (International Publishers, 1970), 7–8, 23, 135–6.
61. "Indian Delegate Raises Racial Issue at Confab: Leaders Attend San Francisco Conference," *New York Amsterdam News*, May 5, 1945, 1A.
62. Marika Sherwood, "'There Is No New Deal for the Blackman in San Francisco': African Attempts to Influence the Founding Conference of the United Nations, April–July 1945," *International Journal of African Historical Studies* 29, no. 1 (1996): 71–94.
63. Davies, *Left of Karl Marx*, xxiv–xxv.
64. Burden-Stelly, "Claudia Jones," 58.
65. Davies, *Claudia Jones*, 6, 8.
66. Davies, *Left of Karl Marx*, 2, 25.
67. Mary L. Dudziak, *Cold War Civil Rights: Race and the Image of American Democracy* (Princeton University Press, 2000), 61–77.
68. Ibid., 155, 186.
69. Manning Marable, "Peace and Black Liberation: The Contributions of W. E. B. Du Bois," *Science and Society* 47, no. 4 (Winter 1983): 399, 401.

7. Antiracism Means Anticapitalism

1. Adom Getachew, *Worldmaking after Empire: The Rise and Fall of Self-Determination* (Princeton University Press, 2019), 2.

2. Martin Luther King Jr., "'A Realistic Look at the Question of Progress in the Area of Race Relations,' Address Delivered at St Louis Freedom Rally, April 10, 1957," in *The Papers of Martin Luther King, Jr.*, vol. 4, *Symbol of the Movement, January 1957–December 1958*, ed. Clayborne Carson et al., kinginstitute.stanford.edu.
3. Coretta Scott King, *My Life, My Love, My Legacy* (Henry Holt, 2017), 70.
4. Ibid., 132.
5. Jeanne Theoharis, *King of the North: Martin Luther King Jr.'s Challenge to Northern Racism and the Limits of Northern Liberalism*, unpublished manuscript, 75, 80–1, 85.
6. Dr. Martin Luther King Jr., "Why We Are in Chicago," *New York Amsterdam News*, March 12, 1966, 21.
7. Martin Luther King Jr., *Where Do We Go from Here: Chaos or Community?* (Beacon Press, 2010), 127.
8. Ibid., 37.
9. Theoharis, *King of the North*, 49, 81, 85.
10. Ibid., 48–9, 83.
11. King, *Where Do We Go from Here*, 59, 179–80, 183, 185.
12. Martin Luther King Jr., "Martin Luther King Jr. Saw Three Evils in the World: Racism Was Only the First," in "King Issue," special issue, *Atlantic*, February 2018, theatlantic.com.
13. Jeanne Theoharis, *A More Beautiful and Terrible Struggle: The Uses and Misuses of Civil Rights History* (Beacon Press, 2018), 16.
14. Scott King, *My Life, My Love, My Legacy*, 37, 90.
15. Sheldon Appleton, "Martin Luther King in Life . . . and Memory," *Public Perspective*, February/March 1995, 11.
16. King, "Martin Luther King Jr. Saw Three Evils in the World."
17. King, *Where Do We Go from Here*, 73, 89.
18. Simon Hall, "On the Tail of the Panther: Black Power and the 1967 Convention of the National Conference for New Politics," *Journal of American Studies* 37, no. 1 (April 2003): 59, 64.
19. Martin Luther King Jr., "The Three Evils of Society: Address Delivered at the National Conference on New Politics, August 31, 1967," nwesd.org.
20. "One Prosecutor Asserts Another 'Fabricated' Rap Brown Charge," *New York Times*, January 16, 1971, 1; "Federal Conviction against Rap Brown Voided on Appeal," *Washington Post*, September 25, 1976, A2; Box 85, Folder 27, Center for Constitutional Rights Records, Tamiment Library/Robert F. Wagner Labor Archives, New York University.
21. "Black Nationalist Hate Groups, 100-448006, Section 1," COINTELPRO: The Counterintelligence Program of the FBI, gale.com.

NOTES FOR PAGES 120 TO 126

22. Memos from J. Edgar Hoover, Director of the FBI, to Mildred Stegall, White House, gale.com.
23. Komozi Woodard, *A Nation within a Nation: Amiri Baraka (LeRoi Jones) and Black Power Politics* (University of North Carolina Press, 1999), 86; author interview with Komozi Woodard, New York City, November 17, 2017.
24. H. Rap Brown, "Speech to Rally at East St Louis, September 10, 1967," *Detailed Report on Student Nonviolent Coordinating Committee (SNCC) Chairman H. Rap Brown*, Federal Bureau of Investigation, January 12, 1968, gale.com.
25. H. Rap Brown, "Speech to Black Caucus of National Conference for New Politics, Palmer House Hotel, Chicago, September 3, 1967," *Detailed Report on Student Nonviolent Coordinating Committee (SNCC) Chairman H. Rap Brown*.
26. "H. Rap Brown Interview with Pierre Loizeau of the Journal *Les Temps Modernes*," unpublished transcript, Box 53, Folder 4, SNCC archives, King Center for Nonviolent Social Change, Atlanta, GA.
27. Kwame Ture and Charles V. Hamilton, *Black Power: The Politics of Liberation in America* (Vintage, 1992), xix, 4–5, 54, 179.
28. Elizabeth Martínez, *De Colores Means All of Us: Latina Views for a Multi-colored Century* (Verso, 2017), 22.
29. H. Rap Brown, "Speech to Black Caucus of National Conference for New Politics."
30. Hall, "On the Tail of the Panther," 65–7, 68, 70.
31. Keith P. Feldman, *A Shadow over Palestine: The Imperial Life of Race in America* (University of Minnesota Press, 2015), 81; James Forman, *The Making of Black Revolutionaries* (Washington University Press, 1997), 498; Matthew Frye Jacobson, *Roots Too: White Ethnic Revival in Post–Civil Rights America* (Harvard University Press, 2006), 222.
32. Forman, *The Making of Black Revolutionaries*, 503.
33. Michael Kazin, "A Patriotic Left," *Dissent*, Fall 2002, 41–4.
34. Jacobson, *Roots Too*, 225.
35. H. Rap Brown, *Die Nigger Die: A Political Autobiography* (Dial Press, 1969), 68, 124–5, 141.
36. "H. Rap Brown, Speech at New York University, December 6, 1967," Box 26, File 1, James Forman papers, MSS85371, Library of Congress, Washington, DC.
37. H. Rap Brown, *Die Nigger Die*, 128–9, 131.
38. "Appeal for Justice by Steering Committee against Repression, 1968," in Box 53, Folder 4, SNCC archives, King Center, Atlanta.
39. Author interview with Jamil Al-Amin, United States Penitentiary, Tucson, Arizona, August 24–25, 2021; *The State of Georgia vs Jamil Abdullah Al-Amin*, transcript of trial proceedings, February 18–March 13, 2002, Superior Court of Fulton County, Georgia.

8. What Is Racial Capitalism?

1. "Letter from Cleveland Sellers to Charles V. Hamilton, July 26, 1971," Box 2, Folder 2, Cleveland L. Sellers Jr. papers, AMN 1017, Avery Research Center, College of Charleston, SC.
2. Karl Marx and Frederick Engels, *Manifesto of the Communist Party*, in *Collected Works*, vol. 6 (Lawrence & Wishart, 1976), 487.
3. Ellen Meiksins Wood, "Class, Race, and Capitalism," in *Political Power and Social Theory*, vol. 15, ed. Diane E. Davis (Emerald Publishing, 2002), 276–81.
4. Martin Legassick, "South Africa: Forced Labor, Industrialization, and Racial Differentiation," in *The Political Economy of Africa*, ed. Richard Harris (Schenkman Publishing, 1975), 229.
5. *Programme of the South African Communist Party: The Road to South African Freedom* (Inkululeko Publications, 1962).
6. Martin Legassick and David Hemson, *Foreign Investment and the Reproduction of Racial Capitalism in South Africa*, Foreign Investment in South Africa: A Discussion Series, no. 2 (Anti-Apartheid Movement, 1976), 3, 12; Bernard Makhosezwe Magubane, *The Political Economy of Race and Class in South Africa* (Monthly Review Press, 1979), 152–3.
7. Legassick and Hemson, *Foreign Investment*, 2, 1, 9–10.
8. Martin Legassick, "South Africa: Forced Labor, Industrialization, and Racial Differentiation," in Harris, *The Political Economy of Africa*; Harold Wolpe, "Capitalism and Cheap Labour-Power in South Africa: From Segregation to Apartheid," *Economy and Society* 1, no. 4 (1972): 425–56; Martin Legassick, "South Africa: Capital Accumulation and Violence," *Economy and Society* 3, no. 3 (1974): 253–91; No Sizwe / Neville Alexander, *One Azania, One Nation: The National Question in South Africa* (Zed Press, 1979); Magubane, *The Political Economy of Race and Class in South Africa*; Bernard Magubane, "The Political Economy of the South African Revolution," *African Journal of Political Economy* 1, no. 1 (1986).
9. Mahmood Mamdani, "Settler Colonialism: Then and Now," *Critical Inquiry* 41, no. 3 (Spring 2015): 608.
10. *The Land: The Report of the Land Enquiry Committee*, vol. 1, *Rural* (Hodder and Stoughton, 1913), lxxii.
11. Marx, *Capital*, vol. 1 (Penguin, 1982), 874, 876, 895, 931.
12. Magubane, *The Political Economy of Race and Class in South Africa*, 96.
13. Mitsuo Ogura, "Urbanization and Apartheid in South Africa: Influx Controls and Their Abolition," *The Developing Economies* 34, no. 4 (December 1996): 405, 408; John Sackur, "Casualties of the

Economic Boom in South Africa," *Times* (April 26, 1971); Legassick and Hemson, *Foreign Investment*, 3; Legassick, "South Africa: Capital Accumulation and Violence," 272.

14. Magubane, *The Political Economy of Race and Class in South Africa*, 92, 96–7.
15. Sackur, "Casualties of the Economic Boom in South Africa."
16. Legassick and Hemson, *Foreign Investment*, 7–8.
17. Wolpe, "Capitalism and Cheap Labour-Power in South Africa," 450.
18. Nicholas Lemann, "Is Capitalism Racist?," *New Yorker*, May 25, 2020; Sean Illing, "How Capitalism Reduced Diversity to a Brand," *Vox*, February 16, 2019.
19. See racialcapitalism.ucdavis.edu.
20. Walter Johnson, "To Remake the World: Slavery, Racial Capitalism, and Justice," in *Race Capitalism Justice*, ed. Walter Johnson and Robin D. G. Kelley (Boston Review, 2017), 20.
21. Peter James Hudson, *Bankers and Empire: How Wall Street Colonized the Caribbean* (University of Chicago Press, 2017), 13.
22. Robin D. G. Kelley, introduction to Johnson and Kelley, *Race Capitalism Justice*, 8.
23. A. Sivanandan, "Race against Time: There Isn't Just One Form of Racism in Britain, but Two," *New Statesman and Society* 6, no. 274 (October 15, 1993).
24. A. Sivanandan, "From Resistance to Rebellion: Asian and Afro-Caribbean Struggles in Britain," *Race and Class* 23, nos. 2/3 (1981/82), 150.
25. Cedric Robinson, *Black Marxism: The Making of the Black Radical Tradition* (Zed Books, 1983); Josh Myers, *Cedric Robinson: The Time of the Black Radical Tradition* (Polity, 2021), 125, 139, 144, 9.
26. Anderson, *Marx at the Margins*.
27. Robinson, *Black Marxism*, 4, 9, 26.
28. Marx, *Capital*, vol. 1, 781.
29. Nikhil Pal Singh, "On Race, Violence, and So-Called Primitive Accumulation," *Social Text* 34, no. 3 (September 2016): 27–50.
30. Inés Valdez, "Socialism and Empire: Labor Mobility, Racial Capitalism, and the Political Theory of Migration," *Political Theory* 49, no. 6 (2021): 906.
31. Lise Vogel, *Marxism and the Oppression of Women: Toward a Unitary Theory* (Rutgers University Press, 1983).
32. Robinson, *Black Marxism*, xxxi, 66.
33. Cedric J. Robinson, *Forgeries of Memory and Meaning: Blacks and the Regimes of Race in American Theater and Film before World War II* (University of North Carolina Press, 2012), xii.
34. Ibid.
35. Robinson, *Black Marxism*, 4.

36. Robinson, *Forgeries of Memory and Meaning*, xv.
37. Robinson, *Black Marxism*, 308.
38. Ibid., 4–5, 309, 168.
39. Stuart Hall, *Familiar Stranger: A Life between Two Islands* (Duke University Press, 2017), 22, 44, 132, 225, 265, 228, 229, 240–2.
40. Stuart Hall, "Race, Articulation, and Societies Structured in Dominance," in *Sociological Theories: Race and Colonialism* (UNESCO, 1980); Stuart Hall et al., *Policing the Crisis: Mugging, the State, and Law and Order* (Macmillan, 1978).
41. Hall, "Race, Articulation, and Societies Structured in Dominance," 314, 330–1.
42. Ibid., 320, 338.
43. Ruth Wilson Gilmore, "Abolition Geography and the Problem of Innocence," in *Futures of Black Radicalism*, ed. Gaye Theresa Johnson and Alex Lubin (Verso, 2017), 438.
44. Hall, "Race, Articulation, and Societies Structured in Dominance," 342.
45. Samir Amin, *The Law of Worldwide Value* (Monthly Review Press, 2010), 84.
46. Jayati Ghosh, "Interpreting Contemporary Imperialism: Lessons from Samir Amin," *Monthly Review* 48, no. 167 (2021): 8–14; Lucas Chancel et al., *World Inequality Report 2022* (World Inequality Lab, 2021), 56–7.
47. Hall, "Race, Articulation, and Societies Structured in Dominance," 338–9.
48. Ibid., 308.
49. Nikole Hannah-Jones, "Our Democracy's Founding Ideals Were False When They Were Written; Black Americans Have Fought to Make Them True," *New York Times Magazine*, August 14, 2019.
50. A. Sivanandan, *Communities of Resistance: Writings on Black Struggles for Socialism* (Verso, 1990), 64.
51. Hall, "Race, Articulation, and Societies Structured in Dominance," 339.
52. Hall et al., *Policing the Crisis*, 348–9, 331, 340, 342.
53. Ibid., 341, 345–94.

9. The Neoliberal Idea

1. David Harvey, *A Brief History of Neoliberalism* (Oxford University Press, 2005), 12, 13, 15.
2. Ibid., 2, 10–11, 19.
3. Pierre Dardot and Christian Laval, *The New Way of the World: On Neoliberal Society* (Verso, 2017), 6–12.

4. Dieter Plehwe, introduction to *The Road from Mont Pèlerin: The Making of the Neoliberal Thought Collective*, ed. Philip Mirowski and Dieter Plehwe (Harvard University Press, 2015), 1–3.
5. Harvey, *A Brief History of Neoliberalism*, 168.
6. David Harvey, *Seventeen Contradictions and the End of Capitalism* (Oxford University Press, 2014), 8.
7. David Harvey, "Response to Alex Dubilet," *Syndicate*, April 1, 2015.
8. Magnus Hirschfeld, *Racism* (Kennikat Press, 1973), 35.
9. Wendy Brown, *In the Ruins of Neoliberalism: The Rise of Antidemocratic Politics in the West* (Columbia University Press, 2019), 175, 177, 187–8, 180.
10. Ibid., 1, 171, 165, 118, 173, 121, 180, 182.
11. Beverly J. Silver, *Forces of Labor: Workers' Movements and Globalization since 1870* (Cambridge University Press, 2003), 162.
12. Milton Friedman, "Neo-liberalism and Its Prospects," *Farmand*, February 17, 1951.
13. Eqbal Ahmad, "Pioneering in the Nuclear Age: An Essay on Israel and the Palestinians," in *The Selected Writings of Eqbal Ahmad*, ed. Carollee Bengelsdorf, Margaret Cerullo, and Yogesh Chandrani (Columbia University Press, 2006), 299.
14. Eqbal Ahmad, "From Potato Sack to Potato Mash: The Contemporary Crisis of the Third World," in *Selected Writings*, 126–7.
15. Lars Cornelissen, "Neoliberalism and the Racialized Critique of Democracy," *Constellations* 27, no. 3 (September 2020): 351.
16. Leo Panitch and Sam Gindin, *The Making of Global Capitalism: The Political Economy of American Empire* (Verso, 2012), 133–4.
17. Charter of Economic Rights and Duties of States, General Assembly Resolution 3281 (XXIX), New York, December 12, 1974.
18. Adom Getachew, *Worldmaking after Empire: The Rise and Fall of Self-Determination* (Princeton University Press, 2019), 12.
19. Frantz Fanon, *Les Damnés de la Terre* (Éditions La Découverte & Syros, 2002), 99.
20. F. A. Hayek, *Law, Legislation, and Liberty*, vol. 2, *The Mirage of Social Justice* (Routledge and Kegan Paul, 1976), 91.
21. Quinn Slobodian, *Globalists: The End of Empire and the Birth of Neoliberalism* (Harvard University Press, 2018), 99.
22. Timothy Mitchell, *Carbon Democracy: Political Power in the Age of Oil* (Verso, 2013), 173.
23. James M. Buchanan, "America's Third Century in Perspective," *Atlantic Economic Journal* 1, no. 1 (November 1973): 6–7, 9, 11.
24. James M. Buchanan, "Afraid to Be Free: Dependency as Desideratum," *Public Choice* 124, nos. 1–2 (July 2005): 19, 24.
25. Melinda Cooper, *Family Values: Between Neoliberalism and the New Social Conservatism* (Zone Books, 2017), 37.

26. Ibid., 38; Elizabeth Hinton, *From the War on Poverty to the War on Crime: The Making of Mass Incarceration in America* (Harvard University Press, 2016), 20–1.
27. Johnnie Tillmon, "Welfare Is a Women's Issue," *Ms.*, Spring 1972, 111.
28. Premilla Nadasen, "'We Do Whatever Becomes Necessary': Johnnie Tillmon, Welfare Rights, and Black Power," in *Want to Start a Revolution? Radical Women in the Black Freedom Struggle*, ed. Dayo F. Gore, Jeanne Theoharis, and Komozi Woodard (New York University Press, 2009), 317, 319–320, 323–6.
29. Alejandra Marchevsky and Jeanne Theoharis, *Not Working: Latina Immigrants, Low-Wage Jobs, and the Failure of Welfare Reform* (New York University Press, 2006), 38.
30. Tillmon, "Welfare Is a Women's Issue," 114.
31. Nadasen, "'We Do Whatever Becomes Necessary,'" 329.
32. Gary S. Becker, *A Treatise on the Family* (Harvard University Press, 1981), 357.
33. Cooper, *Family Values*, 19.
34. Friedman, "Neo-liberalism and Its Prospects."
35. Milton Friedman, *Capitalism and Freedom* (University of Chicago Press, 2002), 24.
36. Ronald Butt, "Mrs Thatcher: The First Two Years," *Sunday Times*, May 3, 1981.
37. Friedman, "Neo-liberalism and Its Prospects."
38. F. A. Hayek, *Law, Legislation, and Liberty*, vol. 1, *Rules and Order* (Routledge and Kegan Paul, 1973), 42.
39. F. A. Hayek, "The Principles of a Liberal Social Order," *Il Politico* 31, no. 4 (1966): 602; F. A. Hayek, *Law, Legislation, and Liberty*, vol. 3, *A New Statement of the Liberal Principles of Justice and Political Economy* (Routledge and Kegan Paul, 1982), 155.
40. F. A. Hayek, "Freedom, Reason and Tradition," *Ethics* 68, no. 4 (1958): 238; Hayek, *Law, Legislation, and Liberty*, vol. 1, 42, 107.
41. Hayek, *Law, Legislation, and Liberty*, vol. 1, 104–5.
42. Hayek, *Law, Legislation, and Liberty*, vol. 2, 31–2.
43. Hayek, "The Principles of a Liberal Social Order," 611.
44. Hayek, "Freedom, Reason and Tradition," 232; Hayek, *Law, Legislation, and Liberty*, vol. 1, 70.
45. Ibid., 45, 55.
46. Hayek, "Freedom, Reason and Tradition," 233.
47. F. A. Hayek, *The Constitution of Liberty* (University of Chicago Press, 1960), 407–9; Hayek, *Law, Legislation, and Liberty*, vol. 3, 166.
48. Hayek, *The Constitution of Liberty*, 1–4; Louis Auguste Paul Rougier, *The Genius of the West* (Nash Publishing, 1971), xvi;

Hayek, *Law, Legislation, and Liberty*, vol. 2, 135–6; Hayek, *Law, Legislation, and Liberty*, vol. 3, 164; David Gress, *From Plato to NATO: The Idea of the West and Its Opponents* (Free Press, 1998).
49. John Gray, "Hayek on Liberty, Rights, and Justice," *Ethics* 92, no. 1 (1981): 79.
50. Hayek, *Law, Legislation, and Liberty*, vol. 2, 133; Hayek, *Law, Legislation, and Liberty*, vol. 3, 165.
51. Hayek, *Law, Legislation, and Liberty*, vol. 2, 147.
52. Jessica Whyte, *The Morals of the Market: Human rights and the Rise of Neoliberalism* (Verso, 2019), 35.
53. Rougier, *The Genius of the West*, xviii.
54. F. A. Hayek, "Free Market," *Times*, March 18, 1980, 18; Whyte, *The Morals of the Market*, 14.
55. Milton Friedman, *Capitalism and Freedom* (University of Chicago Press, 2002), 21.
56. Hayek, *The Constitution of Liberty*, 406.
57. Norman Barry, "Hayek's Theory of Social Order," *Il Politico* 60, no. 4 (1995): 569.
58. Hayek, *Law, Legislation, and Liberty*, vol. 3, 76.
59. Slobodian, *Globalists*, 9, 12, 20.
60. Ibid., 42.
61. Quinn Slobodian, "Perfect Capitalism, Imperfect Humans: Race, Migration and the Limits of Ludwig von Mises's Globalism," *Contemporary European History* 28, no. 2 (May 2019): 148, 152.
62. Slobodian, *Globalists*, 50.
63. Hayek, *Law, Legislation, and Liberty*, vol. 2, 128–9.
64. Ibid., 147.
65. F. A. Hayek, "The Politics of Race and Immigration," *Times*, February 11, 1978, 15; R. W. Apple Jr., "Mrs. Thatcher Touches a Nerve and British Racial Tension Is Suddenly a Political Issue," *New York Times*, February 22, 1978, A10.
66. Hayek, *Law, Legislation, and Liberty*, vol. 3, 56.
67. Julian L. Simon, "Are There Grounds for Limiting Immigration?," *Journal of Libertarian Studies* 13, no. 2 (Summer 1998): 142.
68. Hayek, *Law, Legislation, and Liberty*, vol. 2, 57.
69. Hayek, "The Politics of Race and Immigration," 15; F. A. Hayek, "Integrating Immigrants," *Times*, March 9, 1978, 17.
70. Bernard Semmel, *Imperialism and Social Reform: English Social-Imperial Thought 1895–1914* (Anchor Books, 1968), 18.
71. Dardot and Laval, *The New Way of the World*, 32–5.
72. Étienne Balibar and Immanuel Wallerstein, *Race, Nation, Class: Ambiguous Identities* (Verso, 1988), 22, 25.
73. Martin Barker, *The New Racism: Conservatives and the Ideology of the Tribe* (Junction Books, 1981).

74. Cornelissen, "Neoliberalism and the Racialized Critique of Democracy," 354.
75. Whyte, *The Morals of the Market*, 58–9.
76. Slobodian, *Globalists*, 45, 108–9, 111.
77. Ibid., 149.
78. Cornelissen, "Neoliberalism and the Racialized Critique of Democracy," 352.
79. Slobodian, *Globalists*, 149–50, 180; Phillip Becher et al., "Ordoliberal White Democracy, Elitism, and the Demos: The Case of Wilhelm Röpke," *Democratic Theory* 8, no. 2 (Winter 2021): 70–96.
80. Cornelissen, "Neoliberalism and the Racialized Critique of Democracy," 354.
81. Milton Friedman, "Some Impressions of South Africa and Rhodesia," *Sunday Times*, May 2, 1976.

10. Policing the Wastelands

1. Robert D. Putnam, "Samuel P. Huntington: An Appreciation," *PS: Political Science and Politics* 19, no. 4 (Fall 1986): 838–43; Samuel P. Huntington, "The Bases of Accommodation," *Foreign Affairs* 46, no. 4 (July 1968).
2. Samuel P. Huntington, *Political Order in Changing Societies* (Yale University Press, 1973), 2–5, 8, 45, 56, 289.
3. Ibid., 28.
4. Ibid., 261, 307, 347–57.
5. Michel Crozier, Samuel P. Huntington, and Joji Watanuki, *The Crisis of Democracy: Report on the Governmentality of Democracies to the Trilateral Commission* (New York University Press, 1975), 64, 102–3, 113.
6. Vincent Bevins, "What the United States Did in Indonesia," *Atlantic*, October 20, 2017.
7. Peter Dale Scott, "North American Universities and the 1965 Indonesian Massacre: Indonesian Guilt and Western Responsibility," *Asia Pacific Journal* 12, no. 2 (December 2014): 7.
8. David Ransom, "Ford Country: Building an Elite for Indonesia," in *The Trojan Horse: A Radical Look at Foreign Aid*, ed. Steve Weissman (Ramparts Press, 1975), 93–116.
9. Ian Morison, "Suharto Returns Plantations," *Times*, June 12, 1967, 17.
10. Intan Suwandi, *Value Chains: The New Economic Imperialism* (Monthly Review Press, 2019), 37–8, 59, 99, 164–5; Charles P. Wallace, "New Shots Fired in Indonesia Wage War," *Los Angeles Times*, September 22, 1992; Fahmi Panimbang, "Indonesia Cracks

Down on Organized Labour," *New Internationalist*, January 11, 2018.
11. Michael T. Klare and Cynthia Arnson, *Supplying Repression: US Support for Authoritarian Regimes Abroad* (Institute for Policy Studies, 1981), 4.
12. Eqbal Ahmad, "The Neofascist State: Notes on the Pathology of Power in the Third World," in *Selected Writings*.
13. Andrew Farrant and Edward McPhail, "Can a Dictator Turn a Constitution into a Can-Opener? F.A. Hayek and the Alchemy of Transitional Dictatorship in Chile," *Review of Political Economy* 26, no. 3 (2014).
14. Rashid Khalidi, *The Iron Cage: The Story of the Palestinian Struggle for Statehood* (Oneworld, 2007), 192.
15. Elaine Hagopian, "Minority Rights in a Nation-State: The Nixon Administration's Campaign against Arab-Americans," *Journal of Palestine Studies* 5, nos. 1/2 (Autumn 1975–Winter 1976): 97–114.
16. Timothy Mitchell, *Carbon Democracy: Political Power in the Age of Oil* (Verso, 2013), 151–4.
17. James E. Akins, "The Oil Crisis: This Time the Wolf Is Here," *Foreign Affairs* 51, no. 3 (April 1973): 476.
18. Arnold Hottinger, "The Depth of Arab Radicalism," *Foreign Affairs* 51, no. 3 (April 1973): 500, 504.
19. Akins, "The Oil Crisis," 469, 481.
20. Mitchell, *Carbon Democracy*, 176, 197–9.
21. Ronald Stockton, "Ethnic Archetypes and the Arab Image," in *The Development of Arab-American Identity*, ed. Ernest McCarus (University of Michigan Press, 1994), 146.
22. Eqbal Ahmad, "Pioneering in the Nuclear Age," 301.
23. Eqbal Ahmad, "Yet Again a New Nixon," in *Selected Writings*, 230.
24. Justin Akers Chacón and Mike Davis, *No One Is Illegal: Fighting Violence and State Repression on the US-Mexico Border* (Haymarket, 2006), 115.
25. Raúl Delgado Wise, "Migration and Labour under Neoliberal Globalization," in *Migration, Precarity, and Global Governance: Challenges and Opportunities for Labor*, ed. Carl-Urik Schierup et al. (Oxford University Press, 2015).
26. Suwandi, *Value Chains*, 23.
27. Data from the Hunt Institute for Global Competitiveness, University of Texas at El Paso, utep.edu/hunt institute.
28. Zahid Hussain, "Financing Living Wage in Bangladesh's Garment Industry," blogs.worldbank.org, August 3, 2010.
29. Samir Amin, "The New Imperialist Structure," *Monthly Review* 71, no. 3 (July–August 2019): 32–45; Suwandi, *Value Chains*, 48, 152.

30. Jason Hickel, Dylan Sullivan, and Huzaifa Zoomkawala, "Plunder in the Post-colonial Era: Quantifying Drain from the Global South through Unequal Exchange, 1960–2018," *New Political Economy* 26, no. 6 (2021): 1030–47.
31. Jason Hickel, "Is Global Inequality Getting Better or Worse? A Critique of the World Bank's Convergence Narrative," *Third World Quarterly* 38, no. 10 (2017): 217.
32. Jessica Whyte, *The Morals of the Market: Human Rights and the Rise of Neoliberalism* (Verso, 2019), 154, 216.
33. Leo Panitch and Sam Gindin, *The Making of Global Capitalism: The Political Economy of American Empire* (Verso, 2012), 239.
34. Ibid., 157.
35. Maurizio Lazzarato, *The Making of the Indebted Man: An Essay on the Neoliberal Condition* (Semiotext(e), 2012), 45–6.
36. Daniel Patrick Moynihan, "The United States in Opposition," *Commentary*, March 1975.
37. Giovanni Arrighi, "World Income Inequalities and the Future of Socialism," *New Left Review* 181 (Sept/Oct 1991): 39–40, 51, 59–60.
38. Yao Graham, "Ghana: The IMF's African Success Story?," *Race and Class* 24, no. 3 (Winter 1988): 41–52.
39. Walden Bello, with Shea Cunningham and Bill Rau, *Dark Victory: The United States, Structural Adjustment, and Global Poverty* (Pluto Press, 1994), 63.
40. George Monbiot, *The Age of Consent: A Manifesto for a New World Order* (Flamingo, 2003), 151.
41. Bello, *Dark Victory*, 46.
42. Sylvia Federici, "The Debt Crisis, Africa, and the New Enclosures," in Midnight Notes Collective, *Midnight Oil: Work, Energy, War, 1973–1992* (Autonomedia, 1992), 308–9.
43. Susan Ferguson and David McNally, "Precarious Migrants: Gender, Race and the Social Reproduction of a Global Working Class," in *Transforming Classes*, ed. Leo Panitch and Greg Albo (New York University Press, 2014).
44. Mike Davis, "Planet of Slums: Urban Involution and the Informal Proletariat," *New Left Review* 26 (March–April 2004): 23.
45. *Slums of the World: The Face of Urban Poverty in the New Millennium?* (United Nations Human Settlements Programme, 2003), 1.
46. Achille Mbembe, *Critique of Black Reason* (Duke University Press, 2017), 3.
47. Kalyan Sanyal, *Rethinking Capitalist Development: Primitive Accumulation, Governmentality and Post-colonial Capitalism* (Routledge, 2007), 53, 55.
48. Folasade Iyun, "The Impact of Structural Adjustment on Maternal and Child Health in Nigeria," in *Women Pay the Price: Structural*

Adjustment in Africa and the Caribbean, ed. Gloria T. Emeagwali (African World Press, 1995).
49. A. Sivanandan, *Communities of Resistance: Writings on Black Struggles for Socialism* (Verso, 1990), 28.
50. Ibid., 185.
51. Lucas Chancel et al., *World Inequality Report 2022* (World Inequality Lab, 2021), 62.
52. Adam Habib and Vishnu Padayachee, "Economic Policy and Power Relations in South Africa's Transition to Democracy," *World Development* 28, no. 2 (2000): 252.
53. Ibid., 10, 57.
54. Angela Mitropoulos, "Lifeboat Capitalism, Catastrophism, Borders," *Dispatches Journal* 1 (November 2018): 10.
55. Edward W. Said, "The Mirage of Peace," *Nation*, October 16, 1995, 413.
56. Deepa Kumar, "Terrorcraft: Empire and the Making of the Racialised Terrorist Threat," *Race and Class* 62, no. 2 (Autumn 2020): 34–60; Remi Brulin, "Compartmentalization, Contexts of Speech, and the Israeli Origins of the American Discourse on 'Terrorism,'" *Dialectical Anthropology* 39, no. 1 (2015): 69–119.
57. Benjamin Netanyahu, ed., *Terrorism: How the West Can Win* (Farrar, Straus, Giroux, 1986).
58. Joseba Zulaika, "The Self-Fulfilling Prophecies of Counterterrorism," *Radical History Review* 85 (Winter 2003): 191–9; Edward W. Said, *Covering Islam: How the Media and the Experts Determine How We See the Rest of the World* (Vintage, 1997).
59. Bernard Lewis, "The Roots of Muslim Rage," *Atlantic*, September 1990; Samuel P. Huntington, "The Clash of Civilizations?," *Foreign Affairs* (Summer 1993), 22, 31–2, 35.
60. Samuel P. Huntington, *Who Are We? The Challenges to America's Identity* (Simon & Schuster, 2004), 262.
61. Edward Said, "Spurious Scholarship and the Palestinian Question," *Race and Class* 29, no. 3 (Spring 1988): 32.
62. Stuart Hall et al., *Policing the Crisis: Mugging, the State, and Law and Order* (Macmillan, 1978), 59, 166.
63. Julie Bosman, "Secret Iraq Meeting Included Journalists," *New York Times*, October 6, 2006.
64. "Donald H. Rumsfeld Conducts Town Hall Meeting," *FDCH Political Transcripts*, October 7, 2003, nexis.com.
65. Nikhil Pal Singh, *Race and America's Long War* (University of California Press, 2017), 16, 108.
66. David Lloyd and Patrick Wolfe, "Settler Colonial Logics and the Neoliberal Regime," *Settler Colonial Studies* 6, no. 2 (2016): 111.

67. Omar Jabary Salamanca et al., "Past Is Present: Settler Colonialism in Palestine," *Settler Colonial Studies* 2, no. 1 (2012): 1–8.
68. Michael Rogin, "'Make My Day!': Spectacle as Amnesia in Imperial Politics," *Representations* 29 (Winter 1990): 109.
69. Amos Barshad, "Extraordinary Measures," *Intercept*, October 7, 2018.
70. Todd Miller and Gabriel M. Schivone, "How Israeli High-Tech Firms Are Outfitting the US-Mexico Border," *openDemocracy*, January 26, 2015.
71. Researching the American-Israeli Alliance, with Jewish Voice for Peace, *Deadly Exchange: The Dangerous Consequences of American Law Enforcement Trainings in Israel* (September 2018), iv.
72. Deposition by Thomas Galati in *Handschu v. Special Services Division* (United States District Court, Southern District of New York, June 28, 2012), 31.

11. A War on the Urban Dispossessed

1. Utsa Patnaik and Prabhat Patnaik, *A Theory of Imperialism* (Columbia University Press, 2017), 2.
2. A. Sivanandan, *Communities of Resistance: Writings on Black Struggles for Socialism* (Verso, 1990), 28.
3. *Economic Report of the President: Transmitted to the Congress February 1988* (United States Government Printing Office, 1988), 282.
4. Coretta Scott King, *My Life, My Love, My Legacy* (Henry Holt, 2017), 243–4, 205–6, 254–5.
5. David P. Stein, "'This Nation Has Never Honestly Dealt With the Question of a Peacetime Economy': Coretta Scott King and the Struggle for a Nonviolent Economy in the 1970s," *Souls* 18, no. 1 (2016): 81.
6. Richard Nixon, "Remarks on the CBS Radio Network: Bridges to Human Dignity, the Concept," The American Presidency Project, presidency.ucsb.edu.
7. Keeanga-Yamahtta Taylor, *Race for Profit: How Banks and the Real Estate Industry Undermined Black Homeownership* (University of North Carolina Press, 2019), 127.
8. Ibid., 3, 17, 125–7; Junia Howell and Elizabeth Korver-Glenn, "The Increasing Effect of Neighborhood Racial Composition on Housing Values, 1980–2015," *Social Problems* 68, no. 4 (November 2021).
9. Nixon, "Remarks on the CBS Radio Network."
10. H. Rap Brown, *Die Nigger Die: A Political Autobiography* (Dial Press, 1969), 142.
11. Combahee River Collective, "The Combahee River Collective Statement," in *Available Means: An Anthology of Women's Rhetoric(s)*,

ed. Joy Ritchie and Kate Ronald (University of Pittsburgh Press, 2001), 295.
12. Stuart Hall, *Familiar Stranger: A Life between Two Islands* (Duke University Press, 2017), 16.
13. Philip Gleason, "Identifying Identity: A Semantic History," *Journal of American History* 69, no. 4 (March 1983): 914–15, 919–20, 924.
14. Frantz Fanon, "Racism and Culture," *Presence Africaine* 8–10 (June–November 1956): 124.
15. *Economic Report of the President*, 288, 293.
16. Richard Cockett, *Thinking the Unthinkable: Think-Tanks and the Economic Counter-revolution 1931–1983* (Fontana Press, 1995), 306; John Blundell, "Hayek, Fisher and *The Road to Serfdom*," in *The Reader's Digest Condensed Version of* The Road to Serfdom (Institute of Economic Affairs, 1999), 24.
17. Charles Murray and Richard Herrnstein, *The Bell Curve: Intelligence and Class Structure in American Life* (Free Press, 1994).
18. Quinn Slobodian and Stuart Schrader, "The White Man, Unburdened," *Baffler* 40 (July 2018).
19. Charles Murray, *Losing Ground: American Social Policy, 1950–1980* (Basic Books, 1994), xvi, xx, 69, 76–8, 81, 130.
20. Alejandra Marchevsky and Jeanne Theoharis, *Not Working: Latina Immigrants, Low-Wage Jobs, and the Failure of Welfare Reform* (New York University Press, 2006), 5, 27.
21. Ellora Derenoncourt et al., "Wealth of Two Nations: The US Racial Wealth Gap, 1860–2020," NBER Working Paper No. 30101, June 2022, 3.
22. James Q. Wilson, "Black and White Tragedy," *Encounter*, October 1967, 63, 66–7.
23. Peter Levy, *The Great Uprising: Race Riots in Urban America during the 1960s* (Cambridge University Press, 2018), 1.
24. Komozi Woodard, *A Nation within a Nation: Amiri Baraka (LeRoi Jones) and Black Power Politics* (University of North Carolina Press, 1999), 82.
25. Oscar Lewis, *La Vida: A Puerto Rican Family in the Culture of Poverty—San Juan and New York* (Random House, 1965), xliii.
26. J. Edgar Hoover, "Story of US Crime," *Daily Oklahoman*, October 21, 1968, 6.
27. Hinton, *From the War on Poverty*, 87.
28. Stuart Schrader, *Badges without Borders: How Global Counterinsurgency Transformed American Policing* (University of California Press, 2019), 43.
29. Taylor, *Race for Profit*, 98.
30. Daniel P. Moynihan memo to President Nixon, January 16, 1970, nixonlibrary.gov; Hinton, *From the War on Poverty*, 180–2.

31. Ibid., 185–6.
32. Richard Nixon, "Message to the Congress Transmitting Reorganization Plan 2 of 1973 Establishing the Drug Enforcement Administration," The American Presidency Project, presidency.ucsb.edu.
33. Schrader, *Badges without Borders*, 2.
34. Hinton, *From the War on Poverty*, 164, 173–4.
35. George L. Kelling and James Q. Wilson, "Broken Windows: The Police and Neighborhood Safety," *Atlantic*, March 1982.
36. William J. Bratton et al., "This Works: Crime Prevention and the Future of Broken Windows Policing," *Civic Bulletin* 36 (April 2004): 6.
37. Kelling and Wilson, "Broken Windows."
38. Schrader, *Badges without Borders*, 255.
39. Jamie Peck, "Liberating the City: Between New York and New Orleans," *Urban Geography* 37, no. 8 (November 2006): 681–2.
40. Christina Heatherton, "The Broken Windows of Rosa Ramos: Neoliberal Policing Regimes of Imminent Violability," in *Feminists Rethink the Neoliberal State: Inequality, Exclusion, and Change*, ed. Leela Fernandes (New York University Press, 2018).
41. Naomi Murakawa, *The First Civil Right: How Liberals Built Prison America* (Oxford University Press, 2014), 5–6.
42. Loïc Wacquant, "The Global Firestorm of Law and Order: On Punishment and Neoliberalism," *Thesis Eleven* 122, no. 1 (June 2014): 73–7; Loïc Wacquant, *Prisons of Poverty* (University of Minnesota Press, 2009), 2.
43. Ruth Wilson Gilmore, *Golden Gulag: Prisons, Surplus, Crisis, and Opposition in Globalizing California* (University of California Press, 2007), 70, 77.
44. Murakawa, *The First Civil Right*, 5–6.
45. Barbara Ransby, *Making All Black Lives Matter: Reimagining Freedom in the 21st Century* (University of California Press, 2018), 33, 160.

12. Why Neoliberals Build Borders

1. John Blundell, "Hayek, Fisher and *The Road to Serfdom*," in *The Reader's Digest Condensed Version of* The Road to Serfdom (Institute of Economic Affairs, 1999).
2. Camilla Schofield, *Enoch Powell and the Making of Postcolonial Britain* (Cambridge University Press, 2013), 165.
3. J. Enoch Powell, speech delivered at Town Hall, Kidderminster, March 31, 1967, GBR/0014/POLL 4/1/2, *The Papers of Enoch Powell* (Churchill Archives, University of Cambridge); Schofield, *Enoch Powell*, 177.

4. Richard Cockett, *Thinking the Unthinkable: Think-Tanks and the Economic Counter-revolution 1931–1983* (Fontana Press, 1995), 98–9, 140, 163–4, 167.
5. J. Enoch Powell, speech delivered at Dulwich Conservative Association, February 29, 1964, GBR/0014/POLL 4/1/1, *The Papers of Enoch Powell*.
6. Cockett, *Thinking the Unthinkable*, 139.
7. Iain Macleod, "Enoch Powell," *Spectator*, July 16, 1965, 7.
8. Paul Corthorn, *Enoch Powell: Politics and Ideas in Modern Britain* (Oxford University Press, 2019), 124.
9. Peter Hennessy, *Never Again: Britain 1945–51* (Jonathan Cape, 1992), 711.
10. Schofield, *Enoch Powell*, 55–6, 78, 121.
11. Ibid., 163.
12. J. Enoch Powell, speech delivered at Wolverhampton South West Conservative Association, December 13, 1963, GBR/0014/POLL 4/1/1, *The Papers of Enoch Powell*.
13. Schofield, *Enoch Powell*, 173.
14. Robbie Shilliam, "Enoch Powell: Britain's First Neoliberal Politician," *New Political Economy* 26, no. 2 (2021): 7.
15. Ibid., 6.
16. Schofield, *Enoch Powell*, 113, 164, 168.
17. Peregrine Worsthorne, "Powell and the Tory Party: The Pariah and the Election," *Spectator*, October 10, 1970, 8.
18. "Skin-Colour Is Like a Uniform," *New Statesman*, October 13, 1978, 461.
19. Shilliam, "Enoch Powell," 6.
20. J. Enoch Powell, speech delivered at Turves Green Girls School, Birmingham, June 13, 1970, GBR/0014/POLL 4/1/6, *The Papers of Enoch Powell*.
21. Clive Webb, "Enoch Powell's America / America's Enoch Powell," in *Global White Nationalism: From Apartheid to Trump*, ed. Daniel Geary, Camilla Schofield, and Jennifer Sutton (Manchester University Press, 2020), 109.
22. Douglas Massey, "Economic Development and International Migration in Comparative Perspective," *Population and Development Review* 14, no. 2 (1988): 385.
23. Edward P. Thompson, *The Making of the English Working Class* (Pelican, 1968), 469.
24. Kathleen Paul, *Whitewashing Britain: Race and Citizenship in the Postwar Era* (Cornell University Press, 1997), 164, 166.
25. Carole Boyce Davies, ed., *Claudia Jones: Beyond Containment* (Ayebia Clarke Publishing, 2011), 169.
26. Étienne Balibar and Immanuel Wallerstein, *Race, Nation, Class: Ambiguous Identities* (Verso, 1988), 22.

27. J. Enoch Powell, speech delivered at Midland Hotel, Birmingham, April 20, 1968, GBR/0014/POLL 4/1/3, *The Papers of Enoch Powell*.
28. Anthony Lester, ed., *Essays and Speeches by Roy Jenkins* (Collins, 1967), 267.
29. Andrew Sparrow, "Howard's 'Liberal' Defence of Asylum Policy," *Daily Telegraph*, April 23, 2005.
30. "Heath's Four-Point Plan for Immigrants," *Sunday Telegraph*, January 26, 1969, 4.
31. Justin Akers Chacón and Mike Davis, *No One Is Illegal: Fighting Violence and State Repression on the US-Mexico Border* (Haymarket, 2006), 173.
32. Manu Karuka, *Empire's Tracks: Indigenous Nations, Chinese Workers, and the Transcontinental Railroad* (University of California Press, 2019), 82–3.
33. Mae M. Ngai, *Impossible Subjects: Illegal Aliens and the Making of Modern America* (Princeton University Press, 2005), 3.
34. Ibid., 64, 72.
35. Chacón and Davis, *No One Is Illegal*, 140.
36. Selene Rivera, "A Former Bracero Shares His Story," *Los Angeles Times*, July 18, 2022, A1.
37. Ngai, *Impossible Subjects*, 261–2.
38. Chacón and Davis, *No One Is Illegal*, 202.
39. Elizabeth Martínez, *De Colores Means All of Us: Latina Views for a Multi-colored Century* (Verso, 2017), 4, 18–19.
40. Samuel P. Huntington, *Who Are We? The Challenges to America's Identity* (Simon & Schuster, 2004), 243, 253–4.
41. Deepa Fernandes, *Targeted: Homeland Security and the Business of Immigration* (Seven Stories Press, 2007), 215.
42. Allan Bloom, *The Closing of the American Mind* (Simon & Schuster, 1987); Dinesh D'Souza, *Illiberal Education: The Politics of Race and Sex on Campus* (Free Press, 1991).
43. Julian L. Simon, "The Case for Greatly Increased Immigration," *Public Interest* 102 (Winter 1991): 89–103; Ben J. Wattenberg and Karl Zinsmeister, "The Case for More Immigration," *Commentary* 89 (April 1990): 19–25.
44. Harsha Walia, *Border and Rule: Global Migration, Capitalism, and the Rise of Racist Nationalism* (Haymarket, 2021), 14.
45. Hannah Cross, *Migration beyond Capitalism* (Polity Press, 2021), 10.
46. Bhaskar Sunkara, "Let Them Eat Diversity: An Interview with Walter Benn Michaels," *Jacobin* (January 2011).
47. Bobby Hunter and Victoria Yee, *Dismantle, Don't Expand: The 1996 Immigration Laws* (Immigrant Justice Network and New York University School of Law, 2017).

48. Mizue Aizeki et al., *Smart Borders or a Humane World?* (Immigrant Defense Project and the Transnational Institute, 2021), 3; American Civil Liberties Union, "Customs and Border Protection's (CBP's) 100-Mile Rule," 2014.
49. Todd Miller, *Empire of Borders: The Expansion of the US Border around the World* (Verso, 2019), 157.
50. Maria Sacchetti, "Border Numbers Jump in March, with Striking Increase in Ukrainians," *Washington Post*, April 18, 2022; "Nationwide Enforcement Encounters: Title 8 Enforcement Actions and Title 42 Expulsions 2022," US Customs and Border Protection, July 15, 2022, cbp.gov.
51. Susan Ferguson and David McNally, "Precarious Migrants: Gender, Race and the Social Reproduction of a Global Working Class," in *Transforming Classes*, ed. Leo Panitch and Greg Albo (New York University Press, 2014), 6–7, 15.
52. Chacón and Davis, *No One Is Illegal*, 151, 157.
53. Walia, *Border and Rule*, 7–8.
54. Adam Hanieh, "The Contradictions of Global Migration," in *The World Turned Upside Down? Socialist Register 2019*, ed. Greg Albo and Leo Panitch (Monthly Review Press, 2018).

13. A Darker Red

1. Frantz Fanon, "Racism and Culture," *Presence Africaine* 8–10 (June–November 1956): 126.
2. Molly Molloy, "Homicide in Mexico 2007–March 2018: Continuing Epidemic of Militarized Hyper-violence," *Small Wars Journal*, April 27, 2018.
3. Mahmood Mamdani, *Good Muslim, Bad Muslim: America, the Cold War, and the Roots of Terror* (Pantheon, 2004).
4. Fanon, "Racism and Culture," 124.
5. A. Sivanandan, *Communities of Resistance: Writings on Black Struggles for Socialism* (Verso, 1990), 78.
6. Ibid., 80.
7. Keeanga-Yamahtta Taylor, *From #BlackLivesMatter to Black Liberation* (Haymarket, 2016), 100.
8. Oliver Cromwell Cox, *Caste, Class, and Race: A Study in Social Dynamics* (Monthly Review Press, 1959), 537.
9. Stuart Hall et al., *Policing the Crisis: Mugging, the State, and Law and Order* (Macmillan, 1978), 347, 394.
10. "A. Sivanandan on Racism Awareness Training," excerpt of talk in Manchester, UK, 1982, youtube.com.

11. Barbara Ransby, *Making All Black Lives Matter: Reimagining Freedom in the 21st Century* (University of California Press, 2018), 158–9.
12. Sivanandan, *Communities of Resistance*, 114.
13. Ibid., 51, 58.
14. Aimé Césaire, "Letter to Maurice Thorez," *Social Text* 28, no. 2 (Summer 2010): 152.
15. Sivanandan, *Communities of Resistance*, 75–6.

Index

bold denotes photo

A

Abu Gharib, carceral site at, 18
AFDC (Aid to Families with Dependent Children), 168–9, 170, 214
Africa. *See also* South Africa
   anticolonial movement in, 92, 102, 105, 113, 125, 145
   authoritarian regimes in, 189
   colonialism in, 30–1, 36, 54, 56, 58, 65–6, 68
   consequences of neoliberal transformation in, 197
   genocide in, 76
   independence of countries in, 112, 163
   modernization policies in, 99, 184
   revolts in, 71, 81, 84, 101
   success stories in, 198
African Blood Brotherhood, 63
African diaspora, 67
African National Congress, 200
"The African Roots of War" (Du Bois), 58
Ahmad, Eqbal, 99, 163
Aid to Families with Dependent Children (AFDC), 168–9, 170, 214
Akins, James F., 192–3
Al-Amin, Jamil Abdullah (aka H. Rap Brown), 6, 119–26, 127, 129, 153, 166, 206, 209, 216, 221, 245, 247
Albright, Madeleine, 87–8, 89, 90
Alcatraz, 14–15
Alexander, Neville, 132–3, 134
Algemene Inlichtingen- en Veiligheidsdienst (AIVD), 13, 22
Algeria
   French occupation of, 77, 78, 79, 80
   national liberation movement in, 163
   overthrow of colonialist regime in, 185
   revolutionary violence in, 183

Algerian National Liberation Front, 78
Aliens Restriction (Amendment) Act (1919) (UK), 227
Allende, Salvador, 156, 189
An American Dilemma (Myrdal), 38
American Creed, 38, 39
Amery, Leopold S., 51
anti-apartheid movement, 132
anticapitalism, 62, 118, 124
anticolonial freedom movement, 52
anticolonialism, 62, 63, 77, 92, 135, 162
anticolonial nationalism, 58, 165
Anti-Coolie Act (California), 235
anti-imperialism, 59, 118, 247
anti-Muslim racism, 22, 24, 200–5
antiracism
   according to James, 73
   according to Jones, 105–6
   according to Myrdal, 87, 116
   collective force of, 69
   emergent ideas of, 103
   first stage of, 77
   liberal antiracism, 207–8, 244, 247
   radical antiracism. *See* radical antiracism
   as radicalizing class struggle, 251
   use of education in, 23
anti-Semitism, 22, 29, 30, 36, 59, 76, 85
Antiterrorism and Effective Death Penalty Act (1996) (US), 238
apartheid
   in South Africa, 86, 114, 130–7, 182, 200, 239
   in US, 37, 85, 86
Arafat, Yasser, 191
Aron, Ralph, 16
Ash, Timothy Garton, 19
Asia
   anticolonial movement in, 92, 113
   authoritarian regimes in, 189

INDEX

Asia *(continued)*
  colonization in, 36, 50, 54
  emigration from, 232, 235, 236
  growing political participation in, 184
  independence of countries in, 112, 163
  revolts in, 101, 183
Asia-Africa Conference in Bandung (1955), 188
Atatürk, Mustafa Kemal, 186
Atlantic, on broken windows policing, 219
Attica, 15

B

Bagram, carceral site at, 18
Baldwin, James, 78
Balibar, Étienne, 180
Becker, Gary, 156, 170
The Bell Curve (Murray), 212
Benedict, Ruth, 35–6, 36, 38, 75, 81, 86, 118, 160, 210, 246
Berkeley mafia, 188
Bernstein, Eduard, 55–6
Biden, Joe, 239
bin Laden, Osama, 204
Black capitalism, 207, 209
Black freedom movement, 5, 72, 102–12, 119, 125, 158, 166
Black identity
  according to Hall, 210
  co-opting upsurge in affirmations of, 209
The Black Jacobins (James), 68, 69
Black Left, 103, 108, 112, 117, 207
Black Lives Matter, 1, 250
Black Marxism (Robinson), 139
Black Panther Party, 145
Black Power movement, 73, 121, 123, 125, 127, 139, 209
Black Reconstruction in America (Du Bois), 71
BlackRock, 2–3
Black Skin, White Masks (Fanon), 81
Blair, Tony, 21
Bloom, Allan, 237
Blumenbach, Johann Friedrich, 28
Boas, Franz, 32, 33–4, 35, 38, 75, 81, 86, 210, 231
border
  crisis of in Britain, 227
  culture war at, 235
  expanding infrastructure of enforcement at, 238–9, 244
  necessity of, 231
  as racial battleground, 233
  strengthening of, 232
Border Patrol (US), 236
Bracero Program (US), 236
Bretton Woods conference (1944), 97
A Brief History of Neoliberalism (Harvey), 156, 158
Britain
  emergence of neoliberalism in, 223–7, 234
  free movement policy, 236
  immigration policy in, 227–8, 229, 230, 232–3
  Labour Party, 95, 96, 162, 224, 231, 232, 247
  "new patriotism" in, 226, 229, 230
  reconfiguration of structural racism in, 225
  broken windows policing, 212, 218, 219–22, 243
Brown, Bertram S., 15
Brown, H. Rap, 119, 216. *See also* Al-Amin, Jamil Abdullah (aka H. Rap Brown)
Brown, Wendy, 160–1
Buchanan, James M., 167
Bureau of Prisons (US), 15, 16
Burke, Edmund, 173
Butler, Rab, 229

C

Cama, Bhikaji, 55
Capital (Marx), 133, 134, 140
capitalism
  according to Nkrumah, 101–2
  according to Woods, 128–9
  Black capitalism, 207, 209
  neoliberal restructuring of, 158, 159, 190, 221
  racial capitalism. *See* racial capitalism
  survival strategy of, 93
  welfare-state capitalism, 95, 96, 103, 170, 172
Caribbean
  anticolonial movement in, 9, 53, 92
  capitalist modernity in, 66
  colonialism in, 36, 50, 54, 66–70, 108
  emigration from, 152, 226, 227, 228, 230

INDEX

independence of countries in, 163
insurrectionaries in, 67
Carmichael, Stokely, 73, 121, 216. *See also* Ture, Kwame (aka Stokely Carmichael)
Carter, Jimmy, 236
Casey, William J., 212
Castro, Fidel, 118
Center on Racial Equity, 2
Césaire, Aimé, 6, 66, 74–8, 88, 89, 90, 91, 108, 129, 218, 245, 247, 248, 250–1
Charter of Economic Rights and Duties of States (UN), 164
Chauvin, Derek, 1
Chávez, Hugo, 88
cheap labor, 114, 135, 189, 190, 194, 237, 239
Chicago, IL, living conditions for Kings in, 113–14
Chile
  neoliberal restructuring of economy in, 156
  overthrow of Allende's socialist government in, 156, 189
China
  communist revolution in, 96
  as one of two richest countries (1400 to 1700), 44
  opium exports to, 41–2
  revolutionary violence in, 183
  transformation of position of in world system, 200
Churchill, Winston, 51–2
CIA (US), 98, 101, 188, 191
Civil Rights Act of 1964 (US), 116
civil rights campaign/movement/struggle, 63, 72, 76, 112, 113, 116, 118, 119, 123, 125, 168, 208
Civil Rights Congress, 109
civil rights legislation, 116, 215
"clash of civilizations," 202
class exploitation, 59, 128, 146, 248
class struggle, 55, 59, 62, 69, 71, 73, 102, 103, 104, 125, 131, 160, 166, 250, 251
Clinton, Bill, 214, 238, 245
The Closing of the American Mind (Bloom), 237
collective imperialism, 96–102
colonialism. *See also specific locations*
  according to Lenin, 58

domestic colonialism, 113
internal colonialism, 63, 107, 113, 115, 125, 131
neocolonialism. *See* neocolonialism
structural relationships between racism, fascism, and, 74–8
color prejudice, 31
Combahee River Collective, 105, 209
Comintern (Third International), 59, 61, 63, 131
Commonwealth Immigrants Act (1962) (UK), 229
Commonwealth Immigrants Act (1968) (UK), 232
Communist Manifesto (Marx and Engels), 54, 128
Communist Party of India, 64
communists/communism, 59, 61, 62, 63, 64, 77, 96, 103, 104, 131, 188
Convention on the Prevention and Punishment of the Crime of Genocide (UN), 109
Cooper Jackson, Esther, 103
COVID, racially differentiated effects of, 4
Cox, Oliver Cromwell, 85–6, 246
"crimmigration," 239
The Crisis (journal), 31
Cuba, revolution of (1958), 163, 183
cultural determinism, 35
cultural diversity, 5, 80, 182, 208, 231
cultural evolution, 172, 173, 174, 180, 243
cultural relativism, 34
culture
  according to Boas, 32–4, 231
  according to Hayek, 179
  according to Huntington, 185, 202
  according to Mises, 181
  according to Powell, 231, 232
  "collectivist" culture/"communal" culture, 196, 226
  as having color, 237
  investigation of, 146
  "minority" culture, 231
  neo-racist idea of, 180, 182, 222, 230, 243, 244
  racial concept of, 244
  respect for native cultures, 49, 77
  role of in political development, 202

INDEX

culture (*continued*)
  "sustained death agony" of, 80
  theories of, 210
  use of term, 32–4
  and welfare capitalism, 172
Customs and Border Protection agency (US), 205, 238

D

The Damned of the Earth (Fanon) (usually translated as *The Wretched of the Earth*), 81, 83–4
Darwin, Charles, 179
Davis, Angela, 6, 18
Davis, Mike, 51
Dayan, Colin, 17
decolonization, 78, 92, 95, 157, 158, 162, 165, 166, 190, 191, 239, 250
De Kom, Anton, 6, 9–10, 10, 22, 23, 24, 25, 31, 53, 66, 77
DiAngelo, Robin, 2, 3–4, 39
Discourse on Colonialism (Césaire), 74, 77
diversity
  as anxious politics, 246
  as conditional on deradicalization, 244
  cultural diversity, 5, 80, 182, 208, 231
  emphasis on, 210
  politics of, 231–2
  use of term, 48
domestic colonialism, 113
Drug Enforcement Administration (US), 218
D'Souza, Dinesh, 237
Du Bois, Shirley Graham, 117
Du Bois, W. E. B., 6, 31–2, 38, 58, 71–2, 92, 108, 109, 112
Duterte, Rodrigo, 88

E

East India Company, 41, 45, 46–7, 49
Egypt, nationalization of Suez Canal, 164, 224
Eighteenth Brumaire of Louis Bonaparte (Marx), 67
Elbit Systems, 205
Elkabetz, Roei, 205
Engels, Frederick, 54, 128
Erdoğan, Recep Tayyip, 88
Erikson, Erik, 210

F

Fanon, Frantz, 6, 66, 78–84, 87, 90, 91, 129, 153, 155, 158, 164, 190, 210, 216, 232, 241, 244–5, 247
fascists/fascism, 74–8, 87–9, 108–9
FBI (US), 191, 216
Federal Housing Administration (US), 93–4, 207
Ferguson, Adam, 174
Fink, Larry, 2–3
First International Congress of Black Writers and Artists, 78
Fischer, Eugene, 30
Fisher, Antony, 212, 223
Five Mualimm-Ak, 17
Floyd, George, 1
Ford Foundation, 98, 188
Foreign Affairs (journal), 192
Foreign Investment and the Reproduction of Racial Capitalism in South Africa (Legassick and Hemson), 132
Foreign Investment Law, 189
Forgeries of Memory and Meaning (Robinson), 143–4
Forman, James, 123
France
  colonies of, 77, 163
  coup in (1851), 67
  French Revolution (1789), 63, 69–70
Frankel, S. Herbert, 196
free markets, 155, 157, 162, 164, 173, 174, 181, 189, 193, 207, 208, 210, 214, 237
free movement policy, 57, 178, 228, 235, 236
French Communist Party, 63, 77
French Revolution (1789), 63, 69–70
Friedman, Milton, 155, 156, 162, 171, 175, 182, 189, 224

G

Gaddis, John Lewis, 203
Gandhi, Mohandas K., 62
Garner, Eric, 222
Garvey, Marcus, 67
Garvin, Vicki, 103
gender liberation, 102
gender struggle/oppression, 103, 104–5, 123, 129, 142, 167, 170, 250
genocidal violence, 22

290

INDEX

Ghana
  CIA role in military coup in, 101
  independence of, 92
  neocolonialism in, 93
  structural adjustment programs of, 197–8
Gilmore, Ruth Wilson, 149, 221
Giuliani, Rudy, 220
global markets, 180, 193
Golden Gulag (Gilmore), 221
Graham, Shirley, 108
Guantánamo, carceral site at, 18

H

Hall, Stuart, 6, 146–54, 147, 202, 210, 246
Hamilton, Charles V., 121–2
Haney, Craig, 13
Hannah-Jones, Nikole, 151
Hart-Celler Act (1965) (US), 236
Harvey, David, 156, 157, 158–9, 161
hate crimes, 87
hate speech, 87
Hayek, Friedrich, 155, 165, 172–4, 175, 176, 177, 178, 179, 180, 189, 190, 223, 224, 226, 243
Heath, Edward, 232
Hemson, David, 132, 136
Himes, Chester, 78
Hirschfeld, Magnus, 26–9, 27, 30, 32, 75, 76, 159
Hitler, Adolf, 26, 27, 30, 35, 51, 52, 75, 76, 110
Ho Chi Minh, 63
Hoover, J. Edgar, 14, 120, 216
The House I Live In (film), 37
Hudson, Peter, 138
Humphrey-Hawkins Full Employment Act (US), 207
Huntington, Samuel P., 183–8, 202, 212, 217, 237, 242

I

identity
  according to neoliberalism, 245
  Black identity, 209, 210
  defined, 123–4
  introduction of term, 210
identity politics, 59, 123, 209, 245
ideological racism, 68
IEA (Institute of Economic Affairs), 164, 212, 223

Illegal Immigration Reform and Immigrant Responsibility Act (1996) (US), 238
"illegals," 240, 242
Illiberal Education (D'Souza), 237
IMF (International Monetary Fund), 189, 196–7, 198
Immigration Act (1971) (UK), 233
Immigration and Customs Enforcement (US), 240
immigration policy
  in Britain, 227–8, 229, 230, 232–3
  racisms as embedded in, 90
  in US, 90, 235, 236, 237–8
  worldwide changes in, 234–5
Immigration Reform and Control Act (1986) (US), 236
imperialism. *See also specific locations*
  according to Lenin, 58
  collective imperialism, 96–102
  connection to fascism, 108–9
  liberal imperialism, 248
  racism as tied to history of, 149
  Wall Street imperialism, 108
  welfare imperialism, 99
Imperialism: The Highest Stage of Capitalism (Lenin), 57–8
imperial racism, 229
Inayat, Shah, 44
India
  census in, 48–9
  colonialism in, 41–53
  Communist Party of India, 64
  creation of independent nation, 52
  1857 uprising, 46–7, 55
  famine in, 50–1, 55
  freedom struggle in, 44–5
  indirect rule in, 48–9
  industrial decline of, 45–6
  manufacturing productivity in, 44–5
  as one of two richest countries (1400 to 1700), 44
Indian National Congress, 64
Indonesia
  coup in, 101
  defeat of Dutch colonialism in, 188
  Dutch imperialism in, 9, 106
  revolutionary violence in, 183
  transformation of colonial structures in, 188–9

inflation, according to Huntington, 188
Institute of Economic Affairs (IEA), 164, 212, 223
institutional racism, 121, 122, 152–3
integration, racial, 19, 107, 122, 208, 231
internal colonialism, 63, 107, 113, 115, 125, 131
International Center for Economic Policy Studies (later Manhattan Institute), 212
International Monetary Fund (IMF), 189, 196–7, 198
Iran, nationalization of oil production in (1951), 100, 163–4
Iraq
   invasion, occupation, and destruction of, 20–1, 90, 203
   overthrow of puppet monarchy in (1958), 100–1
Islam. *See also* Muslims
   as "ideal enemy" of US, according to Huntington, 202
   perceptions of by others, 13, 15, 18, 19, 20, 21–2, 24, 48, 80, 125, 192, 202, 203
Israel
   new imperial strategy in, 194
   and Palestine, 123, 165, 190–1, 201, 204, 205
   and US, 202, 205
Israel Defense Forces, 205

J

Jackson, George, 15–16
Jackson, Otis, 126
Jacobson, Matthew Frye, 123
James, C. L. R., 6, 65–7, 68, 69, 71, 72–3, 74, **74**, 83, 88, 90, 91, 101, 129, 153, 166, 245, 247
January 6, 2021, US Capitol attack, 88
Jenkins, Roy, 231
Jews, genocide of European Jews, 8, 11, 18, 36, 66, 76–7, 110
Jim Crow, 104, 108, 144, 166, 239
Johnson, Lyndon B., 101, 166–7, 215, 216, 217, 220
Johnson, Walter, 138
Johnson-Reed Immigration Act (1924) (US), 235
Jonathan Institute conference (1984), 202
Jones, Claudia, 6, 103–11, **106**, 112, 113, 118, 129, 229, 245, 247

K

Kagan, Robert, 88, 89, 90
Kalani, Hemu, 44
Kaplan, Robert, 203
Kautsky, Karl, 55–6
Kelley, Robin, 138
Kelling, George L., 219, 222
Kemalist model, 186
Kenyatta, Jomo, 139
Kerner Commission, 216
Khrushchev, Nikita, 118
Kim Jong-un, 88
Kincaid, Jamaica, 66
King, Martin Luther, Jr., 6, 113, 114–18, 119, 125, 127, 129, 166, 208, 245
Kipling, Rudyard, 50
Kirkpatrick, Jeane, 202
Knox, Robert, 33, 34
Koch, Charles, 238
Koch, David, 238

L

labor
   cheap labor, 114, 135, 189, 190, 194, 237, 239
   racial division of, 239
labor movements, 60, 72, 93, 97, 102, 104, 105, 155, 200, 206
Lamming, George, 78
Latif, Shah Abdul, 44
Latin America
   authoritarian regimes in, 189
   colonialism in, 97
   modernization policies in, 99, 184
   racist imperialism in, 115
   revolt in, 101, 163, 183, 185
La Vida (Lewis), 216
Law Enforcement Assistance Administration (US), 217
Legassick, Martin, 132–3, 134, 136
Lenin, Vladimir, 57–9, 61, 62, 63–4, 69, 83, 94, 104, 107, 131, 166
Lewis, Bernard, 21, 202
Lewis, Oscar, 216
liberal antiracism, 5–6, 37, 40, 74, 85, 86–7, 90, 112, 116, 118, 182, 207–8, 245, 246, 247
liberal imperialism, 248
Liberalism (Mises), 181

INDEX

"liberal" society, 19, 24
Lohia, Ram Manohar, 44
López, Jesse, 16
Losing Ground (Murray), 212, 213
L'Ouverture, Toussaint, 67

M

macro-aggressions, 2, 243, 247
Magubane, Bernard, 132–3, 134–5
Malcolm X, 103, 120, 138–9
Mamdani, Mahmood, 48
Manhattan Institute, 212, 220, 221
Manley, Michael, 164
Marion, Illinois, federal penitentiary in, 15, 16–17
market order, 172–3, 177, 178, 179, 180, 182, 183, 201, 208, 210, 211, 219, 226, 231, 241, 243. *See also* free markets; global markets
Martínez, Elizabeth, 237
Marx, Karl, 46, 54–5, 67, 82, 128, 133–4, 140, 147, 198
Marxists/Marxism, 54–7, 59, 63, 67, 73, 78, 82, 103, 124, 127–8, 130–1, 132, 133, 137, 139–40, 141, 145, 156
mass incarceration, 17, 73, 159, 221, 222, 243, 244
Mbembe, Achille, 199
McCarran Act (US), 111
McNamara, Robert, 196
Mellon Foundation, 138
Méndez, Juan E., 13
Mengele, Josef, 30
Mexico, US policy at border with, 235–6
micro-aggressions, 1, 2, 241
militarized policing, 244
Mises, Ludwig von, 155, 177, 178, 181, 226
Model Cities Task Force (US), 218
modernization
  according to US policy-makers, 98
  policies of, 99, 100, 163, 184, 187, 193
modernization theory, 98–9, 184
Modi, Narendra, 44
Monmouth University, poll by, 1
Mont Pèlerin Society, 155, 164, 174, 196, 223, 224
Moynihan, Daniel Patrick, 167, 197, 213, 214, 216, 217–18, 242
Mualimm-Ak, Five, 17

multiculturalism, 210, 230, 237
multinational corporations, 101, 189, 194–5, 197, 239
Murray, Charles, 212–14, 220, 242
Muslim extremists/extremism, 18, 20, 22, 202, 204, 242
Muslims. *See also* Islam
  global policing of, 242
  incarceration of, 13, 14, 15, 18
  "Muslim problem," 192
  radicalization of, 22
  as suspect, 19–20
  War on Terror and, 21, 126
Myrdal, Gunnar, 38–9, 86, 112, 116, 118, 246

N

Naoroji, Dadabhai, 50, 55
Napier, Charles, 41–4, 42
Narayan, Jayaprakash, 44
"narcos," 242
Nasser, Gamal Abdel, 164, 224
National Association for the Advancement of Colored People (NAACP), 31
National Bureau of Economic Research, on racial wealth disparities, 214–15
National Committee for a Sane Nuclear Policy, 119
National Committee for Full Employment, 207
National Conference for New Politics (NCNP), 119–21, 122–3
National Welfare Rights Organization (NWRO), 168, 169
Naturalization Act (1790) (US), 235
Nazis/Nazism, 8–12, 19, 22–3, 24, 26, 28, 29, 32, 35, 37, 51, 65–6, 75, 76, 85, 88, 110, 112, 229, 231
Négritude movement, 77, 81
The Negro Family: The Case for National Action (Moynihan), 167
Nehru, Jawaharlal, 62
neocolonialism, 93, 96, 97, 98, 99, 102, 108, 115, 159, 164, 171, 197
Neo-Colonialism: The Last Stage of Imperialism (Nkrumah), 93, 101
"Neo-liberalism and Its Prospects" (Friedman), 171
neoliberal racism, 241, 243–4

293

INDEX

neoliberals/neoliberalism
   as attacking "collectivism," 250
   in Britain, 223–7, 234
   and decolonization and antiracism, 162–3
   empire of, 187, 190
   form of imperialism of, 239
   ideology of, 243
   impacts of, 170
   implementation of policies of in South Africa, 200
   imposition of on Third World countries, 177
   influence of, 156–7
   and markets, 162, 181, 182, 193, 194
   as project, 157–8, 171–2, 176–7, 178, 184, 186, 188, 206, 234, 244
   redefining of integration by, 208
   restructuring of capitalism by, 158, 159, 190, 221
   and surplus populations, 204, 221, 222, 241
   transformation of Third World countries by, 190, 197–9
   and welfare reform, 212
neo-racism, 179–80, 230
Netanyahu, Benjamin, 202
New Deal (US), 93, 94, 97, 99, 102, 103, 104, 108, 155–6, 166–8, 208, 211, 214, 216, 247
New Left, 119, 122, 123
New Left Review (journal), 146
New Yorker, use of term racial capitalism in, 138
1917 revolution (Russia), 58, 59, 63, 64, 69
Nixon, Richard, 123, 127, 191, 207, 208, 209, 217, 218, 220
Nkrumah, Kwame, 6, 92–6, 97–8, 99, 101–2, 113, 115, 118, 129, 149, 164, 166, 197, 245, 247
Not Everything Is What It Seems (film), 12
Notting Hill carnival (UK), 111
NWRO (National Welfare Rights Organization), 168, 169
Nyerere, Julius, 164

O

Obama, Barack, 205
Operation Boulder, 191
Oppenheimer, Harry F., 132

Orbán, Viktor, 88
Orwell, George, 52
Oslo accords (1993), 201

P

Pakistan, creation of independent nation, 52
Palestine, and Israel, 123, 165, 190–1, 201, 204, 205
Palestine Liberation Organization (PLO), 191, 201
Pan-African Congress (1945), 92
Papanek, Gustav, 101
Partido Comunista Mexicano, 61
Patnaik, Utsa, 52
Patterson, William L., 109–10, 139
Pentonville Five case (1972), 251
Personal Responsibility and Work Opportunity Act (1996) (US), 214
petrodollars, 193
The Philadelphia Negro (Du Bois), 31, 38
Pinochet, Augusto, 156, 189, 190
PLO (Palestine Liberation Organization), 191, 201
Political Order in Changing Societies (Huntington), 183
Powell, Enoch, 223, 224–8, 229, 230–1, 232–3, 234, 236, 237, 242, 251
primitive accumulation, 133, 134, 141, 198
prisons. *See also* mass incarceration
   Alcatraz, 14–15
   Attica, 15
   expansion of in US, 218
   incarceration of Black people (US), 120, 218, 221–2
   long-term control unit, 16–17
   Marion, Illinois, federal penitentiary, 15, 16–17
   population of (US), 220
   racist regimes at, 24
   rebellions in, 15, 23
   San Quentin, 15, 16
   supermax prisons, 14, 17, 18, 126
   use of isolation in, 13, 14, 15, 17, 18, 22, 24
   use of solitary confinement in, 13, 16, 17–18, 126
   Vught, Netherlands high-security unit, 12–14, 18–19, 22–3
Progressive Party (US), 107–8

INDEX

Public Affairs Committee, 37
Putin, Vladimir, 88

R

race
  according to Fanon, 129
  according to Harvey, 159
  according to Murray, 213–14
  and capitalism, 142
  characterization of politics of under neoliberalism, 244
  as "civic status," 128
  and culture, according to Boas, 32–4
  as detached from culture, 34–5
  historical specificity of, 151
  as "modality in which class is lived," 154
  organization through, 141, 148
  reconfiguring of, 143–4
  relationship between race, gender, and class struggles, 103, 105
  relationship between race and class, 59, 72, 153
  super-race, 37
  use of term, 181
Race and Class (journal), 139
race prejudice/race hatred, 31, 39, 75, 86
Race: Science and Politics (Benedict), 35–6
race science experiments, 30
The Races of Men (Knox), 33
race war, 28, 160
racial capitalism, 7, 132, 134, 135–6, 137–8, 139, 140, 141, 142, 143, 144–5, 146, 150, 161, 170, 171, 190, 211, 239, 241, 244, 247
racial exclusion, 244
racial incorporation, 244
racialism, 143
racial oppression, 59, 97, 104, 107, 113, 153, 245, 248
racial reckoning, 1–2
racial sensibilities, 143
racial theory, 28–9
racism
  according to Al-Amin, 121, 129
  according to Benedict, 35, 118
  according to Césaire, 129
  according to De Kom, 23–4
  according to Fanon, 129
  according to Hall, 146–54
  according to Harvey, 159
  according to Hirschfeld, 159–60
  according to James, 73, 129
  according to Jones, 129
  according to King, 113, 115, 118
  according to Kings, 129
  according to Myrdal, 118
  according to Robinson, 144–5
  according to Sivanandan, 151–2
  according to Woods, 128–9
  in Africa, according to James, 65–6
  anti-Muslim racism, 22, 24, 200–5
  candidates for history "founding moment" of, 151
  of Churchill, 51–2
  and culture, according to Fanon, 78–84
  differing concepts of, 25
  distinct and opposed personalities of, 85
  as enabling state violence, 243
  history of word, 27–32, 36–7
  ideological racism, 68
  imperial racism, 229
  institutional racism, 121, 122, 152–3
  linking of to structures of colonialism, 90–1
  in neoliberal era, 170–1
  and neoliberalism, 162
  neoliberal racism, 241, 243–4
  neo-racism, 179–80, 230
  in Netherlands, 12
  problem with liberal version of, according to Cox, 85–6
  recasting of word by Black Caribbean writers, 66
  redefined, 245
  relocating of to unconscious mind, 87
  state racism, 90, 137, 251
  as structural phenomenon, 53
  structural racism. *See* structural racism
  structural relationships between colonialism, fascism, and, 74–8
  as structure, 74–91
  systemic racism, 2, 3
  as tied to history of imperialism, 149
  use of term, 23
  use of term in US liberalism, 110
radical antiracism, 5, 117, 118, 126, 127, 245, 247
Ransby, Barbara, 222, 248

295

INDEX

Rassismus (Racism) (Hirschfeld), 27–8, 29, 30, 32, 159
Reagan, Ronald, 123, 157, 214, 236
Research Initiative on Racial Capitalism (University of California, Davis), 138
Rhodes, Cecil, 94
The Road to Serfdom (Hayek), 223
Robinson, Cedric, 6, 138–45, **140**, 146, 150
Rockefeller Foundation, 98
Roebuck, John Arthur, 41
Roosevelt, Franklin D., 93, 99, 155–6
Röpke, Wilhelm, 181–2
Rostow, Walt Whitman, 98–9, 217
Roy, Manabendra Nath, 6, 59, 60–2, **60**, 63, 64, 67, 69, 104, 107, 166, 245, 247
Rumsfeld, Donald, 203
Russia, 1917 revolution, 58, 59, 63, 64, 69

S

Safe Streets Act of 1968 (US), 217
Said, Edward, 201
Saint-Domingue revolution, 66, 67, 68, 69–70, 71
San Quentin, 15, 16
Sanyal, Kalyan, 199
Schein, Edgar, 15
Schultz, George, 202
SCLC (Southern Christian Leadership Conference), 119, 120
Scott King, Coretta, 6, 108, 113–14, **114**, 117, 129, 206–7, 211, 245
Scottsboro Boys case (1931), 104
Second International congress of socialists (1907), 55–7
security infrastructure, transnational, 242
segregation, racial, 93, 104, 108, 110, 113, 115, 116, 144, 167, 207–8, 233, 239, 250
Sellers, Cleveland, 127
Senghor, Léopold, 78
Sharp, Clifford, 94
Shaw, George Bernard, 94
Shenfield, Arthur, 164
Shin Bet, 205
Simon, William, 197
Sindh province (India), British colonization of, 41–4
Sivanandan, A., 6, 139, 151–2, 200, 245, 247, 248–9, **249**, 250, 251
A Small Place (Kincaid), 66–7

Smith, Adam, 171–2, 174
SNCC (Student Nonviolent Coordinating Committee), 119, 122, 123, 127
Snyder, Timothy, 88, 89
socialists/socialism, 55–9, 64, 71, 83–4, 124, 247, 250, 251
Socialist Workers Party, 72, 119
Social Statics (Spencer), 33
Soledad Brother (Jackson), 16
solitary confinement. *See* prison, use of solitary confinement in
South Africa
    apartheid in, 86, 130–7, 182, 200, 239
    neoliberal policies in, 200
    Sharpeville massacre (1960), 130
South African Communist Party, 131
Southern Christian Leadership Conference (SCLC), 119, 120
Spearman, Diana, 223–4
Spectator, on Enoch Powell, 224
Spencer, Herbert, 33, 47, 179–80
spontaneous order, 173, 224
Stanford, Leland, 235
state racism, 90, 137, 251
Sterling, Alton, 222
Strachey, John, 96
structural racism, 2, 3, 4, 6, 68, 69, 73, 75, 80, 81, 90, 91, 105, 109, 112, 113, 115, 118, 122, 129, 130, 131, 150, 158, 159, 161, 182, 208, 225, 232, 246, 247, 248–9
Student Nonviolent Coordinating Committee (SNCC), 119, 122, 123, 127
Students for a Democratic Society, 119
Suharto, 188–9, 190, 194
supermax prisons, 14, 17, 18, 126
"super-predators," 222, 242
surplus populations, 141, 153, 201, 204, 205, 211, 212, 219, 221, 222, 228, 239, 241, 242–3
systemic racism, 2, 3

T

Taylor, Keeanga-Yamahtta, 245
Temple, Richard, 50–1
terrorism. *See also* War on Terror
    Jonathan Institute conference on (1984), 202
    use of term, 201–2
Thatcher, Margaret, 157, 171, 178, 234

INDEX

Theoharis, Jeanne, 116
"Theses on the National and Colonial Questions" (Third International), 59, 62–3, 77, 124
Third International (Comintern), 59, 61, 63, 131
Third Reich, 28. *See also* Hitler, Adolph; Nazis/Nazism
Third World countries
  according to modernization theory, 98–9
  authoritarian regimes in, 194
  "communal values" of, 234
  decolonization of, 157
  displacement of rural masses in, 198–9
  efforts to secure colonial independence by, 111
  emigration from, 227, 228, 229, 230, 231, 236, 237
  foreign investments in, 164, 187, 217
  immigrant presence in US by, 237
  industrialization of, 95–6, 195
  international exploitation of, 164
  liberation movements in, 139, 163, 171, 175–6
  modernization policies in, 184
  neoliberalism as imposed on, 177
  neoliberal transformation of, 190, 197–9
  policing of, 220
  problem of according to neoliberals, 176
  production by multinational corporations in, 194–5
  radicalization of, 163, 192, 200, 201, 204
  raw materials from, 97, 165
  solidarity of, 188
  "structural adjustment" of, 196–7
  wage levels in, 206
  wealth gap between West and, 99–100, 191, 197, 201
Tillmon, Johnnie, 168–70, **169**, 211
tolerance education, 35–40
Trotha, Lothar von, 30
Trump, Donald, 29, 87, 88, 89–90, 123, 150, 160
Ture, Kwame (aka Stokely Carmichael), 73, 121–2, 152–3, 216

U

United Auto Workers, 37
United Kingdom (UK). *See* Britain
United Nations (UN)
  Charter of Economic Rights and Duties of States, 164
  Convention on the Prevention and Punishment of the Crime of Genocide, 109
  Human Settlements Programme, 199
  on using new term "racism," 111
United States (US)
  as antiracist, diversity-celebrating nation, 37
  Antiterrorism and Effective Death Penalty Act (1996), 238
  Black freedom movement in, 102–12, 166
  Black organizations in, 63
  Black struggle in, 72, 73, 113–26
  Border Patrol, 236
  Bracero Program, 236
  Bureau of Prisons, 15, 16
  CIA, 98, 101, 188, 191
  Civil Rights Act of 1964, 116
  Customs and Border Protection agency, 205, 238
  development policy of (1970s), 196
  Drug Enforcement Administration, 218
  FBI, 191, 216
  Federal Housing Administration, 93–4, 207
  foreign policy changes, 186–7, 189–90
  growth of wealth in, 49–50
  Hart-Celler Act (1965), 236
  Humphrey-Hawkins Full Employment Act, 207
  Illegal Immigration Reform and Immigrant Responsibility Act (1996), 238
  Immigration and Customs Enforcement, 240
  immigration policy in, 90, 235, 236, 237–8
  Immigration Reform and Control Act (1986), 236
  intervention of in local revolutions and nationalist regimes, 101
  Johnson-Reed Immigration Act (1924), 235
  Law Enforcement Assistance Administration, 217
  liberal antiracism of, 40
  McCarran Act, 111

INDEX

United States (*continued*)
   Model Cities Task Force, 218
   modernization in, 98
   Naturalization Act (1790), 235
   New Deal. *See* New Deal (US)
   Personal Responsibility and Work Opportunity Act (1996), 214
   policy at Mexico border, 235–6
   Progressive Party, 107–8
   punitive mood in urban policing in, 218
   Safe Streets Act of 1968, 217
   unemployment in (1969), 211
   uprisings organized by Black city-dwellers (1967), 215
   Urban Council, 217
   Violent Crime Control and Law Enforcement Act (1994), 245–6
   waning of manufacturing jobs in, 206–7
   white power movement in, 89
Universities and Left Review (journal), 146
Urban Council (US), 217
urban dispossessed, war on, 206–22

V

Van Herten, Henricus, 11
Van Kol, Hendrik, 56
Vierreck, George Sylvester, 26, 27, 28
Vietnam
   French imperialism in, 108
   national liberation movement in, 163
   revolutionary violence in, 183
   war in, 117, 120, 187, 194, 216, 217
Vinson, John, 237
Violent Crime Control and Law Enforcement Act (1994) (US), 245–6
Voting Rights Act of 1965, 116
Vox, use of term racial capitalism in, 138
Vught, Netherlands
   concentration camp in, 8–12
   high-security prison in, 12–14, 18–19, 22–3

W

wage levels, 149, 206, 214
Walia, Harsha, 238, 240
Wallace, George, 167
Wallace, Henry, 107–8

Wall Street imperialism, 108
Walmart, 2
war on crime, 216
War on Drugs, 89, 218
War on Terror, 19, 20–3, 24, 48, 89, 126, 150, 192, 203–4, 205
Watson Institute for International and Public Affairs (Brown University), 20
wealth disparities/gaps, 100, 201, 214–15
Webb, Beatrice, 94
Webb, Sidney, 94
We Charge Genocide (Patterson), 109–10
welfare capitalism, 95, 96, 170, 172
welfare imperialism, 99
"welfare queens," 222, 242
welfare rights movement, 93, 149, 168
welfare-state capitalism, 95, 103
We Slaves of Suriname (De Kom), 9
West Germany, guest worker migration to, 233–4
West Indian Gazette (newspaper), 111
Where Do We Go from Here: Chaos or Community? (King), 118
white fragility, 39
White Fragility (DiAngelo), 2, 3–4
white Left, 55, 69, 122, 155, 157, 159, 161
white power movement, 89
white power structure, 107, 115
white supremacy, 36, 38, 59, 63, 72, 85, 108, 110, 151, 161, 241, 248
Wilson, James Q., 215–16, 217, 218, 219, 222, 242
Wolpe, Harold, 132–3, 134, 136
women's groups, 104, 105
Women Strike for Peace movement, 117
Woods, Ellen Meiksins, 127–8, 131, 137
World Bank, 196–7
World Trade Organization, 177
Worsthorne, Peregrine, 226
The Wretched of the Earth (Fanon), 81, 83–4, 216
Wright, Richard, 78

Y

Yoo, John, 203
Younge, Gary, 4